Anglo-American
Postmodernity

ANGLO-AMERICAN POSTMODERNITY

Philosophical Perspectives on
Science, Religion, and Ethics

NANCEY MURPHY

WestviewPress
A Division of HarperCollins*Publishers*

Published in 1997 in the United States of America by Westview Press, 5500 Central Avenue, Boulder, Colorado 80301-2877, and in the United Kingdom by Westview Press, 12 Hid's Copse Road, Cumnor Hill, Oxford OX2 9JJ

Library of Congress Cataloging-in-Publication Data
Murphy, Nancey C.
  Anglo-American postmodernity : philosophical perspectives on science, religion, and ethics / Nancey Murphy.
    p.   cm.
  Includes bibliographical references and index.
  ISBN 0-8133-2868-3 (hardcover)—ISBN 0-8133-2869-1 (pbk.)
  1. Postmodernism. 2. Philosophy, English—20th century.
3. Philosophy, American—20th century. I. Title.
B831.2.M87 1997
149'.97—dc21   96-37711
                                                                                CIP

The paper used in this publication meets the requirements of the American National Standard for Permanence of Paper for Printed Library Materials Z39.48-1984.

10   9   8   7   6   5   4   3   2   1

To my son, André Fedán

Contents

Acknowledgments

I am grateful to Spencer Carr at Westview Press for urging me to put this book together. Most of the materials have been reworked from previous publications and oral presentations. Thus, the list of those to whom I am indebted has grown over the years.

The distinction I draw in Chapter 1 between modern and (Anglo-American) postmodern thought was worked out with my husband, James Wm. McClendon Jr., and first published in "Distinguishing Modern and Postmodern Theologies," *Modern Theology* 5 (April 1989):191–214. Our ongoing discussions have been the single most important inspiration for this book. Robert J. Russell made helpful comments on a draft of this chapter.

Chapter 2 was originally published in slightly different form as "Scientific Realism and Postmodern Philosophy," *British Journal for Philosophy of Science* 41 (1990):291–303. Reprinted by permission of Oxford University Press.

Chapter 3 is part of a paper discussed under the auspices of the Boston Colloquium for the Philosophy of Science at Boston University in November 1993. I thank the faculty there for the stimulating discussion. The paper was published as "Postmodern Non-Relativism: Imre Lakatos, Theo Meyering, and Alasdair MacIntyre," *Philosophical Forum* 27 (Fall 1995):37–53. Reprinted by permission.

Chapter 4 is a summary of my first dissertation, at the University of California at Berkeley. I am grateful to Paul Feyerabend, my mentor, for his advice on this project and for much else besides. I also thank Hans Sluga and Gonzalo Munévar. The chapter was published in similar form as "Proliferation of Models and the Quest for Progress in Psychiatry," *Explorations in Knowledge* 1 (1984):89–110.

Chapter 5 is an overview of the first half of my book *Beyond Liberalism and Fundamentalism: How Modern and Postmodern Philosophy Set the Theological Agenda* (Valley Forge, Pa.: Trinity Press International, 1996). This book began as a series of lectures at Rice University. I thank Werner Kelber for the invitation; James McClendon and Charles Scalise were especially helpful in this project.

Chapter 6 is a reworking of a paper presented to the Society of Christian Philosophers at Wheaton College in January, 1994. A version of that paper will be published as "Philosophical Resources for Postmodern Evangelical

Theology," *Christian Scholar's Review* 26 (Winter 1996-1997). Reprinted by permission.

Chapter 7 was originally published as part of "Textual Relativism, Philosophy of Language, and the baptist Vision," in Stanley Hauerwas, Nancey Murphy, and Mark Nation, eds., *Theology Without Foundations* (Nashville, Tenn.: Abingdon Press, 1994), 245–270. Comments by Terry Tilley and James Dunn-Smith were particularly helpful.

Chapter 8 originated as a paper presented at a conference on rationality and spirituality at California State University, Fullerton, in March 1993.

Chapter 9 was originally presented as the plenary address at a regional meeting of the American Academy of Religion in St. Paul, Minnesota, in April 1995. I received helpful responses from faculty members at the University of St. Thomas, St. Paul, when I gave the paper there in February 1996. Some of the material in this paper appears in similar form in a book written with George F.R. Ellis, *On the Moral Nature of the Universe: Theology, Cosmology, and Ethics* (Minneapolis: Fortress Press, 1996).

Chapter 10 is a revision of a paper written for a conference on evolution and divine action sponsored by the Vatican Observatory and the Center for Theology and the Natural Sciences at Castel Gandolfo, Italy, in June 1996. I thank William Alston and the participants at that conference for helpful suggestions.

I thank Dennis Patterson at the School of Law, Rutgers University, for his encouragement in pursuing this project. Were it not for him, I would have given up the attempt to capture the term 'postmodern' to describe the changes in Anglo-American thought that are examined here.

Finally, thanks to the staff of Westview Press for their cheerful and efficient help.

Nancey Murphy

Introduction

Stanley Fish introduces *Doing What Comes Naturally*[1] by warning the reader that the essays, though ostensibly on a variety of topics, all say the same thing. Much the same can be said of this book. Each essay, in its own way, hammers home the point that our Western conceptual scheme, at its most basic level, is in the process of change.

The term 'postmodernity' is now in vogue, and I have taken the risk of using it in the title. It is a risk because French (and some other Continental) thinkers have effectively appropriated it to refer to current work in literary criticism, feminist thought, 'metapsychology.' Despite the modifier 'Anglo-American,' my writings are sure to be associated by some with these trendy moves. I state here and now that I have nothing to do with the Lyotardians, Derridians, De Mannians. Would that they had found a different term, for imagination fails me as I hunt for an alternative, and as the essays following demonstrate, I am not as imaginative as these literary folk.

The reason I persist nonetheless in using the term is that we so badly need it on this side of the Atlantic and English Channel. As I say, drastic changes have occurred in some of the most basic concepts expressed in English. I concentrate here on changes in three areas, designated by the philosophical names attached to each: epistemology, philosophy of language, and metaphysics. My contention is that in the last fifty years whole clusters of terms in each of these domains have taken on new uses, and these changes have radical consequences for all areas of academia and presumably for the living of life as well. The following essays trace these consequences only in the three areas with which I am most familiar: ethics, philosophy of science, and philosophy of religion (with a concentration in Christian thought).

The purpose of this book, then, is to attempt to appropriate the term 'postmodern' to describe emerging patterns in Anglo-American thought and to indicate their radical break from the thought patterns of Enlightened modernity. A deeper concern than that of terminology can be expressed as follows: I hope to induce a gestalt switch in the reader's perception of recent (Anglo-American) intellectual history. If now the reader sees continuity or gradual change from Carl Hempel to Karl Popper to Thomas Kuhn; from

---

[1] Stanley Fish, *Doing What Comes Naturally* (Durham, N.C.: Duke University Press, 1989), ix.

1

C. I. Lewis or Rudolf Carnap to W.V.O. Quine; from Gottlob Frege to J. L. Austin and Ludwig Wittgenstein (and 'back' to Michael Dummett and Saul Kripke), I hope to make radical discontinuity appear. I make the bold claim, already implicit in the term 'postmodern,' that the discontinuity will sooner or later be recognized by historians to be of equal magnitude as that between Descartes and his Jesuit teachers.

My own gestalt switch came about serendipitously. My husband and colleague, James McClendon, and I were invited to a conference on "the church in a postmodern world" (sponsored by the Trinity Institute of Manhattan in 1987). The speakers included George Lindbeck, historical theologian at Yale; Diogenes Allen, philosopher at Princeton Theological Seminary; and Robert Bellah, sociologist at the University of California, Berkeley. We asked ourselves the following question: if these speakers represent postmodernity, then what is the substance of their differences from modern predecessors? Our sense was that the nature of the questions, the very terms of the arguments, had indeed shifted and that a handful of philosophers could be credited with the change. In epistemology and philosophy of science, there was the rejection of foundationalism in favor of the holist views of the likes of Quine and Kuhn. In philosophy of language, there was the shift from theories of meaning based on reference or representation to a focus on the social uses of language, found especially in the works of Austin and Wittgenstein. In ethics, the shift was the rejection of modern 'generic' individualism in favor of Alasdair MacIntyre's more complex theory of the priority of the social. I argue that there has been a similar revision of views of the relation of parts and wholes reflected in science and other branches of philosophy and thus that a metaphysical shift has occurred—the rejection of modern atomism-reductionism in all its forms.

I just said that the *arguments* have shifted. By this I mean to recognize that modern thought was never monolithic. Rather, typical arguments, for example, between 'mainline' epistemologists and their skeptical opponents (including some contemporary deconstructionists!), tend to presuppose the same basic theory of knowledge—foundationalism. Thus, McClendon pointed out that modern epistemologists could be thought of as falling along a spectrum or axis, with radical skeptics (disappointed foundationalists) at one end and optimistic foundationalists at the other. In philosophy of language, if language ordinarily gets its meaning from what it represents in the world, then some account has to be given of nonfactual forms of discourse such as ethics, aesthetics, and religion. The modern answer has generally been some form of expressivist theory, such as that of the emotivists in ethics. So here we have not so much a spectrum of views but correlative theories of language, both assuming that normative meaning must be referential. Again, the individualists in the modern period have always heard from a minority of theorists who favored the social group as a focus of analysis; however, modern forms of holism have tended to assume the same *generic* view of the individual as their reductionist opponents—the view that individuals are all alike for the purposes of social, political, and ethical theory.

So great was the temptation to stop with these three axes, forming a 'Cartesian coordinate system' for locating modern 'positions,' that we have not added other relevant 'dimensions' to our analysis. The foregoing model allowed us to define as postmodern thinkers who managed to escape the intellectual 'space' thus delimited, without their reverting to premodern categories.

I believe I have now said enough to make it possible to give an account of how the various essays relate to the central thesis of this book and to one another. The first chapter spells out in greater detail the differences between modern and postmodern philosophy just discussed. It concentrates especially on what I call the metaphysical shift exemplified in the rejection of modern individualism; more generally it is the calling into question of reductionism in a variety of contexts. The rest of the essays are grouped into three sections: first, philosophy of science; second, issues relating to theology and philosophy of religion; and third, the relation among science, ethics, and religion.

Part I

If it is the case, as I claim, that we are living through a revolutionary period in philosophy, then we must expect the same sorts of confusion that Kuhn reports among scientists trying to communicate across paradigms. On my reading, the most prominent debate in current philosophy of science concerns scientific (critical) realism. This is exactly the sort of issue we should expect to draw fire since scientific realism is an attempt to salvage the referential/representative theory of language and its close kin, the correspondence theory of truth, despite the antifoundationalist arguments of N. R. Hanson, Stephen Toulmin, Thomas Kuhn, and others. So Chapter 2, "Scientific Realism and Postmodern Philosophy," shows how the discussion of realism is confounded by the failure to distinguish arguments between modern realists and antirealists, on the one hand, from arguments between moderns and postmoderns on the other. The latter are suspicious precisely of the modern epistemological and linguistic assumptions that animate the debate.

Modern epistemology was prone to its own peculiar form of skepticism—if there is no solid foundation, or if logical connections upward from the foundation fail, there is no knowledge. Postmodern holists have a different range of options: degrees of relativism that depend on the extent to which one recognizes competing epistemological systems and on whether any means can be found to arbitrate, in a nonarbitrary fashion, between competing, equally coherent wholes. Paul Feyerabend and his favorite dialogue partner, Imre Lakatos, well represent the extreme positions on this spectrum. In Chapter 3, "Postmodern Antirelativism," I consider the strategies that Lakatos, Alasdair MacIntyre, and Feyerabend's student Theo Meyering have developed for making rational comparisons of competing research programs (traditions), each of which (in holist fashion) contains its own theory of rationality. For those who object to unchecked proliferation of theories, these three philosophers offer the best available antidote.

No one in a postmodern intellectual climate will occupy an extreme antirelativist or absolutist position. Thus, it is worthwhile to consider, with Feyerabend, the possible intellectual benefits of proliferation of theories in science. He argued that if data are theory-laden (an antifoundationalist thesis), then the proliferation of theories will result in increased factual knowledge. Chapter 4, "Postmodern Proliferation and Progress in Science," tests this thesis in the field of psychiatry and clinical psychology. The last section of this chapter sketches a nonreductionist model of mental illness, thus illustrating the metaphysical aspect of postmodernity—its metaphysical holism.

Part II

Chapter 5, "Beyond Modern Liberalism and Fundamentalism," shows how the criteria for modern and postmodern thought developed herein can be used to understand the development of theological programs. The foundationalism, representationalism, and reductionism of modern thought produce recognizable patterns in modern theology and, in fact, go a long way toward accounting for the acrimonious split between liberals and conservatives that has plagued the American Protestant religious landscape. I argue that the 'resources' of modernity actually produced insuperable difficulties for theologians.

Chapter 6, "Philosophical Resources for Postmodern Conservative Theology," considers the views of self-designated "postliberal" theologians such as George Lindbeck and Ronald Thiemann and then offers some suggestions regarding the way ahead for theologians of a more conservative stripe. I claim that the Anglo-American postmodern intellectual world offers exciting new possibilities for solving theological problems created by modern philosophy.

One of the most intriguing issues for theologians in a postmodern age is the question of how to interpret the Bible. There are a variety of contributions to literary criticism that, if taken seriously, result in a proliferation of interpretations of texts. I argue in Chapter 7, "Postmodern Philosophy of Language and Textual Relativism," that Austin's philosophy of language offers useful guidance for evading the worst forms of textual relativism.

Part III

A book on philosophy of science and philosophy of religion may seem a peculiar mix of topics. However, I claim that it only appears odd in our day because of specific turns taken by modern thinkers. For example, designing a normative theory of language to fit scientific discourse resulted in the relegation of religious language to the dismissive category of mere self-expression. Then arguments were made to the effect that the language of science and the language of religion, being of such different types, were incommensurable. Thus, although it cannot be said (yet) that the postmodern era will be one in which religion and science are reunited, it can certainly be said that the sharp dichotomy between them is a modern phenomenon. I hope to begin making a case for this reunion in Part III. My claim in Chapter 8, "Theology and Postmodern Philosophy of Science," is that the more sophisticated holist theories of knowledge developed recently (especially by Lakatos) make it possible to argue for striking parallels between theological and scientific reasoning.

The last two chapters together contribute to a hierarchical model for conceiving of the relations among the sciences, both natural and social, and then locate both ethics and theology in the hierarchy as necessary elements for any complete account of reality. The inclusion of ethics among the sciences will appear as misguided to moderns as does the inclusion of theology.

Chapter 9, "Theology and Ethics in the Hierarchy of the Sciences," goes beyond claims for the 'value-ladenness' of the social sciences to claims for the 'theology-ladenness' of the social sciences' basic presuppositions about the character of humans in society. Chapter 10, "Supervenience and the Nonreducibility of Ethics to Biology," develops antireductionist themes introduced in Chapter 1 and uses them to address the claims of the sociobiologists. A brief Postscript ties up some loose ends.

1 • • •

Anglo-American Postmodernity

1. Introduction

The term 'postmodern' is being used more and more frequently in a variety of intellectual circles. It is most often associated with deconstructionism, a literary theory–cum–philosophy whose best-known proponent is French critic Jacques Derrida. Deconstructionism's line of descent is Continental: from Friedrich Nietzsche and also from Swiss linguist Ferdinand de Saussure, whose work gave birth to structuralism.

But is postmodernity merely a Continental phenomenon, or does it make sense to speak as well—or instead—of Anglo-American postmodernity?[1] I argue that it does; it is becoming fairly common on this side of the Atlantic as well to note the passing of modernity. For instance, in Stephen Toulmin's intriguing book *Cosmopolis,* he glances at changes in art, architecture, and politics but concentrates his gaze on epistemology.[2] Modern thought, he says, was characterized by a drive for certitude and universality.

We are now at the point in history where we can see the emphasis on certitude and universality as a particular, historically conditioned episode in Western thought. But what comes next? Toulmin urges a return to the values of the Renaissance: interest in the particular, the timely, and the local. He urges especially the replacement of the seventeenth-century ideal of scientific-logical rationalism with the reasonableness of the Renaissance, which was modest about its own powers and required tolerance of social, cultural, and intellectual diversity. But *is* this the way ahead?

---

[1] I suggest in Chapter 7 that deconstructionism presupposes theories of language that, from an Anglo-American point of view, are typically modern.

[2] Stephen Toulmin, *Cosmopolis: The Hidden Agenda of Modernity* (New York: Free Press, 1990).

7

I claim that the groundwork has already been laid for a postmodern world-view very different from both modern and Continental 'postmodern' thought. The first task of this chapter is to provide a brief characterization of philosophical modernity. Against this background we are able to recognize assorted philosophical moves of the past forty or so years as genuinely *post-modern*. Here we find a way ahead that is in fact modest, that recognizes genuine diversity in intellectual matters but without succumbing to the relativistic conclusions of the Continental postmodernists.

I suggest that modern thought in general, especially modern philosophy, has been characterized by three interrelated positions.

1. Foundationalism in epistemology
2. Referentialism in philosophy of language
3. Atomism and reductionism in metaphysics

This general characterization of modern thought was first worked out in an article I wrote with James Wm. McClendon Jr. titled "Distinguishing Modern and Postmodern Theologies."[3] We claimed that modern thought could be 'mapped' along three interdependent axes: the epistemological axis, representing degrees of optimism regarding the foundationalist project; the linguistic axis, with poles representing referential versus expressivist or emotivist views of language; and what we called the metaphysical axis, where we located thinkers according to their individualist or collectivist accounts of human action and identity. We then argued that thinkers who had managed to transcend all three of these polarities or debates, but without simply returning to premodern modes of thought, should be counted as postmodern.

In this chapter I intend to revisit all of these issues. My chief focus, however, is to make good on the claim that the individualism of the modern period is indeed but an instance of a general *metaphysical* stance and, in addition, to suggest that the epistemology and philosophy of language that we designated as 'modern' are deeply influenced by the same metaphysical assumptions. I argue that metaphysical atomism and reductionism first became embodied in natural science, but very quickly spread, via metaphorical or catachretical extension, to the rest of modern thought.[4] Thus, I am able to claim that (Anglo-American) postmodernity is at its root a rejection of reductionism in all its forms, including rejection of reductionism in science, but also the substitution of holism for foundationalism in epistemology and

---

[3] Nancey Murphy and James Wm. McClendon Jr., "Distinguishing Modern and Postmodern Theologies," *Modern Theology* 5 (April 1989):191–214.

[4] Catachresis is the deliberate use of language from one sphere to describe something in another sphere. Here the language of physics ('atoms,' 'forces') is used in the spheres of political theory, psychology, epistemology, and philosophy of language.

the substitution of a focus on use in social context for a referential account of meaning that was in its own way atomistic.

2. Modern Thought

2.1. Foundationalism

Foundationalism is a theory about knowledge. More specifically, it is a theory about how claims to know can be justified. When we seek to justify a belief, we do so by relating it to (basing it on, deriving it from) other beliefs. If these other beliefs are called into question, then they, too, must be justified. Foundationalists insist that this chain of justifications must stop somewhere; it must not be circular, nor must it constitute an infinite regress. Thus, the regress must end in a 'foundation' of beliefs that cannot themselves be called into question.[5]

The plausibility of the foundationalist theory of knowledge comes from a metaphor: knowledge as a building. Upper stories are built upon lower stories, but the whole structure collapses if it has no solid foundation. This metaphor has so thoroughly imbued our thinking that we can scarcely talk about knowledge without hints of it: good arguments are well grounded and solidly constructed; suspicions are unfounded or baseless; disciplines that explore presuppositions are called foundational.

Some historians (Richard Rorty, for example) trace foundationalism all the way back to Plato, but more commonly it is identified with modern philosophy, beginning with René Descartes. It was a fateful day when Descartes, forced by cold weather to stay in a warm room in Germany, examined his "ideas," while meditating on the architecture visible through his window. "It is true," he said,

> that we never tear down all the houses in a city just to rebuild them in a different way and to make the streets more beautiful; but we do see that individual owners often have theirs torn down and rebuilt, and even that they may be forced to do so when the building is crumbling with age, or when the foundation is not firm and it is in danger of collapsing. By this example I was convinced that . . . as far as the opinions which I had been receiving since my birth were concerned, I could not do better than to reject them completely for once in my lifetime, and to resume them afterwards, or perhaps accept better ones in their place, when I had determined how they fitted into a rational scheme. And I firmly believed that by this means I would succeed in conducting my life much

---

[5] For additional details, see Richard Rorty, *Philosophy and the Mirror of Nature* (Princeton: Princeton University Press, 1979), 157–163; Jeffrey Stout, *The Flight from Authority* (Notre Dame, Ind.: University of Notre Dame Press, 1981), 3–5; and Ronald Thiemann, *Revelation and Theology* (Notre Dame, Ind.: University of Notre Dame Press, 1984), 44–46.

better than if I built only upon the old foundations and gave credence to the principles which I had acquired in my childhood without ever having examined them to see whether they were true or not.[6]

Modern philosophy from then on has been captivated by the architectural picture. This notion of tearing down the house (rejecting tradition) is what distinguishes Descartes's foundationalism from earlier quests for certain knowledge.

Why the anxiety? Why the perceived need to justify all received knowledge? We are so much the children of the modern worldview that this question may not even arise. Yet there is a historical explanation. Toulmin offers plausible speculations regarding the cultural climate that gave foundationalism its appeal. Descartes lived through the Thirty Years' War (1618–1648). The bloodshed and chaos that followed upon differences of belief lent urgency to the quest for universal agreement; the epistemologist could render a service to humanity by finding a way to produce such agreement. Science and religion stood for two paths to knowledge: pure reason versus tradition. If human reason was a faculty shared universally, then a new structure built on the deliverances of human reason must garner universal assent. So since Descartes's time, the ideal of human knowledge has focused on the general, the universal, the timeless, the theoretical—in contrast to the local, the particular, the timely, the practical.[7]

One can do a tidy job of summing up the main currents in epistemology since Descartes by noting successive answers to two questions: What is the nature or source of foundational beliefs—clear and distinct ideas, impressions, sense data? What kind of reasoning is to be used for the construction—deductive, inductive, constructive, hypothetico-deductive?

2.2. Referentialism

If we look at theories of language developed by philosophers in the modern period, the predominant view of language can be described as atomistic and referential (or representative). That is, complex utterances were to be understood by analyzing them into their simplest parts, and the meaning of the parts was to be accounted for in terms of reference.

For John Locke, words referred to or represented ideas—"*words in their primary or immediate signification, stand for nothing but the ideas in the mind of him that uses them.*"[8] Ideas, in turn, stood for things; simple ideas were

---

[6] René Descartes, "Discourse on Method," in *Discourse on Method and Meditations,* trans. Laurence J. Lafleur (1637; reprint Indianapolis: Bobbs-Merrill, 1960), 11–12.

[7] Toulmin, *Cosmopolis,* chap. 1.

[8] John Locke, *An Essay Concerning Human Understanding* (1690; reprint, New York: Dover, 1959), 3.2.2.

"perfectly taken from the existence of things" (3.4.17). Simple ideas were compounded to form complex ideas; sentences represented the connections the mind makes between ideas. Locke's approach stands behind much modern philosophy of language.

Gottlob Frege has been one of the most significant influences on modern philosophy of language. Frege was largely responsible for banishing "psychologism" from theories of language—that is, for the rejection of views such as Locke's that understood language first in relation to mental contents. Michael H. McCarthy points out that when the sense of a sentence is made dependent on individual feelings or beliefs, it loses its ability to provide a basis for collaboration. "If shared inquiry is to be possible, there must be a common ground of objective meaning independent of the psychological reactions of the participants. The sense of language must be separated from the private impressions caused by its use."[9] Here we find another instance of the drive for universal agreement that lies behind foundationalism.

Frege's famous distinction between *Sinn* (sense) and *Bedeutung* (reference) might have distracted modern philosophers from their preoccupation with reference since Frege claimed that *sense* was the primary meaning of 'meaning.' However, he understood the sense of a word in terms of the contribution it makes to the *truth* of sentences, and the truth of sentences, for Frege, depended only on its *reference*—so reference returned through the back door.

The logical atomists—Bertrand Russell, Ludwig Wittgenstein in his early work, and others—followed Frege in supposing that philosophy of language was to be done by devising formal artificial languages rather than by analyzing natural languages. They also followed Frege in recognizing the sentence or proposition as the smallest unit of meaningful discourse. Thus, in place of a referential theory of the meaning of words, we have a representative or 'picture' theory of the meaning of sentences or propositions.

With this very clear expression of a referential-representative approach to language came the recognition that whole realms of discourse, such as religion, ethics, and aesthetics, could not be treated in the same manner as factual discourse. This prompted the elaboration of a second theory of language—or, more precisely, the elaboration of a theory of *second-class* language. For example, A. J. Ayer, in his influential popularization of logical positivism, claimed that ethical judgments, having no factual meaning, serve merely to *express* the attitudes or moral sentiments of the speaker.[10] Hence, we may call this the expressivist theory of language. In general, it stated that language that is not factually meaningful, if significant at all, merely expresses the attitudes, intentions, or emotions of the speaker.

---

[9] Michael H. McCarthy, *The Crisis of Philosophy* (Albany: State University of New York Press, 1990), 51.

[10] A. J. Ayer, *Language, Truth, and Logic* (1936; reprint, New York: Dover, n.d.), 107.

2.3. Reductionism

2.3.1. From Metaphysics to Natural Science When we think of the transition from medieval to modern science, the Copernican revolution is most likely to come to mind. However, the transition from Aristotelian hylomorphism to atomism has had equally significant cultural repercussions. Yet probably because the transition happened more gradually—finally completed in biology only in the nineteenth century—this change has received less attention.

Galileo can be given as much credit for this change as for the revolution in astronomy. He was one of the first modern scientists to reject the Aristotelian theory that all things are composed of matter and form in favor of an atomic or corpuscular theory. His version of atomism hypothesized that all physical processes could be accounted for in terms of the properties of the atoms, which he took to be size, shape, and rate of motion.

The success of the subsequent system of physics developed by Isaac Newton depended on the specification of *inertial mass* as the essential property of atoms and on the development of the concept of a force. Atomism was extended to the domain of chemistry by Antoine-Laurent Lavoisier and John Dalton, who made great headway in explaining the phenomena of chemistry on the assumption that all material substances possessed mass and were composed of corpuscles or atoms. This was a striking triumph for the atomic theory of matter and for *reductionism*, that is, the strategy not only of analyzing a thing into its parts, but also of explaining the properties or behavior of the thing in terms of the properties and behavior of the parts.

The atomist-reductionist program continues to bear fruit in contemporary physics, as particle accelerators have made it possible to continue the quest for true 'atoms' in the philosophical sense: the most basic, indivisible constituents of matter. Silvan Schweber states: "Unification and reduction are the two tenets that have dominated fundamental theoretical physics during the present century." He goes on: "With Einstein the vision became all-encompassing. Einstein advocated unification coupled with a radical form of theory reductionism. In 1918 he said, 'The supreme test of the physicist is to arrive at those universal elementary laws from which the cosmos can be built up by pure deduction.' . . . The impressive success of the enterprise since the beginning of the century has deeply affected the evolution of all the physical sciences as well as that of molecular biology."[11]

The increasingly successful reduction of chemistry to physics raised the expectation that biological processes could be explained by reducing them to

---

[11] Silvan Schweber, "Physics, Community, and the Crisis in Physical Theory," *Physics Today* (November 1993):35.

chemistry and thence to physics. There have been a series of successes here, beginning in 1828, when the synthesis of urea refuted the claim that biochemistry was essentially distinct from inorganic chemistry, and continuing in current study of the physics of self-organizing systems and their bearing on the origin of life. The philosophical question of whether biology could be reduced to chemistry and physics, or whether the emergence of life required additional metaphysical explanation in terms of a "vital force," was hotly debated, but vitalism had almost disappeared by the end of the nineteenth century.

In the twentieth century, a variety of research projects have attempted to carry reductionism into the human sphere. There have been some impressive advances in understanding human psychology by means of biological reduction. We now have clear evidence for biochemical factors in many mental illnesses (see Chapter 3); neuropsychologists have localized a surprising variety of cognitive faculties in the brain;[12] theories regarding genetic determination or influence on a wide assortment of human traits are bound to proliferate with the progress of the Human Genome Initiative. Thus, much of modern science can be understood as the development of a variety of scientific research programs that in one way or another embody and spell out the consequences of what was originally a metaphysical theory. It has been the era in which Democritus has triumphed over Aristotle.

In addition, the reductionist assumption has produced a model for the relations among the sciences. The general tendency of modern science has increasingly been to see the natural world as a total system and to conceive of it in terms of a hierarchy of levels of complexity, from the smallest subparticles (at present, quarks and leptons), through atoms, molecules, cells, tissues, organs, organisms, and societies, to ecosystems and the universe as a whole. Corresponding to this hierarchy of levels of complexity is the hierarchy of the sciences: physics studying the simplest levels; chemistry; the various levels of biology; psychology, understood as study of the behavior of complete organisms; sociology; and then perhaps ecology and cosmology. (The organization of the hierarchy above biology becomes problematic; see Chapter 10, section 3.) Versions of the hierarchy of the sciences go all the way back to Thomas Hobbes at the beginning of the modern period. However, the logical positivists, with their program in the 1920s and 1930s for the unification of science, did a great deal to popularize this hierarchy.

Causation in this view is 'bottom-up'; that is, the parts of an entity are located one rung *downward* in the hierarchy of complexity, and it is the parts

---

[12] See, for example, Paul M. Churchland, *The Engine of Reason, the Seat of the Soul: A Philosophical Journey into the Brain* (Cambridge, Mass.: MIT Press, 1995); Gerald M. Edelman, *Bright Air, Brilliant Fire: On the Matter of the Mind* (New York: HarperCollins, 1992); and Antonio R. Damasio, *Descartes' Error: Emotion, Reason, and the Human Brain* (New York: Putnam's Sons, 1994).

that determine the characteristics of the whole, not the other way around. So *ultimate* causal explanations are thought to be based on laws pertaining to the lowest levels of the hierarchy.

We can distinguish a variety of reductionist theses, all intimately related. *Ontological* reductionism holds that higher-level entities are nothing but complex organizations of simpler entities and is opposed to vitalism and mind-body dualism. *Causal* reductionism holds that ultimate causes (at least in the physical universe) are bottom-up. *Methodological* reductionism holds that the proper approach to scientific investigation is analysis of entities into their parts and that the laws governing the behavior of higher-level entities should be reducible to (shown to be special instances of) the laws of the lower levels. The positivists were especially interested in the reduction of the laws of the higher-level sciences to the laws of physics. The success of methodological reductionism in modern science is what lends credence to these other sorts of reductionism.

The crucial *metaphysical* assumption embodied in this view of the sciences is that the parts of an entity or system determine the character and behavior of the whole and not vice versa. This is metaphysical atomism-reductionism.

2.3.2. Catachretical Extensions of Atomism   The atomism that for the Greeks was pure metaphysics has become embodied in a variety of scientific research programs; it has become scientific theory. Yet, I suggest, it continues to function metaphysically, though in a looser sense than that in which Democritus's thesis is metaphysical. Modern thought, not only in the sciences but also in ethics, political theory, epistemology, philosophy of language, has tended to be *atomistic*—that is, to assume the value of analysis, of finding the 'atoms,' whether they be the human atoms making up social groups, atomic facts, or atomic propositions.

In addition, modern thought has been *reductionistic* in assuming that the parts take priority over the whole—that they determine, in whatever way is appropriate to the discipline in question, the characteristics of the whole. Thus, the common good is a summation of the goods for individuals; psychological variables explain social phenomena; atomic facts provide the justifying foundation for more general knowledge claims; the meaning of a text is a function of the meaning of its parts.

It is widely recognized that the individualism of much political philosophy in the modern period was based on the attempt to extend Newtonian reasoning to the sphere of the social:

> The ideas of Newton, Hobbes, and Locke suggested to the social philosophers of the Enlightenment, like Helvétius and Holbach, that individuals in societies were not only analogous to the atomic constituents of physical wholes but were themselves intelligible in terms of a system of quasimechanical, hedonic attractions and repulsions. Given knowledge of the laws of human psychological

mechanics, individual dispositions could be molded to a socially consistent pattern by an appropriate set of ideal institutions.[13]

So while early modern physicists were developing an atomist account of matter, Hobbes was devising atomist accounts of ethics and politics. Hobbes is best known for his development of social contract theory. The atomistic individualism of social contract theory is clear: individuals are logically (if not temporally) prior to the commonwealth, which is an artificial 'body.' Social facts such as moral obligation and property rights come into existence only as a result of the social contract, which is motivated by the individual drive for self-preservation.

The atomist metaphors and the inherent reductionism of Hobbes's account of individual dispositions, affections, and manners are equally striking. Wallace Matson describes the whole of Hobbes's view of reality as follows: "To the question 'What is there to philosophize about?' Hobbes' answer is starkly simple: Bodies. . . . Bodies move. In doing so they move other bodies; that is all that happens."[14]

Thus, in giving an account of sensation, Hobbes emphasizes the effects of the motions of matter in producing internal motions in the perceiver—motions in the head. Likewise, ratiocination is "motion about the head," whereas pleasure is a "motion about the heart." Motions within the body produce passions. All passions can be resolved into two basic forces: attraction or love and aversion or hatred. Biology, too, is a matter of motion and mechanical causes. Here Hobbes was much influenced by Galen's work on the circulation of the blood.

Matson concludes that for Hobbes the science of motion is the only science:

Geometry Hobbes thought of as the first and most abstract part of science, for he conceived of geometrical figures not as static entities but as paths of motions: the circle as the motion of a point at a fixed distance from another point, the sphere as the motion of a semicircle around its diameter. The second part of philosophy is the contemplation of the effects of moving bodies on one another in altering their mutual motions. Third, we must investigate the causes of seeing, hearing, tasting, smelling, and touching. Fourth, the sensible qualities—such as light, sound, and heat. These Hobbes calls in Aristotelian fashion Physics. Then we may consider more particularly the motions of the mind (i.e., brain): the passions of love, anger, envy, and the like, and their causes, which comprise moral philosophy. Lastly, civil philosophy is the study of the motions of men (including their larynxes and tongues) in commonwealths. (2:288)

---

[13] Stanley I. Benn, "The Nature of Political Philosophy," in Paul Edwards, ed., *The Encyclopedia of Philosophy* (New York: Macmillan, 1967), 6:391.
[14] Wallace Matson, *A New History of Philosophy*, 2 vols. (San Diego: Harcourt Brace Jovanovich, 1967), 2:288.

Here we see already a version of the modern conception of the hierarchy of the sciences.

There are even atomist-reductionist elements in Hobbes's epistemology and theory of language. To understand a concept, one resolves (analyzes) it into its constituents. By synthesis (or composition) one can then understand causal relations. Words are marks that stand for thoughts; these marks or signs are connected together to form speech.

Hobbes's social atomism continues throughout the modern period in later versions of social contract theory. Another clear instance of atomism is the utilitarian account of ethics. Here the *only* concept of the common good is a simple summation of the goods for individuals.

Immanuel Kant's approach to ethics brings out an important feature of modern individualism. One feature of atomic theory is the assumption that when one discovers the true atoms, they will all be alike, essentially interchangeable. That is, the differences in different composite substances are not because there are ultimately different kinds of matter in the universe, but because the identical, interchangeable atoms are arranged differently or are involved in different motions.

The contemporary scientific version of this 'generic' assumption regarding basic particles is expressed by Schweber as follows:

By "approximately stable" I mean that these particles (electrons and nuclei) could be treated as *ahistoric* objects, whose physical characteristics were seemingly independent of their mode of production and whose lifetimes could be considered as essentially infinite. One could assume these entities to be essentially "elementary" point-like objects, each species specified by its mass, spin, statistics (bosonic or fermionic) and electromagnetic properties such as its charge and magnetic moment.[15]

Alex Blair has argued that the modern view of the relation of individuals in society ought, correspondingly, to be called "*generic* individualism" to recognize not only the priority of the individual to society but also the fact that individuals are for such purposes all alike. Thus, the whole is a mere collectivity of identical and interchangeable parts rather than an interaction of parts with different characteristics and complementary functions. Individuals in society are more like marbles in a bag than like parts in a machine.[16] The generic feature of Kant's individualism is the assumption that moral duty for one is, by definition, moral duty for each.

It is important to recognize that not all modern thinkers have been individualists. Georg W. F. Hegel is a notable exception. However, many of the

---

[15] Schweber, "Physics, Community, and the Crisis," 35.
[16] Alexander Blair, "Christian Ambivalence Toward the Old Testament: Corporate and Generic Perspectives in Western Culture" (Ph.D. diss., Graduate Theological Union, 1984).

anti-individualists of the modern period have still retained the generic feature of the mainline position—Karl Marx, for example, in his account of the nature of the social class. Here the class takes priority over the individual, but the class is a mere aggregate of interchangeable parts. Marx promoted his own version of the reduction of the cultural to the material and in this respect also is typically modern.

One factor that has complicated the modern reductionist program has been the recognition of the determinist implications for human behavior when reductionism is coupled with a deterministic account of the laws of physics: if the body is nothing but an arrangement of atoms, whose behavior is governed by the laws of physics, then how can free decisions affect the body? From the very beginning of modernity, there have been two responses. One is a materialist account of the human person that simply accepts the determinism. The other approach is to propose some form of dualism. Dualists have held that essential humanness is associated with the mind and thus is quite independent of the workings of mechanistic nature. Then, of course, the problem of mind-body interaction arises.

Hobbes was thoroughly materialist and accepted the determinist consequences of the reduction of thought and will to physical motions "in the head." The modern dualist account of the person can be traced to Descartes, who argued that material substance was only part of reality. The other basic metaphysical principle was thinking substance. Human bodies were complex machines, but the person—the 'I'—is the mind, which is entirely free.

From dualist roots in Descartes's philosophy has grown the distinction between the natural sciences and the *Geisteswissenschaften* (the social sciences and humanities). One strong tradition throughout the modern period has claimed, prior to and over against the logical positivists' program for the unification of science, that these are two radically different kinds of discipline with different methodologies—one dealing with a mechanistically conceived physical nature, the other dealing with the inner life of the mind and mind's cultural products. The debate over the reducibility of the human sciences continues in contemporary philosophy of the social sciences. Methodological individualists say that social events are the product of aggregates of the actions of individuals, whereas methodological collectivists claim that social wholes obey their own, nonreducible social laws; naturalists hold that social science should aim to reproduce the methodological features of the natural sciences, whereas antinaturalists claim that their subject matter calls for a different methodology.

I believe it is fair to say that most philosophical conceptions of *language* in the modern period have been atomistic. Before Frege, the atoms were generally thought to be words. It is the words that have meaning, because of their association with individual ideas or with objects or classes of objects, whereas sentence meaning is a function of the sentence's constituents. After

Frege, the attention shifts to the sentence or proposition; and so begins the search for atomic propositions.

The most extreme atomism in epistemology appeared in the logical positivists' program. The quest for suitable "protocol sentences" was an attempt to reduce the experiential foundation to its most basic constituents—atomic sentences to describe atomic facts. The manifest failure of Rudolf Carnap's attempt to describe the world in terms of sense qualities at point-instants was one of the factors behind W.V.O. Quine's development of holist theses regarding both meaning and knowledge. It may be the very extremity and thoroughness of the positivists' program that allowed the atomist-reductionist assumptions of modernity to be recognized as assumptions and thereby to be called into question.

2.4. Modern Counterpositions

Before the reader objects that this foundationalist, referentialist, reductionist account of modern philosophy is one-sided, I hasten to point out that, although many modern philosophers can be characterized by their assent to the positions I have described, others can be characterized by reactions against these positive developments, but in ways that share many of the assumptions of their opponents. For example, David Hume's skeptical attack on rationalistic foundationalism is as committed to foundationalism in its own way as is Descartes's positive reconstruction. I have already suggested that Marx's collectivism assumes the generic account of how individuals participate in social groupings. Emotivists in ethics claim that ethical language merely expresses the attitudes of the speaker because they assume that such language would have to have an objective referent in order to possess any other sort of meaning.

So my more nuanced claim is that modern thought has been structured by *debates*—over knowledge, language, and the role of the individual—in which position and counterposition share certain underlying assumptions about the nature of justification, meaning, and the relation between parts and wholes. It is the recent critique and displacement of these underlying assumptions that justifies the claim that modern thought is being supplanted by new, postmodern ways of thinking.

3. An Emerging Postmodern Philosophy

If the positions I have designated as quintessentially modern are closely interrelated, it should not be surprising if the new moves that decisively *shift the debates* in philosophy are also interrelated. We have just seen that atomism in science and metaphysics provided inspiration for modern approaches to knowledge and language, so we may wonder if there is a successor position to atomism that plays a similar role in philosophy of language and epistemology.

My claim in this second half of the chapter is that there are new ways of understanding knowledge, language, and reality itself that are in various senses *holistic* and that *together* constitute a radical enough break with modern atomistic modes of thought to deserve to be called *post*modern. However, not all kinds of holism are postmodern; as I have already intimated, some are merely modern reactions against atomism that share the most basic assumptions of the positions against which they argue.

3.1. Antireductionism in Science and Metaphysics

To see the kind of scientific holism or antireductionism that represents a true break with modernity, we must first distinguish from this authentic break several modern counterpositions. One sort is the denial of *metaphysical* or *ontological* reductionism represented by mind-body dualists and by nineteenth-century vitalists in biology, who argued that something extra needs to be added (a vital force, or entelechy) to get living from nonliving. The other sort of modern reaction accepts the premise that the whole is nothing but the sum of the parts but reverses the priorities and ascriptions of value presumed by the dominant modern position. An example here would be the claim that, as between the social and the individual, it is the social level that is truly 'real,' that individuals apart from social relations are not genuinely human, that individual behavior is socially determined. This is a modern reversal of *causal* reductionism.

Since the atomism of modern thought came from early modern science, it is appropriate that the postmodern challenge to reductionist metaphysics should come from science as well. It is now becoming widely recognized that analysis and reduction provide only a partial understanding of complex entities. Schweber describes a crisis in physical theory brought about by recognition of the failure of the reductionist program:

> A deep sense of unease permeates the physical sciences. We are in a time of great change. . . . The underlying assumptions of physics research have shifted. Traditionally, physics has been highly reductionist, analyzing nature in terms of smaller and smaller building blocks and revealing underlying, unifying fundamental laws. In the past this grand vision has bound the subdisciplines together. Now, however, the reductionist approach that has been the hallmark of theoretical physics in the 20th century is being superseded by the investigation of emergent phenomena. . . .
>
> The conceptual dimension of the crisis has its roots in the seeming failure of the reductionist approach, in particular its difficulties accounting for the existence of objective emergent properties.[17]

---

[17] Schweber, "Physics, Community, and the Crisis," 34, 39.

The demise of reductionism can be attributed to the recognition of several related features of the relations among levels of analysis in science: emergence, decoupling, and top-down causation. 'Emergence' or 'emergent order' refers to the appearance of properties and processes that are describable only by means of concepts pertaining to a higher level of analysis. New levels of order appear that require new levels of description. Neil A. Campbell describes the emergence of complexity in biology as follows:

> With each step upward in the hierarchy of biological order, novel properties emerge that were not present at the simpler levels of organization. These emergent properties result from interactions between components. A molecule such as a protein has attributes not exhibited by any of its component atoms, and a cell is certainly much more than a bag of molecules. If the intricate organization of the human brain is disrupted by a head injury, that organ ceases to function properly even though all of its parts may still be present. And an organism is a living whole greater than the sum of its parts.[18]

The new concepts needed to describe the emergent properties are neither applicable at the lower level nor reducible to (translatable into) concepts at the lower level. The irreducibility of concepts entails the irreducibility of laws. Thus, many say that there are "emergent laws" at higher levels of the hierarchy.

'Decoupling' is a technical term in physics, but it can be used more loosely to describe the relative autonomy of levels in the hierarchy of the sciences. Schweber says, "The ideas of symmetry breaking, the renormalization group and decoupling suggest a picture of the physical world that is hierarchically layered into quasiautonomous domains, with the ontology and dynamics of each layer essentially quasistable and virtually immune to whatever happens in other layers."[19]

So the causal connections among levels in the hierarchy of complexity are being called into question in two ways. First, there are some changes at the microlevel that make no difference at the macrolevel. A familiar example is the behavior of a gas in a container. Some average properties of the gas particles (the microlevel) matter for purposes of description at the macrolevel—average kinetic energy of the molecules is proportional to the temperature of the gas, and the change in momentum of the gas molecules colliding with the walls of the container is related to the pressure of the gas. However, the exact paths of individual molecules do not matter; there is an uncountable

---

[18] Neil A. Campbell, *Biology*, 2d ed. (Redwood City, Calif.: Benjamin Cummings, 1990), 2.

[19] Schweber, "Physics, Community, and the Crisis," 36.

number of microstates that are equivalent at the macrolevel, so changing these has no causal implications at the macrolevel.

Second, while these causal relations from below are being loosened, emergent laws (laws relating variables at the higher level) are coming to be seen as significant in their own right and not merely as special cases of lower-level laws. "A hierarchical arraying of parts of the physical universe has been *stabilized,* each part with its quasistable ontology and quasistable effective theory, and the partitioning is fairly well understood" (38).

If strict causal reductionism is denied and autonomous, higher-level laws governing emergent properties and processes are recognized, the door is opened to an even more thorough rejection of reductionism: the recognition of top-down or whole-part causation. It is now recognized in a variety of sciences that interactions at the lower levels cannot be predicted by a look at the structure of those levels alone. Higher-level variables, some of which cannot be reduced to lower-level properties or processes, have genuine causal impact. Biochemists were among the first to notice this: chemical reactions do not work the same in a flask as they do within a living organism. The science of ecology is based on the recognition that organisms behave differently in different environments. Thus, in general, the higher-level system, which is constituted by the entity and its environment, needs to be considered in a complete causal account.

Donald T. Campbell describes relations within the hierarchical orders of biology as follows:

(1) All processes at the higher levels are restrained by and act in conformity to the laws of lower levels, including the levels of subatomic physics.

(2) The teleonomic achievements at higher levels require for their implementation specific lower-level mechanisms and processes. Explanation is not complete until these micromechanisms have been specified.

But in addition to these reductionistic requirements, he adds:

(3) (The emergentist principle) Biological evolution in its meandering exploration of segments of the universe encounters laws, operating as selective systems, which are not described by the laws of physics and inorganic chemistry, and which will not be described by the future substitutes for the present approximations of physics and inorganic chemistry.

(4) (Downward causation) Where natural selection operates through life and death at a higher level of organisation, the laws of the higher-level selective system determine in part the distribution of lower-level events and substances. Description of an intermediate-level phenomenon is not completed by describing its possibility and implementation in lower-level terms. Its presence, prevalence or distribution (all needed for a complete explanation of biological phenomena) will often require reference to laws at a higher level of organisation as well. Paraphrasing Point 1, all processes at the lower

levels of a hierarchy are restrained by and act in conformity to the laws of the higher levels.[20]

Campbell acknowledges that 'downward causation' (or 'top-down causation') is an awkward term for what he is describing. I hope to shed some light on what one really needs to say here by making a detour through philosophical developments in epistemology, philosophy of language, and ethics.

3.2. Excursus: The Concept of Supervenience

A variety of philosophers have used the concept of *supervenience* to attempt to give naturalistic but nonreductionist accounts of morality and of mental events. Supervenience is a relation between properties of different types or levels such that if something instantiates a property of the higher level, it does so in virtue of (as a noncausal consequence of) its instantiating some lower-level property.[21] In such a case, the higher-level property is said to supervene on the lower. There is no consensus on the proper definition of 'supervenience'; I believe R. M. Hare's use is the most enlightening. In connection with moral ascriptions, Hare writes: "First, let us take that characteristic of 'good' which has been called its supervenience. Suppose that we say, 'St. Francis was a good man.' It is logically impossible to say this and to maintain at the same time that there might have been another man *placed exactly in the same circumstances* as St. Francis, and who behaved in exactly the same way, but who differed from St. Francis in this respect only, that he was not a good man."[22]

A critical ingredient in Hare's understanding is the recognition of the role of circumstances. This, I claim, will turn out to provide the requisite degree of 'decoupling' of the levels of analysis to avoid a confusion of supervenience with identity and thus to explain the failure in some instances of reducibility of the supervenient level to the subvenient level. Thus, I define supervenience as follows: for any two properties A and B, where B is a higher-level property than A, B supervenes on A if and only if something's being A in circumstance c constitutes its being B.

To illustrate, consider the act of killing an animal. Depending on circumstances or context, this lower-level, basic act could constitute a variety of

---

[20] Donald T. Campbell, "'Downward Causation' in Hierarchically Organized Systems," in Francisco J. Ayala and Theodosius Dobzhansky, eds., *Studies in the Philosophy of Biology: Reduction and Related Problems* (London: Macmillan, 1974), 180. See also Roger Sperry, *Science and Moral Priority* (Oxford: Basil Blackwell, 1983), chap. 6. For a summary of the literature, see Arthur Peacocke, *Theology for a Scientific Age*, 2d, enl. ed. (Minneapolis: Fortress Press, 1993), chap. 3.

[21] See Terence E. Horgan, "Supervenience," in Robert Audi, ed., *The Cambridge Dictionary of Philosophy* (Cambridge: Cambridge University Press, 1995), 778–779.

[22] Quoted in ibid., 778; italics added.

higher-level acts: in one circumstance, it could be a religious sacrifice; in another, wanton cruelty; in another, merely the preparation of food. We can add a third layer of description, a moral layer. Presumably under most circumstances, offering sacrifice is morally good, and preparing food is (ordinarily) morally neutral, whereas under any circumstances wanton cruelty is morally wrong. So the property of being an evil act supervenes on the property of being an act of cruelty, and both supervene on the act of killing. As John Heil points out, the supervenience relation is asymmetrical and transitive.[23]

A related point is that higher-level properties or states are "multiply realizable." For example, there are a variety of different basic acts that are capable of constituting the higher-level act of cruelty or of religious sacrifice. We can relate these concepts by saying that there are often a variety of *subvenient* states or properties, each of which is capable of realizing the supervenient state or property.

The value of recognizing both the supervenience relation and the multiple realizability of subvenient states is that it allows us to understand how properties (actions, events) of a *single* system but pertaining to *different* levels of analysis are related. A causal relation is inappropriate (my being cruel to animals does not *cause* me to be morally evil). Nor is identity the proper relation (there are more ways to be morally evil than by the killing of animals, and killing animals is not always wrong).

We now look at uses of the supervenience relation to define what I claim are postmodern versions of linguistic holism, epistemological holism, and ethics. Then we return to the vexing question of causal reductionism.

3.3. Linguistic Holism

I claim that at least two sorts of linguistic holism can be differentiated. One is a typical modern counterposition to linguistic atomism, called semantic holism. The other, paying attention to the context and use of language, thereby recognizes hierarchical levels of analysis and provides an analog to top-down causation in science. There are a variety of versions of semantic holism, but, roughly, it is the thesis that the meanings of all terms or sentences in a language are so interconnected that the meaning of each part is dependent on the meanings of all others.

A radically different sort of holism has appeared in the writings of J. L. Austin and the later Wittgenstein. I claimed previously that the shift from a focus on meaning as reference to a focus on meaning as use (as in the writings of these two philosophers) is a change revolutionary enough to mark the shift from modern to postmodern in philosophy of language. I expect this claim to be controversial since the most influential contemporary philosophers

---

[23] John Heil, *The Nature of True Minds* (Cambridge: Cambridge University Press, 1992), 65.

of language in current Anglo-American philosophy are still very much concerned with meaning and reference. So perhaps I should claim that a revolution in philosophy of language has been narrowly averted!

Wittgenstein's later work and Austin's speech-act theory are postmodern, I claim, not because they deny that language is (sometimes) used to refer to or describe things or states of affairs, but because reference enters only as a function of use. Meaning depends on the role language plays in a system of conventions, both linguistic and nonlinguistic, of practices, performances, "forms of life."[24]

Notice that this approach to language is holistic in its own way, but in a way very different from semantic holism. Wittgenstein is famous for arguing that the meaning of an expression is its use in a language game and that language games are bound up with forms of life. So language is situated in social context, and it is this very different sort of whole, the whole game, or the whole form of life—not the rest of the language—that matters for establishing its meaning.[25]

My claim is that this latter form of linguistic holism is analogous to the rejection of reductionism in science; it involves recognition of a hierarchy of levels, and the different levels employ concepts displaying supervenience relations. This hierarchy of levels is very clear in Austin's distinction among locutionary, illocutionary, and perlocutionary acts. To speak, that is, simply to utter sounds, is only a locutionary act; for example, merely saying some word such as 'out.' The social context (along with an intention related to that context) *constitutes* the locution as an illocutionary act—something one does in uttering the sentence. Thus, saying, "Out" *under proper circumstances* may constitute an umpire's call in a baseball game. Illocutionary acts may also have perlocutionary force. For example, this call may be the third out in the ninth inning and thus *result in* the game ending.

If we think of these acts (or forces, to use Austin's term) as hierarchically ordered, it is clear that the predicate 'is a call in the game' supervenes on the predicate 'is the utterance of the word "out."' We could also say that the very utterance of a recognizable word supervenes on the lower-level act of making a particular sound. The property of *being the call that ended the game* supervenes on the illocutionary act.

The same locution in a different setting (different language game) will almost always constitute an entirely different illocutionary act. Imagine that

---

[24] The relevant works are primarily Ludwig Wittgenstein, *Philosophical Investigations*, trans. by G.E.M. Anscombe (New York: Macmillan, 1953); and J. L. Austin, *How To Do Things with Words* (Cambridge, Mass.: Harvard University Press, 1962).

[25] I take it that Wittgenstein's emphasis on the completeness of language games (e.g., *Investigations*, § 18) and the claim that all one needed to know to understand an expression was the way it figured in a language game were intended to *block* the sort of semantic holism found in his *Tractatus*—the assumption that to understand one proposition is necessarily to understand a *whole* language.

the setting involves a wet dog padding into the kitchen. This example shows that there is no bottom-up determination of illocutionary acts by locutionary acts. Also, whether the dog indeed reverses course (Austin's perlocutionary effect) depends on yet a broader set of circumstances; for example, how well trained it has been in the past. Notice that there are both constitutive and causal relations involved. The locutionary act of shouting "Out" *constitutes* under circumstances *c* the illocutionary act of ordering the dog out. The illocutionary act of ordering the dog out *causes* the dog to leave under circumstances *c'* and thereby *constitutes* the higher-order acts of keeping the dog out and keeping the kitchen clean. At both levels, the higher-order act was multiply realizable. "Scat!" might have served as well as "Out!" and pitching a bone out the door might have served as well as shouting.

The important thing to notice is the *simultaneous contribution* to the illocutionary act by the locutionary act and by the setting with its rules or expectations. It is the setting of the baseball game that makes 'Out!' a call, that sets up the possibility for the call to mean anything at all: "As actions rise in grade to the level of meaningful human utterance they necessarily rise also to a setting in complex human structures (languages, linguistic institutions) and occur in connection with complex human practices in such a way that their meaning presupposes these structures and practices."[26]

Yet the call-in-context has one meaning and not another because of the specific word uttered. The social context makes the umpire's judgment a possible move but does not determine what that judgment will be. This is determined (in the happy case) by the way the world is. Out is still out and not in, and this difference makes a difference to the outcome of the game. So interpreters of Anglo-American postmodern philosophy of language are wrong to conclude that because reference has been rejected as the sole source of meaning, the way the world is has no bearing on what we may legitimately say.

We might say that the whole is partially constitutive of the part, whereas the part acts upon (affects, partially determines) the whole. In this light we can see that modern forms of reductionism and their modern counterpositions are simplistic in that they assume a linear model: either part determines whole, or whole determines part. Consequently, I wish to distinguish what I call 'top-down holism' (as in Austin's theory) from 'flat holism,' which fails to take into account this interaction of levels of analysis necessitated by broader sets of circumstances—circumstances of a different type or level.

Most, if not all, versions of semantic holism are of the flat type since they recognize only widespread interaction among entities of the same level: meanings of words or sentences. Flat semantic holism represents a typically

---

[26] James Wm. McClendon Jr. and James M. Smith, *Convictions: Defusing Religious Relativism* (Valley Forge, Penn.: Trinity Press International, 1994), 52.

modern way of thinking. It is interesting in light of this claim that Ernest Lepore, coauthor of an overview of positions on semantic holism,[27] defines it in terms of *representation*. Semantic holism is "a metaphysical thesis about the nature of representation on which the meaning of a symbol is relative to the entire system of representations containing it."[28] This supports my thesis that such forms of semantic holism are merely modern counterpositions to referential/representative atomism.

3.4. Postmodern Epistemological Holism

Perhaps the clearest and cleanest break with modern thought is the replacement of foundationalism by holism. If the story of modern philosophy has been that of a quest for certain and universal knowledge it is a sad story, for it has yielded a series of disappointments. Ideas that were clear and distinct to Descartes appear to others hopelessly vague or just plain false—for example, the premise in his argument for the existence of God stating that "there must be at least as much reality in the total efficient cause as in its effect."[29] Empirical foundations have proved to be less troublesome in themselves, but here the problem of construction looms large. David Hume showed that from a foundation in immediate experience, no certain conclusions could be drawn regarding anything but immediate experiences. So there appears to be an epistemological corollary of Murphy's law at work: whenever the foundations are suitably indubitable, they will turn out to be useless for justifying any interesting claims; when we do find beliefs that are useful for justifying the rest of the structure, they always turn out to be questionable.

Two other internal problems have undermined (note the metaphor!) the foundationalist project. One is that beliefs that are in fact usable for purposes of justification often turn out to presuppose beliefs that belong to the upper stories of the building. For example, scientific data are now widely recognized to be theory-laden, dependent upon theories of instrumentation and theoretical interpretation. Thus, the foundationalist picture of linear reasoning (bottom to top) is an oversimplification; if one of the rationales for having a foundation was to avoid circular reasoning, this is a devastating criticism.

Second, Descartes's supposition that it was possible to begin philosophy with a clean slate turns out to have been mistaken. One thing he failed to doubt was the wealth of knowledge (or error) enshrined in language (recall the connection between 'causation' and 'reality' in the premise just quoted).[30]

---

[27] Jerry Fodor and Ernest Lepore, *Holism: A Shopper's Guide* (Oxford: Basil Blackwell, 1992).

[28] Ernest Lepore, "Semantic Holism," in Audi, ed., *The Cambridge Dictionary of Philosophy*, 724.

[29] René Descartes, *Meditations*, in Lafleur, trans., *Discourse*, 97.

Also, reasonably to call a belief into question requires reasons, and those reasons must be unquestioned, at least for the time. For instance, one of Descartes's most powerful arguments against the reliability of sensory knowledge was based on the supposition that he might be dreaming—but this presupposes that there are such things as dreams. Only one beguiled by a picture could imagine that the whole had been called into question by means of such arguments.

Just as modern epistemology was dominated by an image, that of a building needing to be supported, so postmodern epistemology is dominated by a picture: W.V.O. Quine's image of knowledge as a web or net. There are no sharp distinctions among kinds of beliefs in the web, and so there is no distinction between basic (foundational) beliefs and nonbasic beliefs. Beliefs differ only in their 'distance' from experience, which provides the 'boundary conditions' for knowledge. The requirement of consistency transmits experiential control throughout the web.[31]

Now, I am counting Quine as postmodern, yet I am often surprised to hear it said that his view is no different from those of modern coherentist theorists. This suggests that there are two versions of epistemological holism and that Quine is being read as a proponent of a *flat* holism.

However, the holism of much contemporary philosophy of science (and, I suggest, Quine's own position) is a top-down holism. Here the hierarchy is one of both interpretation and justification (and involves meaning-truth holism as well). It is widely recognized that data are not just *given*, as the etymology of the word would suggest; they are made ('facts' comes from *facere*) by means of their interpretation in light of "ideals of natural order" (Toulmin) or theoretical assumptions (Hanson, Kuhn). In addition, the role of data in supporting a particular scientific theory is justified by means of theories of instrumentation—those theories that go into construction of the instruments by which the data were obtained (Kuhn, Lakatos).

Thus, it is the theoretical structure (paradigm, research program) that serves as a context for interpreting the observations or experimental results and thus *constitutes* them as supporting evidence for the theoretical structure. But just as the context of the baseball game cannot alone determine the content of the umpire's call, neither does the theoretical structure determine the content of the facts that support it.

There is another level in the hierarchy of complexity of science itself: theories of scientific rationality constitute certain kinds of relations between a theory and a set of facts as justificatory or confirmatory relations. So, for instance, before the recognition of hypothetico-deductive reasoning as a

---

[30] See Matson, *A New History*, 2:280.
[31] See W.V.O. Quine, "Two Dogmas of Empiricism," *Philosophical Review* 40 (1951):20–43; and W.V.O. Quine and J. S. Ullian, *The Web of Belief*, 2d ed. (New York: Random House, 1978).

legitimate form of scientific inference, the claim that a theory is supported by a fact that *follows from it* would have been seen as a mere logical error, the fallacy of affirming the consequent (see Chapter 3 for an extended treatment of the hierarchical relations between theory justification in science and justification of theories of scientific method).

So we find in these views of science and philosophy of science the same sort of interlevel, asymmetrical, mutual conditioning that I have described in postmodern theories of language. A raw datum (if there is such a thing) is constituted a scientific fact when described in light of a theoretical interpretation of reality. This involves placing it within a broader context, a context including the theories of instrumentation that give it meaning. Yet the theory does not determine the facts; the partial circularity is not vicious. In light of the next higher order of analysis, scientific methodology, those empirical findings become confirmation or justification for the theoretical structure itself. This involves the much broader context of the language game of science itself. The fact that Quine includes logic in the web of beliefs makes it clear that his holism is of this top-down sort rather than mere modern coherentism.

3.5. Postmodern Ethics

I hope that I have succeeded in showing that the individualism of modern ethics and political theory is but an instance of the broader metaphysical assumption of atomism-reductionism. I now intend to make good on the claim that Alasdair MacIntyre's approach to ethics is postmodern in that it moves beyond the atomism/individualism of the modern period.

According to MacIntyre, the modern fact-value distinction (or the attempt to sever moral reasoning from tradition) has led to emotivism and moral relativism. Relativism can be avoided only through the recovery of a corporate view of society that will support the notion of a common good, not reducible to a summation of individual goods. Such a society is no mere collection of like individuals; rather, in virtue of their different roles and historically constituted relationships, individuals participate in it through complementary interaction.

MacIntyre's goal is to provide an account of corporate life that will illumine the concept of *virtue*. If the virtue tradition from Homer, through Aristotle and Aquinas, to Jane Austen can be rescued from internal problems, it will provide a framework for rational ethical debate. He begins with the notion of a *practice*. By 'practice,' he means "any coherent and complex form of socially established cooperative human activity through which goods internal to that form of activity are realized in the course of trying to achieve those standards of excellence which are appropriate to, and partially definitive of, that form of activity, with the result that human powers to achieve excellence, and human conceptions of the ends and goods involved, are systematically extended."[32]

Architecture, farming, physics, medicine, chess, portrait painting, and music are all examples of such practices. Human qualities required for successful participation in practices are *candidates* for virtues. However, not all such qualities are virtues; MacIntyre must find a way to rule out such 'qualities' as skill in bank robbery or seduction.

Thus, definition of a virtue requires consideration of even broader contexts than the practices in which a person may engage. The first is the context of the whole of a single human life; before one can call a quality a virtue, one must see how it and the practice it supports contribute to an individual's life story from birth to death. This means that one must consider how the quality and the practice contribute to that person's life not as self-defined individual but as daughter or son, citizen of a city, member of a profession, tribe, nation.

However, a still broader context of analysis is required. How is one to judge life stories? MacIntyre's answer is that *traditions* generally provide answers to the question "What is the *telos* of human life?" In light of this telos—this answer to the question of what human life is for—life stories can be judged as successful or not in achieving their ultimate goal. The traditions MacIntyre has in mind here are large-scale traditions such as the world religions or philosophical traditions such as Aristotelianism.

MacIntyre's ethical theory escapes the modern individualist-collectivist debate in several ways. First, his account of the role of traditions in human life runs counter to the modern (Hobbesian) assumption that the individual is logically prior to the community. Individuals can be who they are only by virtue of the roles they fill and the ongoing traditions that shape those roles. Second, the opposition between individual and collective good that we find in modern debates has disappeared in MacIntyre's thought. Individual good is unintelligible apart from the goods inherent in practices, which are essentially communal. Finally, as mentioned previously, the generic view of society is abandoned. One's participation in society is by means of roles and skills complementary to others' roles and skills. This view of society is not new; perhaps it has been the most common account over the course of history. As MacIntyre points out, it was Aristotle's view; it also appears to have been the biblical view of community, and it appeared again in modern Romanticism. Thus, alone, it cannot serve as a mark of postmodern thought, and some may accuse MacIntyre of simply attempting to turn back the clock.

However, despite similarities between Aristotle and MacIntyre, the latter's thought exhibits the same sort of top-down holism that I have argued is the

---

[32] Alasdair MacIntyre, *After Virtue*, 2d ed. (Notre Dame, Ind.: University of Notre Dame Press, 1984), 187.

hallmark of Anglo-American postmodern thought. The supervenience relations among the levels of analysis in MacIntyre's ethics can be described as follows. The property of being a virtue supervenes on the property of being an acquired human quality in virtue of the following hierarchical set of circumstances: (C_1) the human quality is necessary for attaining the goods internal to some practice; (C_2) the practice itself is an appropriate practice for the person in question to engage in, given the circumstances of the whole of the person's life story; and (C_3) the person's life story is the story of a good life considered in light of the (or a) tradition's concept of the telos of human life in general.

This hierarchical ethical analysis intersects the holist epistemological hierarchy since to avoid relativism, MacIntyre must next answer the question of how one is to justify a moral tradition. He offers a tradition-constituted metajustification of his reconstruction of the virtue tradition (see Chapter 3; for further discussion of MacIntyre's ethical theory, see Chapters 9 and 10).

3.6. Top-Down Causation Revisited

To expect to undo the reductionist assumptions of the modern period in one short chapter would be unrealistic, but let us see what light we can shed on the issue by employing the concept of supervenience as herein defined. As indicated in section 3.1, the empirical failure of reductionism to give complete scientific accounts is now fairly widely recognized. Yet no one is suggesting a return to vitalism.[33] So the question arises, How can it *not* be the case that the causal laws governing the parts also determine the whole? I believe that the answer to this question must go something like this: different sciences (or different subdisciplines within a science) provide descriptions of reality pertaining to different levels of scale or different levels of complexity. These levels of analysis are necessarily related because they are analyses of more or less the same physical systems.

However, properties or event descriptions at one level are related to properties or event descriptions at the other level neither by equivalence (identity) relations nor by causal relations but rather by supervenience relations. This means that (1) when one considers the relation between a lower-level property and its supervenient property, there will always be the broader circumstances or context, described at the higher level, to be taken into account.

Laws of nature are always statements of relations among variables within a closed or isolated system. That is, there is a tacit ceteris paribus clause: "so

---

[33] There have always been mind-body or body-soul dualists, but this is generally for other reasons than the recent recognition of the failure of the reductionist program in the physical sciences.

long as nothing else interferes with the system." Thus, (2) the laws of the lower level are only sufficient to describe the lower-level system in isolation from any factors pertaining solely to the higher-level system.

A consequence of (1) and (2) is that the lower-level laws cannot always fully describe relations among supervenient variables. Supervenience (as here defined) involves additional variables (the context or circumstances) that may interfere with the closed system presupposed in the application of the lower-level laws. In other words, the reason the laws of physics are not always the sole determinant of complex processes is that they apply in isolated systems, and by definition the level that supervenes involves added variables. These added variables may not themselves be describable in terms of physics and thus not capable of being incorporated into the laws of physics. So the supervenience relation, as here defined, provides just enough *decoupling* of the levels of description to account for the failure in some instances of causal reductionism.

Because it is the context or circumstances involved in the supervenience relation that violate the ceteris paribus clause and disrupt the system described by the lower-level laws, we can see the rationale for referring to the phenomenon as 'whole-part' causation. Since these circumstances are often only describable at the higher level of analysis, we can see the rationale for speaking of this failure of reductionism as 'top-down' or 'downward' causation.

3.6.1. Examples Donald Campbell's example of downward causation in the development of the jaws of worker termites and ants is often repeated in the literature on top-down causation. Here is Campbell's account:

> It seems worthwhile to try to make these points more clearly and strikingly by use of a concrete biological example. Consider the anatomy of the jaws of a worker termite or ant. The hinge surfaces and the muscle attachments agree with Archimedes' laws of levers, that is, with macromechanics. They are optimally designed to apply the maximum force at a useful distance from the hinge. A modern engineer could make little if any improvement on their design for the uses of gnawing wood, picking up seeds, etc., given the structural materials at hand. This is a kind of conformity to physics, but a different kind than is involved in the molecular, atomic, strong and weak coupling processes underlying the formation of the particular proteins of the muscle and shell of which the system is constructed. The laws of levers are one part of the complex selective system operating at the level of whole organisms. Selection at that level has optimised viability, and has thus optimised the form of parts of organisms, for the worker termite and ant and for their solitary ancestors. We need the laws of levers, *and organism-level selection* (the reductionist's translation for 'organismic purpose'), to explain the particular distribution of proteins found in the jaw and *hence* the DNA templates guiding their production. (The occasional nonfunctional mutant forms of jaws conform just as loyally to the laws of levers and biochemistry as do the more frequent functional forms.) Even the *hence* of the previous sentence implies a reverse-directional 'cause' in that, by natural selection,

it is protein efficacy that determines which DNA templates are present, even though the immediate micro determination is from DNA to protein. (It is a further complexity that this determination too is by a back-handed selective-retention process.)[34]

Let us see if we can translate Campbell's account into the terms of supervenience relations. The upward causation here is from the DNA of each individual ant to jaw structure (from the biochemical level to the biological level). Campbell's point is that this alone is an inadequate account since it does not explain the DNA distribution and thus why this particular distribution of proteins is found in the jaw. There are two supervenient levels of description: one is something like "mechanically advantageous distribution of proteins"; the other is something like "adaptive jaw structure," which can be defined only through a consideration of the ant's environmental niche. That is, a particular jaw structure can be described as an *adaptive* jaw structure only within the broader circumstances of the ant's environment—something that cannot be accounted for at the molecular level or even at the mechanical level. (To complete the explanation for the protein distribution, we need to include opportunity for natural selection to have taken place in the past, but this complication is not intrinsic to instances of top-down causation.)

For another example of top-down causation, consider a well-known experiment in which subjects receive a small electrical shock on the back. Depending on what they have been led to expect (their mental set), they will experience the sensation either as a burn or as ice. It is common now to speak of mental events as supervenient on brain or neurological or bodily events. So at the subvenient level, there is a series of physical events including the application of the shock, the transmission of a nerve impulse to the brain, and then the set of brain events that realize the sensation of heat or cold. The experience itself, the supervenient mental event, is an effect of both the original stimulus and whatever environmental events created the subject's mental set. So environment has a top-down causative effect on the mental event since the series of neurological and other physical events alone cannot explain why one person experiences heat and another cold.

3.6.2. Flat Holism Versus Top-Down Holism
It is necessary to emphasize the difference between genuine top-down causation (a variety of top-down holism) and the causal analog of flat holism. Reductionists in the past have always recognized that an entity is often influenced by its environment. The level that considers the interaction between an organism and its environment is a higher level of analysis than that of a study of the organism in abstraction;

---

[34] Campbell, "'Downward Causation,'" 181.

indeed this is a special case of a hierarchy of increasing complexity since the entity in its environment is necessarily a more complex system than the entity alone. The interactions between any specific entity and its environment will be more loosely coupled than those operating within the entity, for it is precisely the tight nature of the internal coupling that leads us to identify the entity as an entity of a particular kind. Consequently, only some of the variables in an environment will affect the entity, and they will usually affect the internal variables of the entity in an imprecise way.

Thus, it is always necessary in characterizing hierarchical systems to define clearly the boundary of each entity, the nature of the environment in which it exists, and the interactions that take place across that boundary—thereby defining the larger system consisting of the entity and its environment. We are always at liberty to consider this system (the entity and its environment) as the system of interest rather than just the entity with which we began. However, this progression, too, will happen in a hierarchical fashion: each environment is itself contained in a larger environment (an ecosystem is contained in the biosphere, which is contained in the solar system, and so on) until we reach the environment that consists of the entire universe (the subject of study of cosmology).[35]

The question at issue between a flat holism compatible with reductionism and a top-down holism is whether the environmental variables can be translated into the concepts of the lower level and thus incorporated into the lower-level analysis. For example, many social psychologists would concede that individuals are affected by the social environment, but these psychologists would point out that the social variables have no effect unless they are realized by means of some individual variable. So, for instance, it is the individual's perception of the social environment (realized neurologically) that is causally efficacious, not the social environment itself.

This sort of reductionist reply is sometimes perfectly in order. The interesting cases are the ones where the environmental variables can be described *only* at the higher level of analysis, when they cannot be reduced to factors at the lower level. *This will be the case when the circumstances involved in the supervenient level are multiply realizable.*

Because there are these two different sorts of cases—when the higher-level circumstances are or are not themselves reducible—the term 'whole-part' causation is not ideal for our purposes. It could equally well apply to cases where the environmental variables are reducible to variables at the subvenient level.

For an illustration, let us return to the example of the electric shock. The circumstances that account for the subject's mental set (the expectation of

[35] I am grateful to George F.R. Ellis for this analysis of the relation between an entity and its environment; see our jointly authored book, *On the Moral Nature of the Universe: Theology, Cosmology, and Ethics* (Minneapolis: Fortress Press, 1996).

either heat or cold) are multiply realizable. That is, the experimenter could set up the subject to expect to be burned in countless ways: by saying that it was an experiment on heat sensitivity, by leaving burn ointment in sight in the room, and so on.

Let us grant the reductionist assumption that whatever these environmental variables may be, they must be realized neurologically. That is, the subject must notice the clues, and that noticing is somehow realized neurologically. However, the reductionist cannot go on to claim that all of the causes of the subject's experience (of heat in this case) are neurological since there is no conceivable law connecting stimulus plus neurological realization of the environmental variables with the realization of the experience. There is no way to describe the disjunctive set of neurological states, all of which constitute the expectation of heat, except by means of this higher-level (mental-level) description, 'the expectation of heat.'

Now, I have just argued that there can be no such laws at the neurological level and that therefore the reductionist's argument for determination at the neurological level cannot go through. This raises a question about the connection between causation and lawful regularity. These concepts have been associated for centuries, but one might still try to save the reductionist program by arguing that absence of laws does not entail absence of causation. That is, there may well be neurological causes even if there is no law that describes them. But this is a point that the antireductionist can gladly grant. If we were to say that there are *no* neurological causes in operation, this would be too strong a claim; it would entirely sever the relations between the mental and physical levels and would go against much empirical evidence. So neurological causes (or at least necessary conditions) there must be. But the sting of reductionism is drawn if we can show that there are no *laws* at the neurological level sufficient to determine all mental events, or put the other way around, if we can show that events at the mental level truly make a difference causally—that the causal relations described at the mental level really matter.

4. Conclusion

In this chapter I have claimed that a variety of significant changes in the Anglo-American intellectual world can be understood as various instances of a new 'thinking strategy.' The predominant strategy in modern science as well as in modern philosophy has been analysis and reduction. Of course, there has always been a reaction that emphasizes the whole, such as in idealism. The new strategy differs from such reactions by recognizing *a complex mutual conditioning between part and whole.* It recognizes different levels of complexity and recognizes as well that no one level can be thoroughly understood in isolation from its neighbors.

This new strategy, I suggest, is essential for an understanding of language, the justification of knowledge claims, the relation between individuals and society, and, finally, the relations among the sciences. It represents a significant enough departure from the predominant modes of modern thought to mark the beginning of a new, postmodern era.

PART I

Philosophy of Science

2 • • •

Scientific Realism and Postmodern Philosophy

1. Introduction

In recent years 'scientific' or 'critical' realism, along with various forms of 'antirealism,' has become a topic of lively debate. The literature makes good reading—authors from a variety of fields displaying skill in argument and employing interesting illustrations from the history of science. My plan in this chapter is to highlight one feature of this debate and then to explain it in a way that I hope will shed fresh light on the entire issue. This feature is the *lack of convergence* in the discussion. There are numerous positions on both sides. "Scientific realism," says Jarrett Leplin, "is a majority position whose advocates are so divided as to appear a minority."[1] There are even more radical divisions among the realists' opponents—each attempt at classification of the antirealists produces different results. For that matter, it is not entirely clear who is on which side. Arthur Fine lists supporters of his own "nonrealist" position that include both avowed realists and antirealists.[2]

The *status* of the realist thesis is subject to debate. Is it a metaphysical claim descendant from earlier denials of idealism? Is it an empirical hypothesis supported by its ability to account for the success of science? Is it a tautology?

Finally (and this is most significant for my thesis), participants in the discussion claim not to understand one another. The purpose of this chapter is to show that the distinction made in this book between modern and postmodern thought will serve to explain a great deal of the confusion in this

---

[1] Jarrett Leplin, ed., *Scientific Realism* (Berkeley and Los Angeles: University of California Press, 1984), 1.
[2] Arthur Fine, "The Natural Ontological Attitude," in ibid., 102–103.

debate. There are both modern and postmodern positions represented here, along with differences between realists and antirealists. Just as scientists tend to "talk past one another" during the transition from one paradigm to another,[3] it is the moderns and postmoderns in this debate who talk past one another.

I mentioned in the Introduction that modern thinkers can be placed on three 'axes,' representing dominant modern position versus modern counter-position. Since these axes (epistemological, linguistic, and metaphysical) are interrelated, it is possible to imagine their intersection mapping a three-dimensional 'space' wherein to locate modern thinkers, using (appropriately) an imaginary Cartesian coordinate system. This space is represented in Figure 2.1.

Modern scientific realists disagree among themselves about their exact location in the upper-right-hand quadrant, distancing themselves from the extreme representationalist position of the "naive realists" but never clear about *how far* they are from the naive realists. I suspect that this ambiguity concerning exactly *how* representative scientific language is supposed to be is what allows critical realists to avoid the horns of a dilemma: If no claims are made for representation—if it is never specified in what sense knowledge corresponds to reality—then the position is safe from all the criticisms of correspondence theories of truth and of representational theories of language, but it is vacuous. But if one does claim to know how the sentence, model, or theory does and does not correspond with reality, one runs into all the same problems that confront the naive realist. Modern opponents of the scientific

FIGURE 2.1   Modern intellectual 'space'

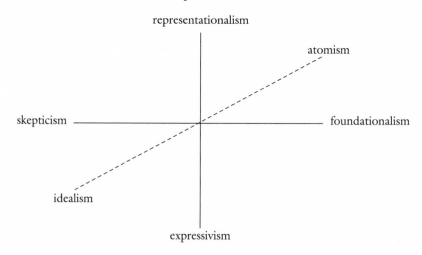

[3] See Thomas Kuhn, *The Structure of Scientific Revolutions,* 2d ed. (Chicago: University of Chicago Press, 1970).

realists can be positioned in the lower-left-hand quadrant. (All are atomists rather than idealists, so we can ignore the z axis.)

In sharp contrast, postmodern participants are searching for ways to express their recognition that there is something wrong with the very terms of the (modern) realist debate. They are attempting to distance themselves entirely from this modern conceptual space.

2. Scientific Realisms

I hope to show in this section that there are both modern and postmodern variants of realism. Although I cannot claim to have examined all the literature, it appears that most realism is modern, whereas opponents attack from both modern and postmodern perspectives.

The difference between modern and postmodern realism can be stated roughly as follows: modern realists (attempt to) speak of the relation between language and the world. Assuming a modern representational or referential theory of language, modern realists seek referents for theoretical terms, employ correspondence theories of truth, or make claims for relations of approximate resemblance between theoretical language and some aspects of the world. Yet unlike the earlier 'naive' realists, 'critical' realists have pulled back some distance from the extreme representational position on the linguistic axis; they highlight the metaphorical nature of scientific language, and they see scientific models and theories not as literal pictures of reality but as partial, tentative representations of what there is. Critical realists are chastened moderns.

Proponents of postmodern realism, in contrast, restrict discussion of the words 'real' and 'exists' to the linguistic framework. An example of postmodern realism can be found in Wilfrid Sellars's work.[4] Sellars proposes that to know molecules exist is to be justified in asserting that there is an x such that it is $\phi_1 \ldots \phi_n$ where $\phi_1 \ldots \phi_n$ is a sufficient condition in the framework of the theory for satisfaction of the concept of a molecule. The theory provides a license to move from statements in the observation language asserting the existence of a certain state of affairs to asserting the presence of molecules. "To know that molecules exist is to be entitled to the observational premises, and to be entitled to the license to move from this premise to the theoretical conclusion. To be entitled to this license is for the theory to be a good theory" (117–118). In short, Sellars defines existence of theoretical entities in terms of correspondence rules and support for theories.

This is just the sort of caution one should expect in light of the writings of Ludwig Wittgenstein and J. L. Austin. Wittgenstein emphasized the fact that one cannot *talk* about the relation between language and the world. In

---

[4] Wilfrid Sellars, *Science, Perception, and Reality* (London: Routledge and Kegan Paul, 1963).

light of his later work especially, one cannot expect there to be a *general theory* about such matters. Austin makes us wary of words like 'real.' We only know what the word means in cases where we can specify imaginable kinds of *failures* to be real, as in real cream versus nondairy creamer.[5] Sellars's work leads us to ask, What could it possibly mean to say that we have a well-confirmed theory involving, say, molecules, which specifies their properties and the observational criteria for their presence, that these criteria are fulfilled, and yet to say that molecules do not exist? In general, to be is to be the value of a variable: postmodern realism confines itself to proposing conventions for the use of the words 'real' and 'exists' in the new territory of science.

Sellars's is a rather unexciting realism, not worth fighting over except, perhaps, when it is seen as the only sensible alternative to the more shocking versions of antirealism. The kind of realism that excites its adherents is the modern kind where claims are made in the material mode about extralinguistic entities and their correspondence with theoretical terms. Realists such as Ernan McMullin claim that the long-term success of a scientific theory gives reason to believe that *something like* the entities and structures postulated in the theory actually exist.[6] Richard Boyd's version asserts that typically and over time, the operation of the scientific method results in the adoption of theories that provide increasingly accurate accounts of the causal structure of the world.[7] A common argument for current versions of modern realism is that only realism can account for the success of science.[8]

Modern realism is interesting; it satisfies the urge that David Pears claims is the source of philosophy—the urge to transcend the sphere of human experience and language.[9] However, I predict this position will become increasingly difficult to defend as modern theories of language become increasingly discredited.

By comparison, postmodern realism seems entirely unproblematic, but relatively uninteresting. As a proposal for use of language in a domain where clear criteria have not yet been established, it may be compared to the following: the debate over the ethics of abortion often turns on the question of when human life begins—at conception, when the fetus is viable, or sometime in between. Some participants in the debate believe there is some fact of the matter to be discovered or accepted; these correspond to modern realists

---

[5] See J. L. Austin, "Other Minds," in J. O. Urmson and G. J. Warnock, eds., *J. L. Austin: Philosophical Papers* (Oxford: Clarendon Press, 1961), 44–84; see esp. 54–57.

[6] Ernan McMullin, "A Case for Scientific Realism," in Leplin, ed., *Scientific Realism*, 8–40; see esp. 14–15.

[7] Richard Boyd, "Scientific Realism and Naturalistic Epistemology," *PSA 1980:* 613–662; see esp. 613.

[8] See, for example, Hilary Putnam, *Meaning and the Moral Sciences* (London: Routledge, 1978).

[9] David Pears, *Wittgenstein* (London: Collins, 1971), 21.

and antirealists. Postmodern realists are like those who would say that there really is no fact to be discovered here. We as yet have no established criteria for applying the term 'living human being' to the unborn. What is needed is a convention defining the point at which we shall say human life has begun.

To someone who believes that there is a fact to be discovered, whether about the beginning of human life or about the relation of scientific terms to the world, the existence of a conventional solution will not be at all appealing—in fact, it may seem outrageous. To others for whom there is no fact at issue, the degree of interest attached to the convention will depend on its repercussions—which are a matter of life and death in the abortion dispute but minimal in the debate over scientific realism. Thus, I claim that Sellars's and other similar proposals are unobjectionable but rather uninteresting.

3. The Controversy

Just as there are both modern and postmodern realist positions, so there are both modern and postmodern antirealist arguments. The stimulus for the entire debate in philosophy of science came from the positivists' instrumentalism. The argument goes like this: theories are underdetermined by observation; thus, an indefinite number of theories can be equally well confirmed and, if treated realistically, would provide a number of possible pictures of unobserved reality. Therefore, only the observation statements can be treated realistically. The theories, then, must be given some other status such as instruments for calculating further predictions from a set of data.[10]

Many current antirealists buy into modern assumptions when they take at face value the question of whether theoretical terms refer or whether well-supported scientific theories are "typically approximately true" in the correspondence sense of 'true.'[11] Thus, McMullin (a critical realist) and Larry Laudan (an antirealist) are both relying on modern modes of thought when they debate whether the history of science supports the claim that successful theories have generally been approximately true and have generally contained referring terms. So here it is skepticism regarding current scientific knowledge that drives the antirealist conclusion, a result of the intersection between theories of language and theories of justification that we find in the correspondence theory of truth.

Between modern advocates and adversaries of realism, there are no communication failures, no confessions of puzzlement at one another's positions. It is in debates between modern realists and postmodern opponents that

---

[10] For a summary of the development of instrumentalism, see Boyd, "Scientific Realism," 650.

[11] Larry Laudan, "A Confutation of Convergent Realism," in Leplin, ed., *Scientific Realism*, 219.

confusion appears. One expression of puzzlement comes from McMullin. He distinguishes between "strong antirealists" (classical instrumentalists) and more recent "weak antirealists," who, he says, are "often hard to place. . . . Their rhetoric is antirealist in tone, but their position often seems compatible with the most basic claims of scientific realism. . . . This gives the weak antirealists' position a puzzling sort of undeclared status."[12]

An instance of communication failure is found in the work of biochemist Arthur Peacocke. Peacocke claims that the greatest threat to the new scientific realism is now the "strong program" in the sociology of science, especially as formulated by David Bloor and Barry Barnes at Edinburgh.[13] The strong program, based on postmodern philosophy of science and Durkheimian sociology of knowledge, maintains that the underdetermination of theory by experience allows room for causal (sociological) explanation of all scientific theories—of true, or accepted, science as well as of false theories. This program regards all of the products of science as social constructions. Critical realists such as Peacocke claim that their own position is a middle way between an untenable naive realism and the sociologists' position, which they regard as a purely relativistic, irrationalist account of science.

The sociologists of science are clearly operating with a postmodern conception of knowledge. Consistent with W.V.O. Quine's "Two Dogmas of Empiricism," Bloor sees all knowledge to be determined by the 'boundary conditions' of experience and (socially transmitted) prior belief. In fact, Bloor's and Quine's descriptions of knowledge could profitably be combined. To Quine's account, symbolized by his net metaphor, Bloor adds precision regarding the kinds of factors that govern decisions about changes necessary to maintain consistency within the web of belief. Also, Bloor points out that social factors often account for "patterns of relevance that connect experiences to some beliefs rather than others" (28). Along with the pragmatic criteria Quine mentions (conservatism and simplicity), the sociologists' research shows the influence of sociological forces on the selection of concepts for organizing and interpreting experience—for example, Bloor notes romantic themes in Thomas Kuhn's theory of scientific development (54–70); Barnes notes the ties between Mendelian genetics and political conservatism in Great Britain from 1890 to 1910 (60–62).

Bloor continues to speak of true and false beliefs, noting that our everyday understanding of truth is in terms of correspondence: when we talk of truth, we suppose that "some belief, judgment or affirmation corresponds to

---

[12] McMullin, "A Case for Scientific Realism," 25–26.
[13] Arthur Peacocke, *Intimations of Reality* (Notre Dame, Ind.: University of Notre Dame Press, 1984). See, for example, David Bloor, *Knowledge and Social Imagery*, 2d ed. (Chicago: University of Chicago Press, 1991); and Barry Barnes, *Interests and the Growth of Knowledge* (London: Routledge and Kegan Paul, 1977).

reality and that it captures and portrays how things stand in the world" (32). However, this is a vague idea; no one has been able to make clear what exactly is meant by "picturing," or "fitting," or "matching," or, for that matter, "the world."[14] Without some direct access to the hidden aspects of reality to which theories are supposed to correspond, there is nothing more to be said about the truth of a theory than to display the justification for holding that theory.[15] Thus, Bloor suggests that we attend to actual uses of the word 'true' rather than merely invoke the old correspondence theory of truth. (For more on Bloor's account of truth, see Chapter 6.)

I claimed previously that the debate over scientific realism contains some confusions. We can see instances of this in Peacocke's reactions to the strong program. One instance is his claim that critical realism represents a middle position between naive realism and the strong program.[16] However, if we pursue the metaphor in section 1, there can be no midpoint between positions that are not located in the same conceptual 'space.' Furthermore, Peacocke interprets the positions of his opponents in terms of his own modern axes: the sociologists do not hold to the foundationalist-representational view of knowledge and language; therefore, they must be placed in the skeptical-expressivist quadrant of modern conceptual space and hence the claim that the sociologists provide an *irrationalist* account of science (22). And again, Bloor points out that the naturalistic account of scientific theories must be applicable to theories in the sociology of knowledge, or else the sociology of knowledge would provide a counterexample to its own theses. Peacocke, commenting on this self-reference, suggests that it is a case of sawing off the branch one is sitting upon (20). What for Bloor is evidence of the universal applicability of this approach is for Peacocke a reduction to absurdity. When one operates with the picture theory of knowledge, social determination of theory suggests falsity. With a Quinian view of knowledge as a web attached to experience only at the edges, social influences on theory choice are perfectly compatible with truth.

Modern realists accept the same facts about science as do the sociologists: the underdetermination of theory by data; the theory-ladenness of data; the effects on perception of prior belief; the influence, in theory construction, of ideals of natural order, of tacit assumptions embedded in paradigms; the constant shift in conceptual frameworks from one era to another. The sociologists go on to demonstrate by means of historical examples the value of sociological factors for explaining the decisions scientists make within the area

---

[14] Cf. Richard Rorty, *The Consequences of Pragmatism* (Minneapolis: University of Minnesota Press, 1982).

[15] Cf. Fine, "The Natural Ontological Attitude."

[16] Peacocke, *Intimations of Reality*, 26.

permitted by rational constraints. The critical realists reject this move and represent the sociologists as having, according to Peacocke, "firmly barred the way of science to reality" (26). In short, I suggest that modern realists and certain of their opponents are able to agree about the facts of the matter, yet talk past one another because they operate with different 'paradigms' of rationality.

From a postmodern point of view, neither modern realism nor its modern denial makes sense. Arthur Fine suggests that the "natural ontological attitude" is to accept the results of science as on a par with the things for which we have the evidence of the senses; it is (merely) to adjust our behavior, practical and theoretical, to accommodate these 'truths.' Realists and antirealists alike hold such an attitude, he claims, but differ in what they add to this 'nonrealist' position. Whereas antirealists add various sorts of qualifications, the realist merely adds a "desk-thumping, foot-stamping shout of 'Really!'"[17] The added 'really' is (really) meaningless.

Michael Levin approaches the question by distinguishing between the real and calculative parts of theories such as special relativity. The instrumentalist can be understood to propose that we take the calculative perspective toward even the ostensibly 'real' parts of theories—a suggestion that Levin finds unintelligible. When realists claim that the realistic parts of theories are more than calculating devices, they are stating a useless tautology. Thus, he concludes, neither the advocacy nor the denial of realism is significant.[18]

4. Exceptions That Prove the Rule

I have claimed that scientific realism is in the main a modern position, an application of a more general representational theory of language to scientific theories. I have also claimed that representationalism and foundationalism together provide two 'axes' of the modern philosophical framework, whereas attention to linguistic usage and epistemological holism together form the basis for a new postmodern scheme. This analysis suggests that typical scientific realism, employing a modern theory of language, should be incompatible with holist epistemology, yet there are several writers who hold to both scientific realism and holism. In this section I show that two such apparent counterexamples—Boyd and Paul Churchland—actually support my claim to the extent that serious problems can be found in their positions. Thus, I hope to show that they are in fact exceptions that prove the rule: one

---

[17] Fine, "The Natural Ontological Attitude," 97.
[18] Michael Levin, "What Kind of Explanation Is Truth?" in Leplin, ed., *Scientific Realism*, 124–139.

cannot be both a holist and a modern realist without running into conceptual difficulties.[19]

Boyd accepts a view of science wherein theories accommodate to the structure of the world by successive approximation; scientific language increasingly provides categories that "cut the world at its joints," while scientific method itself accommodates to the world. "If this picture of science is approximately accurate," he maintains, "then an adequate philosophy of science must be realistic since it must reflect the fact that knowledge of 'theoretical entities' is possible."[20]

The view that scientific theories successively approximate reality used to be taken for granted, but this many years after Kuhn's *Structure of Scientific Revolutions* the burden of proof has shifted. How does Boyd defend this position? He adjusts the instrumentalist argument to take account of holism; instead of answering the objection that more than one theory might be equally well confirmed by a given set of observations he answers the objection that more than one "total science" might be equally acceptable with the following argument: "If T is the actual current total science, and T' is an alternative total science which is profoundly implausible in light of T, then there are *evidential* reasons for preferring T to T'" (651). The justification for counting implausibility in light of T as strong evidence against T' is the *realist* claim that well-confirmed theories are approximately true. And thus Boyd's argument comes (viciously) full circle.

Churchland can also be dealt with summarily. His holism leads him to deny any difference in kind between common sense and scientific knowledge. Commonsense knowledge is itself theoretical. "We cannot, therefore, adopt an instrumentalist or other non-realist attitude towards the doctrines and ontologies of novel theoretical frameworks, unless we are prepared to give up talk of truth, falsity, and real existence right across the board."[21] Yet a few pages later, Churchland finds himself compelled to call into question the status of commonsense ontology: "What status does reason demand we actually assign to the speculative conceptions of reality embodied in our common-sense conceptual framework, if the emerging picture of reality provided by modern-era science is accepted, provisionally, as true?" (42). After characterizing the view that commonsense ontology can be reduced to scientific ontology as "not (quite) wholly mad" (44), he suggests that common

---

[19] One often hears simple counterinstances called rule-proving exceptions. The original use of the phrase was to refer to cases that only seem to be exceptions and turn out to be outside of or reconcilable with the principle they seem to contradict. See Ernest Grover, ed., *Fowler's Modern English Usage*, 2d rev. ed. (Oxford: Oxford University Press, 1983), s.v. "exception."

[20] Boyd, "Scientific Realism," 615.

[21] Paul Churchland, *Scientific Realism and the Plasticity of Mind* (London: Cambridge University Press, 1979), 2.

sense is simply a network of theories that got there first and may in whole or part be displaced by the scientific picture.

So scientific theories must be treated realistically if commonsense theories are, but commonsense theories need not be? One gets the impression reading Churchland's book that the "emerging picture of reality provided by modern-era science," which is "downright stupefying in its power and generality," is simply assumed. When the possibility of multiple 'true pictures' of reality emerges (here, science versus common sense), as it did for the early instrumentalists (competing, equally well-confirmed theories) or for Boyd (competing total sciences), Churchland solves the problem by simply jettisoning the commonsense realism upon which his argument is supposed to be based. I suspect but cannot show that every instance of holist scientific realism must suffer from similar circularity or inconsistency.

5. Conclusion

I began this chapter by noting a prominent feature of the realism debate, which I termed a 'lack of convergence,' evidenced by claims of opponents not to understand one another and by their failure to agree on such basics as the status of the theory and who is on which side. I claimed that this confusion was a result of the authors approaching the issue from both modern and postmodern perspectives. Based on this distinction I claimed, first, that typical forms of scientific realism (seeking referents for theoretical terms or correspondence accounts of the truth of scientific theories) are positions at home only in a modern framework and, second, that the postmodern presuppositions of other participants accounted for the ability of opponents to talk past one another.

I conclude that from a postmodern point of view neither the assertion nor the denial of modern scientific realism makes sense. No single theory of scientific language should be expected to fit everything from continental plates to quarks and ids. In the problematic cases, the realists are arguing about the proper use of 'real' beyond those areas where we have established conventions. We may wish to stipulate how the term's use will be extended (as Sellars, for example, has done), and we may argue about that. But there is no right or wrong in the matter. Thus, I suggest that the best solution to the realist debate in philosophy of science is simply to drop the issue and to attend instead to very pressing questions regarding the justification of scientific claims. To this I turn in the following chapter.

3 • • •

Postmodern Antirelativism

1. Introduction

I have suggested in previous chapters that modern epistemologists can be located along a spectrum or axis according to their degree of optimism or pessimism regarding the possibility of providing a foundational justification for knowledge. René Descartes and Thomas Reid set modern standards for confidence. David Hume is the best known of modern skeptics. It is not clear whether Hume should be placed at the extreme skeptical end of the spectrum or whether his goal was merely to refute the overblown claims of the rationalists.[1]

Throughout the course of the modern era, the *range* of epistemological positions seems to have shifted gradually from the optimistic end toward the skeptical end. This has been due largely to the growing predominance of empirical over rationalist theories: empirical data do not have the foundational certitude of rational first principles;[2] and one cannot *deduce* anything of interest from them (the problem of induction). So most recent foundationalists have long since abandoned Descartes's quest for certain knowledge. A symptom of the change is the proliferation of *critical* realist theories of knowledge and language, which I examined in the previous chapter.

It is the thesis of this chapter that postmodern epistemologists fall along a spectrum as well. Here the poles are not rationalism (optimistic foundationalism) and skepticism, but rather absolutism and relativism. For postmoderns with a holist epistemology, the worry is that there may be a number of competing wholes (webs of belief, paradigms, total sciences, worldviews, traditions) and no nonarbitrary way to choose among them.

---

[1] Wallace Matson distinguishes these possibilities, referring to the hard Hume and the soft Hume, respectively. See Wallace Matson, *A New History of Philosophy*, 2 vols. (San Diego: Harcourt Brace Jovanovich, 1987), 2:353.

[2] An exception is sense data, which do provide an incorrigible foundation, but here the problem of arguing from the foundation to anything interesting is magnified; see Chapter 1, section 3.4.

I doubt that any postmodern epistemologist can support an absolutist position—the view that there is but one consistent and acceptable theory of everything. Nor does it appear that there are any serious thinkers who are complete relativists;[3] such a view is self-referentially incoherent. The interesting positions, then, form a range of those that represent more or less confidence concerning our ability to adjudicate among competing theories or traditions. This chapter focuses on three optimists: Imre Lakatos, Theo Meyering, and Alasdair MacIntyre.

2. Postmodern Relativism

2.1. W.V.O. Quine

The foundationalist metaphor created its own brand of skepticism. One imagines the whole of one's knowledge structured as a building. With this picture in mind, it is obvious that the whole comes tumbling down if there is no adequate foundation. Quine's holism removes the foundationalist worry—there is no 'place' in the web of beliefs for a foundation, so its absence does not lead to skepticism. Unfortunately, Quine's picture almost inevitably produces a new epistemological anxiety: relativism.

Quine himself is no relativist. The web of beliefs is taken to include the whole of knowledge. It is possible gradually to alter the whole (the old image of a ship repaired at sea), but it is impossible to imagine replacing the whole thing at once—this would not be epistemological revolution but madness.

But Quine has a fairly circumscribed view of what counts as knowledge: science, logic, and everyday knowledge of the sensible world. If we apply the holist model to other realms of thought such as the social sciences or theology, it works very nicely except for one factor: alongside the net representing one's own system of thought is a whole row of competitors!

So justification of belief now involves two sorts of questions. Not only is there the question of whether this particular belief is justifiable within the particular web to which it belongs—and here we know how to proceed. But we also have to ask whether this web of beliefs is justified (or justifiable) over against its competitors—and here it is not at all clear how we are to proceed.

Even if we choose not to countenance any competing systems as part of the total web of beliefs (or alongside of the standard web), relativistic worries can arise from Quine's description of knowledge. That is, we *might* get away with saying that there is only one web, but we cannot deny that there

---

[3] Paul Feyerabend, whose views I consider in the next chapter, is often taken as a thorough relativist. However, he used to say that his teaching of methodological anarchism in science did not prevent his throwing away many of the papers that were sent him.

might well have been others or that the one we have *might well have been radically different.*[4] The first factor is the relation Quine proposes between beliefs and experience: he denies the possibility of any one-to-one mapping of beliefs onto experience. There are beliefs *near* the edge—the experiential boundary—but not 'connected' to experience. The connections are conventional—in Quine's view, stimulus-response connections.

The second factor, the pressure to maintain consistency within the web, will sometimes lead to revision of even those beliefs most closely related to experience. If we add a third factor, the recognition of cultural diversity—different worlds of experience—the image of a single experiential boundary gives way to a set of only partially shared or overlapping circles of experience.

These three factors together suggest that the particular way we have chosen to describe and explain experience is severely underdetermined by experience itself. Whether or not we countenance current competitors to our own worldview, it is clear that there could have been, could yet be, a variety of competing accounts of reality.

The fact that logic and philosophy, for Quine, are themselves but parts of the web intensifies the relativist worries: if rational principles as basic as the laws of logic are subject to the same vicissitudes as common theory, then how can one stand outside of competing webs and use criteria such as consistency and logical coherence to evaluate them? So if Quine himself is not worried about relativism, perhaps, we think, he should be!

2.2. Thomas Kuhn

Whether Thomas Kuhn intended it or not, he has provided powerful arguments for relativism in philosophy of science.[5] The language in philosophy of science is a bit different from Quine's, and the unit of analysis is different (paradigms versus total webs of belief), but most of the worrisome claims are the same. Data are theory-laden and hence underdetermined by experience. Theory is underdetermined by data. Radically different theories are supported by different domains of data or at least by differently interpreted data.

In addition, we have in Kuhn's survey of paradigm changes compelling evidence of radical conceptual changes in science; and there is also the claim that the scientific worldviews employing these different concepts are incommensurable. However, the most significant contribution Kuhn makes to the relativist's resources is his claim that standards of rationality themselves are

---

[4] This is the inference Richard Boyd attempts to block with his argument that the existence and confirmation of our existing "total science" provide adequate rational grounds for rejecting any proposed alternative total science; see Chapter 2, section 4.

[5] In Thomas Kuhn, *The Structure of Scientific Revolutions,* 2d ed. (Chicago: University of Chicago Press, 1970).

paradigm-dependent. This is a less radical position than Quine's claim that logical 'beliefs' are themselves but a part of the web and thus subject to revision in light of experience. But Kuhn's claim that at least some standards for evaluation of paradigms are paradigm-dependent has been more widely accepted and thus has had a greater impact on epistemology.

3. Postmodern Nonrelativism

3.1. Imre Lakatos

Lakatos's methodology of science was a response to Kuhn's claim that paradigms involve their own standards of success and that whatever standards *are* universal to science (consistency, empirical fit, fruitfulness) are insufficient to determine the choice among competing paradigms. Lakatos's most influential piece in the philosophy of science is his "Falsification and the Methodology of Scientific Research Programmes."[6] Here he made it plain that he intended to continue in the tradition of Karl Popper's falsificationism, while taking account of criticisms of Popper's work by historicist philosophers of science such as Kuhn.

On Lakatos's view, scientific rationality requires the specification of a criterion for choice among competing "research programs." A research program consists of a set of theories and a body of data. One theory, the "hard core," is central to the research program and is protected from falsification. Conjoined to the core is a set of auxiliary hypotheses that together add enough information to allow the theory to be confirmed by empirical data. Examples of types of auxiliary hypotheses are theories of observation or of instrumentation, lower-level theories that apply the core theory in different kinds of cases, and statements of initial conditions. The auxiliary hypotheses form a "protective belt" around the hard core since they are to be modified when potentially falsifying data are found. A research program, then, is a series of complex theories whose core remains the same while auxiliary hypotheses are successively modified, replaced, or amplified in order to account for problematic observations.

Lakatos claimed that the history of science is best understood not in terms of *successive* paradigms, as it is for Kuhn, but in terms of *competing* research programs. Some of these programs Lakatos described as "progressive" and others as "degenerating." A degenerating research program is one whose core theory is saved by ad hoc modifications of the protective belt—mere face-saving devices or linguistic tricks, as Lakatos called them. We have some sense of what these expressions mean, but it is difficult to propose criteria by

---

[6] In John Worrall and Gregory Currie, eds., *The Methodology of Scientific Research Programmes: Philosophical Papers, Volume 1* (Cambridge: Cambridge University Press, 1978), 8–101.

which to rule out such nonscientific maneuvers. The heart of Lakatos's methodology is his characterization of the kinds of maneuvers that are scientifically acceptable. A research program is said to be *progressive* when the following conditions are met:

1. Each new version of the theory (core theory and its auxiliaries) preserves the unrefuted content of its predecessor.
2. Each new version of the theory has excess empirical content over its predecessor; that is, it predicts some novel, hitherto unexpected facts.
3. Some of these predicted facts are corroborated.

When the first and second conditions are met, a theory is said to be theoretically progressive. When all three are met, a theory is empirically progressive as well. From this the contrary follows: a research program is *degenerating* when the change from one version to the next accounts at most for the one anomaly (or set of anomalies) for which the change was made but does not allow for the prediction and discovery of any novel facts. The choice of a theory thus becomes a choice between or among two or more competing *series* of theories, and one chooses the more progressive of the programs. Consequently, the choice depends on the program' Srelative power to *increase* scientific knowledge. So one might say that what Lakatos's "novel facts" criterion was intended to do was to fashion Kuhn's assorted "maxims" into a single criterion that would provide a clear answer to the question of which of the competitors is the more acceptable.

Paul Feyerabend has criticized Lakatos on the grounds that one never knows when it is fair to eliminate the less progressive program since programs that are progressive overall sometimes degenerate for a time.[7] If this is the case, then Lakatos has merely traded undecidability about how to apply a variety of sometimes-conflicting criteria for the problem of *when* to apply his *single* criterion.

Whether or not Lakatos's criterion works, I claim that he has nonetheless made two crucially important contributions toward a response to relativism. The first is his claim that research programs need to be evaluated on the basis of how they change over time. That is, a look at the data supporting a research program or at its degree of coherence at any temporal cross-section of its history will not reveal the qualities that ought to be considered in evaluating it. *Empirical progress* is an intrinsically historical concept. I submit that this temporal dimension is an essential ingredient for any scientific methodology and, more broadly, for any epistemology that begins with a holist account of knowledge and then proceeds to answer the second-order question of how one justifies an entire web of beliefs (or paradigm or research program).

---

[7] See Paul Feyerabend, "Consolations for the Specialist," in Imre Lakatos and Alan Musgrave, eds., *Criticism and the Growth of Knowledge* (Cambridge: Cambridge University Press, 1970), 197–230.

The second lasting contribution Lakatos has made to postmodern epistemology is his account of what I call the "fractal structure"[8] of justification.
What I mean by this is as follows: Lakatos has described the structure of science in terms of competing research programs. Each research program consists of a temporal succession of theories, each of which is a relatively slight
modification of its predecessor. In the case of a progressive program, each
new theory is better than its predecessor (in that it at least has more empirical content than the predecessor, without simply tacking on ad hoc hypotheses, and occasionally some of this excess content is corroborated).

The labor Lakatos expended in showing his own methodology to be a
minor modification of Karl Popper's (Popper's objections notwithstanding)
can be explained when we recognize that Lakatos intended to cast his own
methodology of scientific research programs not as a single theory but as the
most recent reformulation of a *research program* in the history and philosophy of science—as a progressive problem shift relative to Popper's. Lakatos's
agreement to broaden the definition of 'novel fact' in accordance with Eli
Zahar's suggestion (to count as novel corroborating facts that were previously known but believed to be unrelated to the theory) would then constitute the third version of the program.[9]

So, in effect, Lakatos viewed the history of philosophy of science as *iso-
morphic* with the history of science itself. The justification of his methodology in this manner assumes a metaphilosophical methodology—a theory
about the justification of philosophical theories that is identical in structure
to the theory it is used to justify. The importance of this move can be seen
when we contrast Lakatos's work with that of his predecessors in philosophy
of science. The logical positivists' verification criterion was rejected in part
because of the recognition that when applied self-referentially, the criterion
showed itself to be meaningless; it was self-stultifying. Analogously, Lakatos
argued that the major methodologies in philosophy of science, if considered
as theories about scientific rationality, failed to measure up to their own standards. In particular, Popper's falsificationism is falsified by the history of science.[10] Feyerabend suggests that Lakatos was the first to develop a theory of

---

[8] Fractals are objects or sets with self-similar, nontrivial structure on all scales—for example,
a snowflake shape where successive enlargement of sections of its outline reveal the same pattern as the section itself, only on smaller and smaller scales.

[9] See Imre Lakatos and Eli Zahar, "Why Did Copernicus's Programme Supersede Ptolemy's?"
in Worrall and Currie, eds., *The Methodology*, 168–192. I agree with a number of critics who
deny that this was a 'progressive' move and provide what I believe is a more satisfactory definition in "Another Look at Novel Facts," *Studies in History and Philosophy of Science*, 20, no. 3
(1989):385–388.

[10] Imre Lakatos, "History of Science and Its Rational Reconstructions," in Worrall and
Currie, eds., *The Methodology*, 102–138.

rationality "sly and sophisticated" enough to apply to science;[11] I claim that his real achievement was to develop a theory of rationality sly and sophisticated enough to apply to itself!

3.2. Theo Meyering

A recent book by Theo Meyering shows that further iterations can be added to Lakatos's two-level structure.[12] Here Meyering traces the development of three research programs in cognitive theory whose aim was to explain visual perception: the "identity theory," based on the transmission of Aristotelian forms; the Cartesian mechanicist theory of information transmission; and the closely related information-theoretical conception inaugurated by Hermann von Helmholtz in the nineteenth century.

For Aristotelians up through the Middle Ages, the same *forms* that constitute the essential ontology of the world also in*formed* the percipient in a literal sense. Alhazen (ca. A.D. 1000) was the most significant contributor to the Aristotelian program in the Middle Ages.

A new theory of vision was required by the metaphysical change from hylomorphism to Cartesian corpuscularism. Now, ideas formed in the mind as the effect of sensation are no more than arbitrary constructions of the mind. Hence, an epistemological gap is opened between immediate experience and the external reality of which it is taken to be a *symbolic and partial representation* rather than a qualitatively identical copy.

The theory of (partially) representative ideas, however, turned out to raise more questions than it could answer. These questions were not resolved until Helmholtz formulated an activist theory of the mind in which Immanuel Kant's formal structures of perception were replaced by learned hypotheses. For example, regarding spatial perception, Helmholtz proposed that depth perception depends on learned hypotheses relating retinal disparity to distance, which are constantly tested by interaction with the physical world. Meyering notes that because Helmholtz's perceptual theory had him working on both sides of a fence subsequently erected between the empirical and the philosophical, his contributions have not been fully appreciated, despite the fact that his program was superior to the alternatives of his day.

---

[11] Paul Feyerabend, "Imre Lakatos," *British Journal for the Philosophy of Science* 26 (1975): 1–18.

[12] Theo Meyering, *Historical Roots of Cognitive Science: The Rise of a Cognitive Theory of Perception from Antiquity to the Nineteenth Century* (Dordrecht: Kluwer Academic, 1989). For a somewhat fuller account of Meyering's historical work, see my review essay, "Philosophical Fractals: Or, History as Metaphilosophy," *Studies in History and Philosophy of Science* 24 (1993):501–508.

Now for Meyering's intriguing metaphilosophical argument: the central goal of his book is to provide support for the philosophical thesis of *epistemological naturalism*, whose core assumption is the interdependence of philosophical and empirical knowledge. Naturalism is to be contrasted with what I call the standard account, which regards philosophy as a purely conceptual discipline, inherently distinct from empirical investigations. Meyering's approach to the justification of his thesis is to reconstruct empirico-philosophical histories for both naturalism and the standard account.

The standard account traces its origins to Descartes, but Meyering shows that Descartes's *science* is the driving force behind his philosophy and, more to the point, that apart from the scientific context, Descartes's most influential philosophical moves make little sense. Here we see the use Meyering makes of his account of Descartes's science for his more ambitious project. Descartes inherited from medieval thought the view that optics was the most basic of the sciences. However, because of Descartes's own mechanicist postulates, the identity theory had become untenable. His new theory of perception was based on his corpuscular theory of matter, but the latter led almost inevitably to a sharp dualism of mind and body, within which it may well have been impossible to develop a theory of perception that adequately bridged the gulf between judgment and the physiology of perception. So the Cartesian program in optics created a crisis in philosophy: how to justify the claim to have true knowledge of the world on the basis of interpretations of purely symbolic data from the senses. The problem of the philosophical justification of knowledge has remained central to the standard account ever since.

It is also a commonplace to trace the origin of the analytic conception of philosophy through Kant's formalism to Descartes's mind-body dualism. Meyering's contribution here is to treat Cartesian substantial dualism and Kantian formalism as ingredients in ongoing research programs in the *scientific* study of perception. So by this route Meyering has again shown that the philosophical antecedents of the standard account can be better understood in terms of his naturalist program than on the standard account's own terms.

Meyering's reconstruction of the history of cognitive science is the most ingenious aspect of the book, as this is where it displays its fractal form. Meyering corroborates the naturalist thesis by applying it self-referentially on at least three levels. First is the claim, already discussed, that epistemological naturalism does a better job of accounting for the history of modern philosophy than does the standard account. So here the naturalist thesis in its broadest form is supported in a naturalistic fashion—not by argument from first principles but by 'empirical' testing against the history of thought.

Second, Lakatos's methodology of scientific research programs is a version of naturalism applied to philosophy of science. Meyering provides additional corroboration for Lakatos's methodology by showing that it is in fact useful for reconstructing the history of cognitive science.

Third, using Lakatos's methodology, Meyering argues that the Helmholtzian program was the most progressive and therefore the most acceptable research program in its day. This fact has a double significance. First, Helmholtz's program itself is an instance of a naturalistic approach to perceptual knowledge. Second, the program can easily be seen as an antecedent to contemporary cognitive science, which is the appropriate empirical extension of naturalized epistemology. So naturalism, the characteristic feature of the whole, appears fractal-like on each level of Meyering's analysis of the history of thought.

3.3. Alasdair MacIntyre

MacIntyre's recent work in ethics and epistemology reveals a similarly complex, fractal structure. In *After Virtue,* he reached the conclusion that the justification of an ethical position requires locating the position with respect to its history—that is, locating it within a tradition of moral enquiry. The conclusions of *After Virtue* made it clear that in order to avoid moral relativism, one needed a way to arbitrate among competing moral traditions.[13] But moral traditions are embedded in larger traditions that incorporate their own standards of rationality. So here is an analog to the Kuhnian problem of the paradigm dependence of standards of rationality. The core of MacIntyre's epistemological position is acceptance of the tradition-ladenness of justification: "To be outside all traditions," he says, "is to be a stranger to enquiry; it is to be in a state of intellectual and moral destitution."[14]

I attempt to describe MacIntyre's fractal epistemology by tracing its development through several works.[15] In an early article, he argued that justification of theories in science depends on our being able to construct a historical narrative that makes the transition from the old theory to the new theory intelligible:

What the scientific genius, such as Galileo, achieves in his transition, then, is not only a new way of understanding nature, but also and inseparably a new way of understanding the old science's way of understanding nature. It is because only

---

[13] Alasdair MacIntyre, *After Virtue,* 2d ed. (Notre Dame, Ind.: University of Notre Dame Press, 1984); see esp. the Postscript.

[14] Alasdair MacIntyre, *Whose Justice? Which Rationality?* (Notre Dame, Ind.: University of Notre Dame Press, 1988), 367.

[15] I am treating successive works as cumulative additions to a single, complex theory of rationality, but it would be more appropriate to treat the series of works as a succession of theories in a research program or tradition and then apply his own criteria for evaluating such traditions.

from the standpoint of the new science can the inadequacy of the old science be characterized that the new science is taken to be more adequate than the old. It is from the standpoint of the new science that the continuities of narrative history are re-established.[16]

Thus, he claims, scientific reason turns out to be subordinate to, and intelligible only in terms of, historical reason. This is equivalent to Lakatos's insistence on the historical character of justification in science. Let us call this aspect of justification the diachronic dimension. Here MacIntyre is answering the question of how one justifies a modification within a given tradition.

However, a second question is how one justifies the tradition as a whole over against its rivals. He takes up this issue in *Whose Justice? Which Rationality?* One aspect of the adjudication between competing traditions is to construct a narrative account of each tradition: of the crises it has encountered (incoherence, new experience that cannot be explained, etc.) and how it has or has not overcome these crises. Has it been possible to reformulate the tradition in such a way that it overcomes its crises without losing its identity? Comparison of these narratives may show that one tradition is clearly superior to another: it may become apparent that one tradition is making progress, while its rival has become sterile (this is another echo of Lakatos; compare his concepts of *progress* and *degeneration*). In addition, if there are participants within the traditions with enough empathy and imagination to understand the rival tradition's point of view in its own terms, then "protagonists of each tradition, having considered in what ways their own tradition has by its own standards of achievement in enquiry found it difficult to develop its enquiries beyond a certain point, or has produced in some area insoluble antinomies, ask whether the alternative and rival tradition may not be able to provide resources to characterize and to explain the failings and defects of their own tradition more adequately than they, using the resources of that tradition, have been able to do" (166–167).

Let us refer to this aspect as synchronic justification. Notice that it involves diachronic evaluation of each tradition as an intrinsic element. Now, the self-referential twist: MacIntyre's own account of tradition-constituted enquiry is itself a theory and, as such, is subject to evaluation by the same narrative method—in both its diachronic and synchronic aspects. In *Whose Justice? Which Rationality?* he uses his narrative method to justify his own reformulation of the moral tradition in which the concept of a virtue plays a central role and, at the same time, argues for the narrative method itself by placing

---

[16] Alasdair MacIntyre, "Epistemological Crises, Dramatic Narrative, and the Philosophy of Science," in Gary Gutting, ed., *Paradigms and Revolutions* (Notre Dame, Ind.: University of Notre Dame Press, 1980), 69.

it within a large-scale intellectual tradition—the Aristotelian-Thomist tradition—and then by comparing this tradition to the Enlightenment alternative. To do this, he has to show three things: (1) that the Enlightenment tradition of 'traditionless reason' is incapable of solving its own most pressing intellectual problems—in particular, the problem of the tradition-ladenness of standards of rationality; (2) that his own version of the Aristotelian-Thomist tradition has a good chance of solving the problem; and (3) why we could have been so misled by the tradition that claimed to reject all tradition. He makes his argument by assuming the standpoint of tradition-constituted reason and by then using that perspective to diagnose the mistakes of his predecessors: the Enlightenment tradition cannot tell its own story intelligibly because its own standards of rationality require such standards to be universal and not historically conditioned. His own account is vindicated by the extent to which it sheds new light on this aspect of intellectual history.

So, in sum, MacIntyre's own reformulation of virtue theory is justified because it solves the problems its predecessors in the virtue tradition of moral reasoning could not solve and, furthermore, because it explains why they *could not* solve them. But this approach to the justification of an ethical position is an instantiation of a broader theory of rationality, according to which a tradition is vindicated by the fact that it has managed to solve its own major problems, while its competitor has failed to do so, and by the fact that it can give a better account of its rival's failures than can the rival itself. But this theory itself needs to be justified by showing that it is a part of a large-scale epistemological tradition (the Aristotelian-Thomist tradition) and that this tradition is itself justified—by MacIntyre's narrative, in which he recounts how this tradition has overcome its problems, while its main contemporary competitor, modern Enlightenment reason, has not.

3.4. Evaluation

So what are we to make of this 'fractal' philosophy? MacIntyre has pointed out that in the past philosophers have usually written the history of epistemology as though it were not, in fact, a historical narrative.[17] My suggestion is that when philosophers do take seriously the historical conditioning of epistemology itself, there are four possible responses. The two- or three-layered philosophical arguments I have examined here constitute one possible response, whose essential aspect is the move to a metaphilosophy with a selfsame structure. A second possibility is to invent a different metamethodology, but this strategy either is self-stultifying or calls for an infinite regress of metamethods. A third possibility is to declare one's own stage in the

---

[17] Ibid., 57.

development of historical consciousness the point toward which history has been moving—a Hegelian absolutism. The fourth option, and the one most often chosen, is relativism. Some accept it with great reluctance; others (such as the Continental postmoderns) celebrate it. However, critics of deconstructionism point out that deconstruction is self-referentially incoherent: the only way to accept the theory and use the method is by exempting one's own thought from the method. Jacques Derrida, of course, would not be moved by this criticism since part of his program is to seek freedom from the habits of thought and logical checks of philosophy.

I suggest that fractal philosophy offers the best chance of evading relativism with regard to standards of rationality. It is an attempt (similar to that of chaos theorists) to find order on a higher level of analysis, and—this is the crucial factor—the higher-level findings exhibit coherence rather than self-stultification. In light of the other options, whatever circularity there is in the reasoning appears virtuous rather than vicious. Perhaps this type of philosophical analysis will turn out to be our generation's most important contribution to reflection on the nature of rationality.

4. Conclusion

Let me now try to sum up the argument of this chapter. I have tried to show that we are already in position to see significant development in a holist epistemological *tradition*. If we take Quine's "Two Dogmas" and Kuhn's *Structure* as classic texts, then we see that this approach leads to a crisis that calls for serious reformulation of the tradition. The crisis is relativism; the reformulation involves changing the unit of analysis from that of a static web of beliefs or paradigm to that of a research program or tradition—adding the historical dimension—and, in addition, ensuring self-referential coherence such that the (tradition-laden) standards of rationality involved in the tradition are not violated when applied to themselves.

So I have placed Lakatos, Meyering, and MacIntyre at the forefront of the development of a new philosophical tradition (Anglo-American postmodernity), one of whose essential constituents must be a new theory of knowledge. Insofar as I have constructed an intelligible narrative from Quine through MacIntyre, showing how the later overcame inadequacies in the earlier, I have performed a diachronic justification of the final position (MacIntyre's) and (appropriately) have used MacIntyre's account of the justification of theories in doing so.

(Notice that I am placing MacIntyre in a different tradition than the one he claims as his own: Anglo-American postmodernity rather than a long-awaited restoration of the Aristotelian-Thomist tradition. MacIntyre himself may not appreciate this, but I believe that his work is more *intelligible* against this contemporary background and that I have thus improved on this work in so doing. To use his own terms, I say that MacIntyre has borrowed from a medieval tradition the resources necessary for enriching the Anglo-American conceptual scheme, but the theory these resources allowed him to formulate is in fundamental continuity with the work of Lakatos.[18] That MacIntyre's work is a natural successor to Lakatos's is suggested by the fact that Meyering has, independently of MacIntyre, made comparable moves to extend Lakatos's work.[19])

To return to the issue of justification: I have sketched a diachronic justification of the work of Lakatos, and then of his successors, Meyering and MacIntyre, as the best so far in this fledgling tradition. But what about synchronic justification of this tradition itself? We need to consider two competitors: the most recent version of the modern Enlightenment tradition and Continental postmodernism.

Contemporary Anglo-American philosophy grew out of criticism of modern philosophy, and to know contemporary philosophy is to know the history: what problems were found to be intractable for predecessor positions; how the new moves overcome the problems. It is to know why Kuhn supersedes Carl Hempel; why Quine supersedes Rudolf Carnap and C. I. Lewis. So in this case, synchronic justification *is* diachronic justification.

It is another matter with Continental postmodernism, which grows out of much earlier critiques of Enlightenment thought. MacIntyre has already initiated a critique of Continental postmodernism in *Three Rival Versions of Moral Enquiry: Encyclopaedia, Genealogy, and Tradition*.[20] 'Encyclopaedia' is his name for the Enlightenment tradition since its understanding of rationality was enshrined in the *Encyclopaedia Brittannica* (especially the ninth edition). 'Genealogy' is the name he gives to a tradition stemming from Friedrich Nietzsche's *Zur Genealogie der Moral* (1887) and continued today by the deconstructionists, Michel Foucault, and others. This latter tradition includes a theory of 'antirationality': the great books need to be "unmasked" to show how they conceal the will to power. 'Tradition,' of course, refers to the tradition of tradition-constituted enquiry.

MacIntyre's criticism of genealogy, in brief, is as follows. First, the genealogists always inescapably seek to disown a part of their past. But such 'disowning' presupposes enough continuity to make the disowning possible. "To be unable to find the words, or rather to be able only to find words

---

[18] See MacIntyre, *Whose Justice?* 362.

[19] MacIntyre has pointed out (in personal correspondence, July 27, 1994) that his account of rationality differs significantly from Lakatos's in that MacIntyre requires for the statement of his position a strong conception of truth that is essentially Thomistic. See Chapter 6 for an account of MacIntyre on truth.

[20] Alasdair MacIntyre, *Three Rival Versions of Moral Enquiry: Encyclopaedia, Genealogy, and Tradition* (Notre Dame, Ind.: University of Notre Dame Press, 1990).

incompatible with the genealogical project, in which to express an unironic relationship to a past which one is engaged in disowning, is to be unable to find a place for oneself as genealogist either inside or outside the genealogical narrative and thereby to exempt oneself from scrutiny, to make of oneself the great exception" (214).

Second, the genealogical stance is dependent for its concepts, modes of argument, theses, and style on a set of contrasts between it and what it aspires to overcome. Hence, it is inherently dependent upon, derivative from, that which it professes to have discarded (215).

MacIntyre does not see these as fatal criticisms; he says that it is too soon to tell whether these internal problems can be overcome. In addition, I suggest that MacIntyre may not be taking seriously enough the fact that such internal incoherencies would be seen by some proponents of the genealogical tradition not as problems but as liberation from the domination of philosophy. Perhaps the issue comes down to the simpler but rationally insoluble question "Why be rational?"

So I claim that the epistemology I have described and exemplified here (holist, naturalized, fractal structured) is the way ahead for the Anglo-American philosophical tradition. This approach is partially vindicated by its self-referential coherence, by its history, and by the weakness of its noisiest competitor. However, the most that can be claimed is that sometimes one can use one's own tradition-dependent standards of rationality to argue cogently in the public forum for one's own tradition. This leaves room for some competing theories, research programs, traditions, and so we had better see (in the next chapter) what to make of this proliferation.

4 • • •

Postmodern Proliferation and Progress in Science

1. Introduction

The fields of psychiatric medicine, clinical psychology, and psychiatric social work are notorious for their proliferation of widely divergent points of view regarding mental illness. Not only do these three separate fields themselves represent different approaches, but also within each field there is a vast array of different schools. However, upon closer examination, it appears that many of these schools share certain assumptions about the nature and causes of mental illness. Indeed, most current theories in the mental health sciences can be classed as belonging to one of two major *models* of mental illness: the medical model or the psychosocial model.

The term 'model' has many uses in science. I use it to refer to a set of assumptions about the nature of the subject of enquiry whose purpose is to provide guidelines for research. Models are often simplified representations of reality, as the ellipse is of the actual orbits of the planets. A model of mental illness is a view of the nature of mental illness simplified in a manner intended to allow for optimal focusing of research and clinical practice. The assumptions about mental illness that are most useful for research are those regarding its causes, and speaking rather loosely, we can say that the two major models of mental illness are distinguishable on the basis of their views on this matter.

The medical model considers phenomenal mental illness to be symptomatic of an underlying physiological abnormality. Some of the most exciting theories here are attempts to find imbalances in chemicals called neurotransmitters and to explain mental illness as effects of these abnormalities. The psychosocial model sees mental illness as a response by a physiologically normal person to an abnormal psychological or interpersonal environment.

Adherents of this model range from the Freudians, with their psychodynamic theories; through the behaviorists, who claim that mental illness is simply learned behavior; and the cognitive therapists, who postulate deviant assumptions about self or world; to theorists such as R. D. Laing, who argues that mental illness is not illness in any sense of the word but is a healthy response to an unhealthy environment.[1]

I argue in the following pages that the medical model can be shown to have made a great deal more progress in recent years than the psychosocial model. The question then arises as to whether the mental health sciences would not be better off to abandon the less progressive psychosocial model. A pragmatic argument points out that resources are limited and that they ought not be wasted on a theory or model that is doing poorly.

This argument is in accord with modern philosophy of science, which assumes that the theory that is closest to the truth will be found to excel in any standard measure of acceptability (usually degree of confirmation) and that its competitors could then be dismissed as probably false. Although Karl Popper parts company with much of modern (positivistic) philosophy of science, he concurs in this matter. In fact, his entire methodology of science is based on the rejection of falsified theories, so that by process of elimination, the best one remain alone in the field.[2]

Though differing in many respects from traditional philosophy of science and from Popper, Thomas Kuhn has provided an interesting argument for restriction of proliferation. According to Kuhn, science progresses in two ways: progress is made during periods of "normal science" when researchers concentrate their efforts on working out the details of an accepted paradigm, and progress is also made during revolutionary periods when the accepted paradigm is abandoned in favor of a new one. Progress in either case requires restriction of proliferation, first, because normal science indeed requires a concentrated effort to develop a single paradigm and, second, because without the time and energy spent on this problem-solving phase, a paradigm cannot be made to show its limitations, and it is the encountering of insoluble limitations that brings about scientific revolutions.[3]

In opposition to this view, both Paul Feyerabend and Imre Lakatos have argued that proliferation leads to progress in science. Lakatos has highlighted the importance of the successes of competitors in spurring the development of scientific research programs. In order to remain progressive, a research

---

[1] R. D. Laing, *The Politics of Experience* (New York: Pantheon Books, 1967).

[2] See, for example, Karl Popper, *Conjectures and Refutations: The Growth of Scientific Knowledge* (New York: Harper and Row, 1963).

[3] Thomas Kuhn, *The Structure of Scientific Revolutions*, 2d ed. (Chicago: University of Chicago Press, 1970).

program must account for its competitors' anomalies in a content-increasing, rather than an ad hoc, manner.[4] Feyerabend has argued even more strongly for the value of proliferation: some facts of crucial importance cannot be discovered without the aid of a rival theory. Furthermore, since theories must be given time to develop, and since scientists seldom give up one theory unless another is available, proliferation cannot be restricted to specific revolutionary periods in the course of scientific development, nor can we ever be sure that a degenerating research program will not turn around and become progressive. Feyerabend has argued that for these reasons, any number of competing theories ought not only be tolerated but also encouraged.[5]

Against this background, the questions to be addressed in the following pages can be stated:

1. How can the medical model be shown to be rationally preferable to the psychosocial model? I argue that by the use of increasing success in therapy as a crude measure of progress, the medical model can be shown to be far superior to the psychosocial model.[6]
2. Given this result, what can be said for the value of the psychosocial model? Has it nonetheless made a significant contribution to our understanding of mental illness, as Feyerabend's and Lakatos's arguments suggest it might, or has it simply been a waste of resources?

I argue that despite the limited success of the psychosocial model, it has provided us with information that we would not have had without it, and this information shows us that the more successful medical model is inherently inadequate to guide research and clinical practice in the health sciences. In fact, the combined successes and failures of both standard models point to the need for a new model that integrates physiological, psychological, and social contributors to illness into unified theoretical structures.

The whole of my argument is intended to show that the limited relativity or proliferation that must be accepted in light of even the strictest of Anglo-American postmodern epistemologies is nothing to be lamented.

---

[4] Imre Lakatos, "Falsification and the Methodology of Scientific Research Programmes," in John Worrall and Gregory Currie, eds., *The Methodology of Scientific Research Programmes: Philosophical Papers, Volume 1* (Cambridge: Cambridge University Press, 1978), 8–101.

[5] Paul Feyerabend, *Against Method* (London: New Left Books, 1975).

[6] Note that this crude measure of progress is not to be confused with Lakatos's concept of a progressive research program. Lakatos's concept depends on the derivation of observable consequences from *theories*. Here we are looking at *models*—vague entities guiding theory formation and thus less directly related to empirical observations.

2. Two Models of Mental Illness

2.1. The Medical Model

The medical model of mental illness premises that 'mental' illness is best understood as a disease of the body that adversely affects those aspects of the person that have traditionally been classified as mental, for example, emotions, cognition, personality. Therefore, the model most used in general medicine is expected to apply here as well. According to this model, disease is an abnormal physiological condition that produces unwanted symptoms. Therefore, whatever is found to be the initial cause of the disease condition is also indirectly the cause of the illness-as-experienced—the symptoms or syndrome. It is recognized that these abnormal physiological conditions may be caused by a variety of factors, singly or in combination: genetic endowment, invasion of the body by microorganisms or poisons, injury, stress, poor nutrition. Thus, when the medical model is adopted for mental illness, it entails that mental illness is to be seen as symptomatic of underlying physiological abnormalities. Types of abnormalities most often suggested today are faulty chemical processes in the brain, but gross brain abnormalities, endocrine disorders, disorders of the entire nervous system, and others are sometimes suggested.

The medical model of illness can be represented schematically as follows:

initial cause $\longrightarrow$ disease entity $\longrightarrow$ symptoms
(abnormal physiological (physical or
condition) mental)

Notice how this general view of mental illness provides direction for research and theory development. The first step is to study the physiology of the mentally ill person, seeking to correlate some abnormality with the presence of the symptoms. Once this is done, the remaining steps are to attempt to correct the condition, for if this is done and the illness disappears, it becomes clearer that the research is on the right track. However, before the theory is entirely acceptable, one must be able to give an account of the chain of physiological events leading from the abnormality to the various symptoms, and one must find another chain of physiological events that is taken to have been the initial cause of that abnormality.

Investigation of the initial cause of a disease is obviously dependent upon first ascertaining what the disease consists in. Since psychiatric medicine is at the point where underlying physiological abnormalities have not even been found for many of the illnesses the discipline hopes to treat, it is not surprising that scant attention is paid to the initial causes of the disease entities. (The exception here is that much study has gone into determining the extent to which schizophrenia and bipolar affective disorders are genetically based.) Of course, satisfactory explanation, as well as prevention, requires that the initial causes be investigated, not only what the causes are but also how they effect the physiological and mental changes in the mentally ill person.

A corollary of the premise that disease is a physiological abnormality is that to treat the illness-as-experienced, one must correct the abnormality. Therefore, treatment of mental illness requires, for example, restoration of the balance of neurochemicals rather than an attempt to "talk" the person out of the symptoms. The most common approach to treatment is direct physiological intervention to repair the abnormality or remove the disease entity. It is thought that in general manipulation of the types of variables that figure into the epidemiologist's study (however useful for prevention of future cases) will not be effective for treatment. Once the disease occurs, the effects cannot be reversed by a change in the conditions in the environment that caused the disease.

2.2. The Psychosocial Model

I have classed as variants of the same model a diverse array of schools and theories. Under the psychosocial model, we find psychoanalysis and other depth psychologies, Carl Rogers's psychology of the person and client-centered therapy, family systems therapy, cognitive therapy, and a host of others—in short, all of the schools whose prescribed form of treatment for mental illness consists of what we commonly call psychotherapy. I also include here the behaviorists and learning theorists, whose therapies include behavior modification and systematic desensitization. All these schools have in common the premise that mental illness is caused by harmful interactions with people in one's environment. The illness is a *psychological* one, but 'psychological' can be interpreted in mentalistic or behavioral terms, and it is produced by the *social* environment.

Each school looks to different elements in the person's experience and provides a different account of the causal chain leading ultimately to the mental illness. Also, the approaches to treatment are rather varied in detail and rationale, but most have in common that healing is to be brought about by the establishment of a relationship between the person and the therapist.

2.3. Contrasts Between the Models: What Is Really at Stake?

To examine the contrasts between the medical and psychosocial models of mental illness, some attention must be paid to the matter of causation. On the surface, the issue of the causes of mental illness appears to be what divides the proponents of the two models. Adherents of the medical model, speaking loosely and a bit polemically, say that mental illness is 'caused' by physiological abnormalities.[7] Adherents of the psychosocial model claim that mental illness is caused by life experiences. However, when questioned, adherents on both sides would undoubtedly demonstrate an awareness that many factors are (or at least could be) involved in producing the mentally ill person's symptoms.

Psychologists and like-minded psychiatrists surely admit that all experiences must be realized by or at least be associated with some physiological state, and medical researchers surely know that at least some experiences (such as stress) produce harmful physiological changes. So why do the two opposing camps remain?

The answer, I believe, has to do with the use of the word 'cause.' We distinguish between the cause of an event and mere conditions for its occurrence. The choice of which of the innumerable conditions involved will be elevated to the status of cause depends not only on certain facts of the matter but also on our point of view, and this point of view usually bears some relationship to our reasons for wanting to know what the cause is.

The first basis for distinguishing between a cause and a mere condition for mental illness is, of course, whether or not it is a factor that serves to distinguish people who are mentally ill from those who are not. Being alive is a necessary condition, but since most living people are not mentally ill, this factor can safely be ignored. This is a simple distinction in principle, but in practice it is very difficult to apply. One way of contrasting the two models is to look at their answers to each of the following questions: (1) Are there, in fact, physiological abnormalities that, if detected, would serve to distinguish the mentally ill from others? (2) Are there recognizable patterns of events in the social histories of the mentally ill that would serve to distinguish them from others?

Aside from this factual matter, another determinant of views about the cause of mental illness is interest in curing and preventing it. Thus, the choice about which variables to pursue as possible causes will be influenced by judgments about their manipulability. So another issue dividing proponents of the two models is whether physiological or environmental variables are more easily controlled. Notice that a member of one of the psychosocial schools might be a radical reductionist, holding that mental events are identical with brain events, which makes for a serious involvement (to say the least) of physiological factors in mental illness, but he or she may still deny that mental illness qua physiological condition is detectable, recognizable as abnormal, or treatable. He or she can still claim that what is important to investigate are the environmental factors leading to the problem since these are the ones available to study and manipulation. Many behaviorists take this

---

[7] Recall that with the medical model, the illness *is* the physiological abnormality, phenomenal mental illness is its symptom, and the (initial) cause of the illness is yet another matter.

position, and members of the psychotherapeutic schools could do so if they were willing (as many are) to say that their mentalistic terms apply to hypothetical constructs rather than to real entities. Conversely, an adherent of the medical model might well grant that mental illness appears as a reaction to environmental situations, but he or she might then add either that without the underlying physiological abnormality, the person would have been able to cope with the situation (i.e., suffering from stress does not distinguish the mentally ill from others), or that even if the physiological condition is itself caused by an environmental situation, there is a better chance of correcting the physiology by direct intervention than there is of controlling the environment appropriately and thereby reversing the physiological damage.

It is important to emphasize here that the assumptions of a model are meant to be working assumptions. That is, their aim is not so much to be statements of truth about mental illness (or whatever) but to provide guidelines for practices such as research and therapy. Thus, what appears as a difference of opinion about the causes of mental illness turns out to be more accurately described as a difference of opinion concerning which of several types of factors can most fruitfully be explored.

It is also important to mention that, although there are illnesses classified as psychiatric disorders that appear only to fit the medical model (e.g., psychosis associated with intracranial tumor), and others that appear to fit only the psychosocial model (e.g., adjustment reaction to adolescence), it is not the case that all psychiatric disorders can be simply divided up between the two models. The two models are in hot competition to explain and produce treatments for all of the disorders most commonly thought of as mental illnesses: the neuroses and psychoses. The illnesses that unquestionably fit only one model are actually few in number.

3. Evaluation

3.1. Success in Therapy as a Measure of Progress

The situation in psychiatry is thus a rather unhappy one: two models, differing sharply in crucial respects, are competing for most of the field of mental illness. Both are, on the face of it, quite plausible. Can we choose between them on any reasonable grounds? In this chapter, I use a method of comparing these two models that, to my knowledge, no one has attempted previously; that is, I compare them on the basis of the amount of progress they have made in the recent past, and I use increasing treatment efficacy as a measure of progress. This method needs some explanation.

There is much debate in the mental health sciences concerning what constitutes acceptability of theories (models), but this debate can be bypassed in this discussion, first, because Feyerabend's argument in favor of proliferation is independent of any decision on this matter. His view is that regardless of which methodology of science one chooses, there can always be found instances where one scientific theory is clearly superior to others in the field on the grounds specified, yet upon examination it will also be found that so-called inferior theories will have made contributions to the overall progress of the field.

Second, the methodological debate can be avoided in this case because we are interested not in particular theories here but in the models that guide theory formation as well as practice in the clinic. Fortunately, we have reasonably clear-cut criteria for success in the area of clinical practice: the most successful model is obviously the one that has the most effective treatments for mental illness. Therefore, I rely on this rather crude but practical means of comparing the two models.

The foregoing is the reason for my looking at clinical outcome as a means for evaluating the two models. There are two reasons for looking at *rate* of increasing treatment capability rather than simply at current effectiveness. One is the general shift of emphasis in philosophy of science from a view of theories as static entities with fixed logical relations determining their acceptability, to a dynamic view of theory development emphasizing progress.[8] The second reason is that it is not easy to choose between the two models on the basis of current treatment abilities without a consideration of their histories. Both models provide partially successful treatments for some illnesses. However, adding even as little as forty years of historical perspective, we find that, whereas the psychosocial model has produced little documentable *improvement*, the medical model has added new treatments to its repertoire at an impressive rate.

3.2. Results

3.2.1. The Medical Model   Let us look first at recent gains attributable to the medical approach. Since 1950, a number of drugs have been developed for treatment of psychiatric disorders: (1) the phenothiazines and other antipsychotic drugs for schizophrenia, with some uses for the affective psychoses; (2) the antidepressants for both neurotic and psychotic depression; (3) lithium for mania and sometimes for bipolar manic-depressive illness; (4) the benzodiazepines (minor tranquilizers) for anxiety disorders; and (5) ritalin and other stimulants for hyperkinesis in children. Other medical treatments for mental illnesses (and various illnesses with mental symptoms)

---

[8] Lakatos, Kuhn, and Feyerabend are primarily responsible for this shift in philosophy of science. More recently, MacIntyre has made a similar move in epistemology more generally. See Chapter 3.

include several treatments (surgery, radiation, and drugs) for brain tumors and cerebral arterioschlerosis, dilantin and other anticonvulsants for epilepsy, and dietary compensation for certain metabolic disorders that result in mental retardation.

None of these treatments has been researched thoroughly enough that it can be said exactly how effective it is, but some are known to be relatively ineffective, or the illnesses for which they are prescribed are quite uncommon. The proportion of treatable brain tumors is small (but growing), and so is the proportion of treatable cases of deterioration due to arterioschlerosis. Amphetamine psychosis is rare, and the metabolic disorders causing mental retardation that can be corrected are rare also.[9]

What, then, counts as "significant" progress? Development of the phenothiazines is certainly a major breakthrough. Schizophrenics used to fill the mental facilities and stay for years. To be able to treat effectively even a small proportion of this devastating and common illness is impressive. These drugs often eliminate or reduce hallucinations and delusions. However, they do not affect the negative symptoms of the disease, such as withdrawal and flatness of affect. Thus, it is difficult to quantify the benefits. One early meta-analysis of studies showed that patients treated ranked at the seventieth percentile (i.e., better off than 70 percent) of untreated controls in overall functionality.[10] However, since these studies were done, a new drug, clozapine, has been found effective for a number of patients who were not helped by the early type of antipsychotic medications.

The older antidepressant medications, monoamine oxidase inhibitors, have a success rate of approximately 50 percent. The newer tricyclic antidepressants and the "second-generation" antidepressants (including the now-famous Prozac) have a success rate of approximately 65 percent. These latter classes of drugs have fewer adverse side effects as well.[11] There is a high but unknown spontaneous remission rate for depression, but this success rate is nonetheless a noteworthy achievement even if the drugs do no more than hasten a recovery that would have occurred spontaneously later. Bipolar manic-depressive illness and unipolar mania are relatively rare, but since lithium is almost always (in 70–80 percent of cases) highly effective in treating

---

[9] The best sources for information on current medical treatments for mental illnesses are psychiatry and clinical psychology textbooks. The ones I have found most helpful are A. Freedman, H. Kaplan, and B. Sadock, *Modern Synopsis of Comprehensive Textbook of Psychiatry* (Baltimore: Williams and Wilkins, 1980); and Ronald J. Comer, *Abnormal Psychology*, 2d ed. (New York: Freeman, 1995).

[10] M. L. Smith, G. V. Glass, and T. I. Miller, *The Benefits of Psychotherapy* (Baltimore: Johns Hopkins University Press, 1980); reported in Patricia B. Sutker and Henry E. Adams, *Comprehensive Handbook of Psychopathology*, 2d ed. (New York: Plenum Press, 1984), 323.

[11] Comer, *Abnormal Psychology*, 164.

mania, this should also be considered an important achievement.[12] The minor tranquilizers are very effective in providing symptomatic relief of anxiety and represent an improvement over the opiates used before 1950 in that they are less addictive.

The frequency of hyperkinesis is not known, and although there is controversy over the increased use of ritalin as a treatment, we may include this as a case of improvement. The success rate for control of grand mal seizures among epileptics using dilantin and other anticonvulsant medications is approximately 80 percent. I consider this an important advance for psychiatry, even though epilepsy is not a mental illness, because the disease often produces mental symptoms.

Thus, to sum up, even after we restrict the time period to only the past forty years, and thereby fail to consider several prior contributions of the medical model (such as prevention of syphilitic dementia by means of penicillin, electroconvulsive treatment for depression, and barbiturates for symptomatic relief of anxiety), and we also eliminate the cases judged to be relatively unimportant, we still have the psychoactive drugs for schizophrenia, depression, mania, epileptic symptoms, and hyperkinesis and safer treatments for anxiety.

3.2.2. The Psychosocial Model   During the past forty years, a considerable amount of research has been done on the effects of psychotherapy. The research is difficult to carry out for both practical and theoretical reasons, and for years there was no consensus on whether psychotherapy was beneficial at all. There is still a great deal of controversy and confusion, but a few conclusions are beginning to emerge. The major conclusion is that in general, given all types of psychotherapy and all types of illnesses usually treated, the average patient is typically somewhat better off than a member of a control group receiving no treatment at all. This conclusion is reached not from analyses of single studies but from meta-analyses combining the results of as many as 375 separate pieces of research.[13] This flurry of reviews was provoked

---

[12] Ibid., 165.

[13] The most significant of these reviews are S. Hollon and A. Beck, "Psychotherapy and Drug Therapy: Comparison and Combinations," in A. Bergin and S. Garfield, eds., *Handbook of Psychotherapy and Behavior Change* (New York: Wiley, 1978); L. Luborsky, B. Singer, and L. Luborsky, "Comparative Studies of Psychotherapies: Is It True That 'Everybody Has Won and All Must Have Prizes'?" *Archives of General Psychiatry* 32 (1965):995–1008; D. H. Malan, "The Outcome Problem in Psychotherapy Research," *Archives of General Psychiatry* 29 (1973):719–729; J. Meltzoff and M. Kornreich, *Research in Psychotherapy* (New York: Atherton Press, 1970); M. L. Smith and G. V. Glass, "Meta-analysis of Psychotherapy Outcome Studies," *American Psychologist* 132 (1977):752–760; Smith, Glass, and Miller, *The Benefits of Psychotherapy*; M. J. Lambert, F. D. Weber, and J. D. Sykes, "Psychotherapy Versus Placebo" (poster presented at the annual meeting of the Western Psychological Association, Phoenix, Arizona, April 1993); and P. Crits-Christoph et al., "Meta-analysis of Therapist Effects in Psychotherapy Outcome Studies," *Psychotherapy Research* 1, no. 2 (1991):81–91. Names in parentheses in the following text indicate the studies that best document the information presented.

by Hans J. Eysenck's review in 1952 of 24 studies. He claimed to show that 72 percent of control subjects receiving no therapy managed to improve, while only 44 percent of subjects receiving psychoanalytic therapy and 66 percent of those receiving eclectic therapies improved.[14]

Since our interest here is not in a static view of the average effects of psychotherapy at present but rather in the degree to which the psychosocial model has increased the abilities of its practitioners to treat mental illness, let us use two of these reviews of psychotherapy outcome research. L. Luborsky et al. reviewed 32 studies.[15] Among the first half (done between 1954 and 1963), 13 of the 16 (81 percent) showed some advantage for psychotherapy over no treatment, but of those done between 1964 and 1974, only 8 (50 percent) had a positive outcome. One might first blame the apparent decrease in effectiveness on increased quality of outcome research. However, Luborsky claims that when the poorer half of the studies (methodologically) is compared with the better half, the two subgroups show the same main trends.

The same thing can be done with Meltzoff and Kornreich's 101 studies using the same cutoff date.[16] They have the studies broken down into six categories: all were first classified as adequate or questionable in design and then further subdivided according to results—positive and major, positive but minor, and null or negative. These are the percentages of positive studies before and after 1963, depending on whether the data from the questionable studies are included or not: all positive studies regardless of design: early, 72.5 percent and recent, 88.6 percent; all positive studies, adequate design only: early, 83.3 percent and recent, 85.0 percent. This breakdown shows some improvement, although the amount according to only the adequate studies is very slight. The conclusion to be reached here is that, although at least half of the studies show that some patients benefit to some extent (and this may be only a barely measurable difference from the control group members), there is no discernible trend showing improvement in success with therapy. In fact, Luborsky's study shows a decrease in effectiveness.

This is the general picture. Now let us look at the results in more detail. Although traditional psychotherapy (psychoanalysis and its closer relatives) was developed specifically to treat neurosis, there is, surprisingly, a dearth of methodologically sound research showing its effectiveness in this particular area (Malan). Also, evidence for the effectiveness of any type of psychotherapy in treating psychosis is weak and ambiguous. Some studies show a small advantage for therapy over control group, but a sizable number also show no

---

[14] Hans J. Eysenck, "The Effects of Psychotherapy: An Evaluation," *Journal of Consulting Psychology* 16 (1952):319–354.

[15] Luborsky, Singer, and Luborsky, "Comparative Studies of Psychotherapies."

[16] Meltzoff and Kornreich, *Research in Psychotherapy.*

difference. Most of the studies concern schizophrenia; some concern the affective psychoses, especially depression; and very few concern paranoid psychosis (Meltzoff, Luborsky). So for these two classes of illness that are the most common of mental disorders, psychotherapy has the least documented effect.

Many of the illnesses for which traditional psychotherapy is often found to be helpful are, ironically, not ones that the average person would even consider to be mental illnesses, despite their classification as such by the American Psychiatric Association.[17] Also, behavioral therapies have been found helpful for a variety of ailments not generally thought of as mental: enuresis, headache, irritable bowel syndrome, and sexual dysfunction.[18]

There is also fairly strong evidence for the effectiveness of psychotherapy (Malan, Luborsky) and hypnotherapy (Luborsky) for treating psychosomatic illnesses. Epilepsy (occurring in about 1 per 200 population) results in personality disorders in some cases and in brain damage causing mental deterioration in others. Some of the cases of epilepsy have known factors that trigger the seizures, so if they are precipitated by emotional factors, the illness can sometimes be controlled with the help of psychotherapy. Marital adjustment problems and other adjustment reactions sometimes respond to counseling. Parkinsonism occurs in about 2 per 1,000 population and often produces intellectual impairment, mild dementia, and depression. Supportive psychotherapy, encouraging the patient to stay active, slows the course of the disease. Also, both hypnotherapy and psychotherapy have been shown to aid in treatment of skin conditions such as warts and eczema and of various stress-related illnesses such as ulcers.

There are two relatively new treatments in the field of psychotherapy that merit some attention. One of these, systematic desensitization for phobias, is a product of learning theory, developed in the 1960s. This is definitely an instance of progress for the psychosocial model since it works much better than traditional psychotherapy for this illness. But how significant is it compared to the advances of the medical model? The factors to consider are the frequency and severity of the illness, along with the effectiveness of the treatment. There is no doubt that systematic desensitization is highly effective for typical phobias such as fear of snakes or of heights. However, this type of phobia is seldom a serious impairment to the patient's well-being. In fact, many of the 'patients' for the systematic desensitization studies were college students who were usually not suffering much from their phobias. In contrast,

---

[17] See *Diagnostic and Statistical Manual of Mental Disorders*, 4th ed. (Washington, D.C.: American Psychiatric Association, 1994).

[18] Dianne L. Chambless et al., "Training in and Dissemination of Empirically Validated Psychological Treatments: Report and Recommendations," *Clinical Psychologist* 48, no. 1 (Winter 1995):3–23; see Table 3.

agoraphobia is often quite severe and highly debilitating, but systematic desensitization is not notably effective in treating this serious illness.

Another new treatment (of the 1970s) is cognitive therapy. This is a significant advance; cognitive therapy is as effective for depression as the antidepressants[19] and has been shown to help with agoraphobia and some other anxiety disorders as well.

This is the extent of documentable improvement in the effectiveness of the psychosocial model's treatments over the past forty years. Against a baseline of limited success with psychotherapy for a variety of illnesses, we find only two well-documented new treatments: behavior therapy for phobias, a fairly insignificant illness; and cognitive therapy for a serious disorder. Recall, however, that the medical model already offers two treatments for depression, both more effective and faster than traditional psychotherapy: the antidepressant medications and shock therapy. Cognitive therapy will be an improvement over these treatments if it is shown to have fewer side effects and to result in a lower remission rate. So all in all, this is not an encouraging picture.

To make matters worse, there are two results of research that tend to undermine all at once the positive results for psychotherapy. The first is that with the few exceptions just noted, all of the immense variety of different psychotherapeutic techniques produce nearly the same rate of improvement. One would expect that different treatments based on different explanations of the same illness would have different results, but this is not the case. This has led some theorists to suspect that it is not the specific techniques used in the psychotherapies that help the patients but rather some general factors common to all forms of psychotherapy.[20] The factor most suspected in this role is expectation of cure on the part of the patient.

This has led to a second type of research that tends to undermine the positive results of psychotherapy. Researchers have set up studies of the effects of treatment where the control group is given a bogus treatment intended to increase subjects' expectation for cure to the same level as that of the treatment group. One study so far has found that when the controls are matched with the treatment group on this factor, even systematic desensitization is no longer found to produce significantly better results than a bogus treatment.[21]

---

[19] Comer, *Abnormal Psychology*, 180.

[20] A. Kazdin and L. Wilcoxon, "Systematic Desensitization and Nonspecific Treatment Effects: A Methodological Evaluation," *Psychological Bulletin* 2 (1976):103–107; R. B. Sloane et al., *Psychotherapy Versus Behavior Therapy* (Cambridge, Mass.: Harvard University Press, 1975); Crits-Christoph et al., "Meta-analysis of Therapist Effects"; S. L. Garfield, "Eclectic Psychotherapy: A Common Factors Approach," in J. C. Norcross and M. R. Goldfried, eds., *Handbook of Psychotherapy Integration* (New York: Basic Books, 1992).

[21] J. E. Marcia, B. M. Rubin, and J. S. Efran, "Systematic Desensitization: Expectancy Change or Counter Conditioning," *Journal of Abnormal Psychology* 74 (1969):382–387.

3.3. Overview

In this section we have considered two models of mental illness, perhaps equally plausible on the surface. We have seen that the treatments attributable to both models are at least partially successful in some instances for some illnesses. However, when we look at the two models on the basis of their momentum—the progress they have made in improving their treatment capabilities during the past forty years—the medical model is far superior. In fact, we can reasonably expect to see even greater strides in the future as the basic sciences upon which research in psychiatric medicine depends increase our understanding of the functioning of the human brain and nervous system, and as increasing technological abilities (e.g., positron-emission tomography) allow new and more detailed research. In the period between 1950 and the present, we have seen psychiatric medicine progress from dependence on trial-and-error discovery of treatments (e.g., the effectiveness of both chlorpromazine and convulsive therapy for mental illness was discovered by accident) to the point where elaborate theories regarding the neurochemical defects responsible for mental illnesses are being pieced together. For example, a deficiency in the enzyme dopamine-beta-hydroxylase may be responsible for the symptoms of schizophrenia. The technological capabilities to test such theories are now partially developed, and there is every reason to expect that they will continue to improve at a fast pace. It is also possible that identification of genetic factors in the etiology of mental illnesses will eventually lead to effective interventions. In contrast, the psychosocial model faces new research that may show that its small but steady rate of treatment success has been an illusion created by research practices that are deficient in not granting sufficient attention to the positive effects of ingredients of the therapeutic process common to all forms of psychotherapy.[22]

This issue of momentum is an important one. The question at issue is, Which model is rationally preferable? Present treatment capability is not a suitable measure because we recognize that models and theories need time and favorable external circumstances in order to develop. It may further be objected that rate of improvement of treatment efficacy is not a fair measure either, if the period of time chosen for the comparison finds one model starting near zero (the medical model) and the other already effective (the psychosocial model). If it is the case that during the period in question the medical model only 'catches up' with the psychosocial model, then why is it rationally preferable to the psychosocial model?

---

[22] This, of course, is a highly contested issue. For a recent discussion, see Lisa Grencavage, Richard R. Bootzin, and Varda Shoham, "Specific and Nonspecific Effects in Psychological Treatments," in Charles G. Costello, ed., *Basic Issues in Psychopathology* (New York: Guilford Press, 1993), 359–376.

The answer has to do with momentum, meaning the apparent likelihood of the medical model continuing to progress versus the likelihood that the psychosocial model will continue to show little or no progress. The bases for this judgment are that improvements in research technology and basic sciences can be expected to feed into more and better research on suspected physiological contributors to mental illness, while there is no such help visible on the horizon for the psychosocial model. In fact, the interesting direction for the future of psychotherapy research seems to be the exploration of nonspecific factors that contribute to recovery from illness, which are common not only to all forms of psychotherapy but also to other kinds of treatment. So even if research on nonspecific treatment variables leads to the ability to manipulate them to better advantage, this advantage is expected to be shared by all healing practitioners and is therefore not likely to give the psychosocial model any edge over the medical model. I have more to say on this topic in what follows.

4. The Contribution of the Psychosocial Model

The question to be addressed in this section is whether, despite a lack of progress relative to the medical model, the psychosocial model has made a significant contribution to the overall progress of the field. My thesis is that it has in this respect: without information provided by the practice of therapy using the psychosocial model's assumptions and guidelines, we would not be in as good a position to see the inherent inadequacy of the medical model. This information dramatically increases the anomalies faced by the medical model to the point where they can no longer reasonably be ignored.

To appreciate this contribution of the psychosocial model, let us first examine the situation for the medical model prior to its venturing into the field of psychiatry. Considering physical illness alone, we can already find several anomalies. First, psychosomatic illness is real (physical) illness, apparently generated by a psychological condition. It is generally quite resistant to ordinary medical treatment; if one condition is cured, a new one usually develops to take its place. Psychosomatic illness is anomalous for the medical model in that the condition that seems unavoidably to count as the cause of the illness is a psychological one, and furthermore, direct physiological intervention is not a satisfactory approach to treatment. These patients are generally referred to psychiatrists.

Second, stress-related illnesses such as high blood pressure, asthma, and ulcers are also somewhat anomalous for the medical model for the same reasons. Physiological intervention is less effective in many cases than is psychiatric therapy to reduce stress.

Third, there are other assorted physical conditions that respond to hypnotherapy and psychotherapy. An interesting example is the common wart, known to be caused by a virus, often resistant to direct treatment—it can be removed surgically but often returns. That hypnotherapy—mere suggestion—could cause warts to disappear is totally inexplicable according to a model that sees the microbiological disease entity alone (the virus) to be a complete, adequate explanation of the condition.

Fourth, there is the placebo response. The knowledge that many people improve when given any treatment at all, so long as they believe it to be an effective treatment, has been with us since the days of Hippocrates. 'Placebo' is difficult to define, but we can say that it is a drug or procedure used in treatment that is believed to have no specific physiological action on the condition in question.[23] The most common example of a placebo is a sugar pill given in place of active medication. Placebo effects have been reported in branches of medicine as diverse as dentistry, podiatry, and optometry. The best-known effect of the placebo is pain relief, but it has also been found to induce nausea, relieve anxiety, decrease stomach secretions, and speed recovery from surgery.

What makes the placebo anomalous for the medical model is that the decisive factor in its effectiveness is the patient's *expectation* of what it will do, not the placebo's chemical or other physical properties. There is no place in the medical model for a psychological factor such as this, and as a result we have little understanding of how a psychological state such as the expectation of pain relief can actually cause pain reduction. Apparently, it does so by inducing the body to produce beta-endorphin, a natural opiatelike chemical, since administration of naloxone, which blocks the effects of endorphins, eliminates the placebo effect.[24]

It may be thought that the discovery of a chemical mechanism involved in pain reduction in response to a placebo shows that the placebo response is not anomalous for the medical model after all. This is not the case, however, for the chain of biochemical causes and effects can never be "closed" without the psychological variable of expectation of relief. It is just as much a puzzle for the medical model to explain how expectation of pain reduction can cause increased beta-endorphin production as it formerly was to explain how it could cause pain reduction. Furthermore, those who would have dismissed the placebo response by claiming that the subjects had simply imagined the improvement cannot now claim that the increased beta-endorphin

---

[23] The specific ingredient in a treatment is the one that is expected to produce the desired change; those that form the setting or vehicle for the specific ingredient are called nonspecific. Obviously, what counts as specific and nonspecific is dependent on theory.

[24] See H. Lehman, N. P. Vasavan Nair, and N. S. Kline, "Beta-endorphin and Naloxone in Psychiatric Patients: Clinical and Biological Effects," *Journal of the American Psychiatric Association* 136 (1979):762–766.

production is likewise imaginary. Thus, the anomaly becomes more, rather than less, pronounced when this neurochemical process is found to intervene.

These four anomalies are common knowledge, but it seems quite reasonable that they have been more or less ignored by medical practitioners. In the first place, the history of science shows us that even the best theories have anomalies; a policy of rejecting all theories thus afflicted would bring science to a screeching halt. Lakatos suggests that it is integral to scientific rationality to hold on "dogmatically" to our core theory in the face of anomalies so long as we have some plan in mind to take account of them. The medical practitioners' general strategy along these lines seems to be to refer all such anomalous cases to a psychiatrist. And this is a perfectly acceptable strategy until psychiatrists themselves adopt the medical model, whereupon it finally and unavoidably becomes the medical model's duty to explain these phenomena in terms of physiology and microbiology.

The medical practitioners' strategy for dealing with the placebo anomaly seems to be to deny or ignore it. Research shows that doctors tend to deny their use of placebos.[25] Also, it is noteworthy that researchers in all fields of medicine have implicitly classified the placebo response as an experimental artifact rather than as a response to treatment. This is shown by the fact that in the test of a new treatment, its effects will be compared to that of a placebo, but the placebo response is considered to be a baseline, not an alternate therapeutic effect, and the patients who receive it are called a "no treatment" control group.

Again, I do not intend to imply that there is anything irrational about this strategy of denial. Science could not be done without such maneuvers. There comes a point, however, when an anomaly can no longer be ignored. The contribution the psychosocial model makes is to push the placebo anomaly to that point.

Recall that in section 3.2 I discussed the worry that it is not psychotherapeutic techniques themselves that account for the benefits of psychotherapy, but rather it is the patient's expectancy of cure that is the determining factor. This worry is based on two findings: the similarity of effect size for all types of psychotherapy and the lack of difference between the effects of therapy and of any bogus treatment that generates the same level of expectancy of cure as that of the treatment group. These findings have led a number of people to suggest that the effects of psychotherapy are nothing other than

---

[25] A. K. Shapiro and E. Struening, "A Comparison of the Attitudes of a Sample of Physicians About the Effectiveness of their Treatment and the Treatment of Other Physicians," *Journal of Psychiatric Research* 10 (1974):217–229.

the placebo response.[26] In my judgment, this is a very likely conclusion, but if one wishes to be more guarded, one still has to admit that the effect of psychotherapy is at best only a slight addition to the placebo response that can be obtained when the placebo treatment is convincing. In either event, this new way of looking at the placebo response, developed as a result of psychotherapy outcome research, presents an anomaly of great magnitude for the medical model when applied to mental illnesses. In short, one of the main forms of treatment for a wide spectrum of illnesses within one whole branch of medicine (psychiatric medicine) is either identical with the administration of a placebo or else on the basis of current evidence is indistinguishable from it.

What this means for psychiatry is that, even if the medical model is extremely fruitful for the study and treatment of mental illness, it is not adequate, as it stands, to explain a huge number of cases of recovery from mental illnesses. A new model is required that can integrate psychological factors and physiological factors into unified causal theories.

Now, it may have been obvious from the outset that psychiatry is in need of a new model; the medical model could not account for the successes of psychotherapy in any event. The main effect of the reinterpretation of psychotherapy outcomes as placebo responses (in conjunction with the interpretation of mental illness as a class of physical illness) is that the medical model's adequacy for understanding *any* illness is called into question. To the extent that researchers using the medical model succeed in discovering physiological abnormalities associated with mental illnesses, they are faced with the anomalous cures of (or improvements in) these conditions by psychotherapy. By reinterpreting psychotherapy as a placebo treatment, we find a common phenomenon of a great magnitude throughout all of medicine. This phenomenon points dramatically to the conclusion that an adequate understanding of health and illness must consider psychological factors along with and in interaction with physiological factors. More specifically, what the placebo response suggests is that the organism has rather surprising resources for curing itself of various kinds of illnesses and that these resources can be stimulated through the psychic life of the patient. At this point, it appears that continuing research in any field of medicine with a model that directs our attention only to physiological factors in illness and its treatment and ignores this interesting and promising factor in the recovery from illness would be a grave error.

Thus, we can see that in this particular instance the proliferation of alternative viewpoints has been of great importance to the overall development of the field. The weaker psychosocial model has contributed to our understanding of mental illness, forcing us to adopt a more sophisticated conception of illness *in general* than that offered by the medical model in its original form.

---

[26] The most noted of these is J. D. Frank, *Persuasion and Healing* (Baltimore: Johns Hopkins University Press, 1973).

5. Medical Research of the Future:
An Integrated Model

One way to sum up the foregoing section is to say that there is an inherent contradiction in the thinking of many medical practitioners. The medical model has justified ignoring many anomalies within the field of medicine itself by means of an implicit dualism: psychosomatic illness and the placebo response are *mental* phenomena and as such of no interest to medical practitioners. But when the medical model is applied to 'mental' illness itself, the model assumes the *reducibility* of the mental to the physical.

I argued in Chapter 1 that there is now a third option beyond dualism and reductionism: nonreductive physicalism. We should not be surprised, then, to find a third model of mental illness developing that takes advantage of this new 'thinking strategy.' In the past few years, it has become common in psychiatric or clinical psychology textbooks either to mention the earlier models, with their limitations, and then to urge that their insights be combined, or to propose an entirely new model: a biopsychosocial model.[27]

Such models tend to conceive of mental illness in terms of concepts drawn from systems theory. Systems research studies organizational characteristics of systems at various levels of organization—the biochemical, the organic, the individual, the social—and seeks isomorphies from which fundamental laws and principles applicable to all levels of organization can be constructed.

An excellent example of an isomorphy found in systems at various levels of organization is the feedback loop. This is a concept that applies equally well in numerous kinds of systems, mechanical, biological, interpersonal, ecological. As long ago as the 1930s, physiologist Walter Canon became interested in the mechanisms (which he called homeostatic mechanisms) that regulate bodily functions—maintaining temperature, respiration, heart rate, and others within an acceptable range. He suggested that the physician's role ought to be that of aiding the body in maintenance of its own health by using increased understanding of these mechanisms.[28]

Notice how the concept of the feedback loop encourages recognition of top-down causation. The purpose of a feedback mechanism is to keep tabs on the variation of some condition (e.g., temperature in the room) and to initiate processes of change when the condition varies beyond certain limits (e.g., the thermostat turns on the furnace when the temperature drops below

---

[27] In the former case, see, for example, Comer, *Abnormal Psychology*. In the latter case, see, for instance, David H. Barlow and V. Mark Durand, *Abnormal Psychology: An Integrative Approach* (Pacific Grove, Calif.: Brooks/Cole, 1995); and Ronald W. Pies, M.D., *Clinical Manual of Psychiatric Diagnosis and Treatment: A Biopsychosocial Approach* (Washington, D.C.: American Psychiatric Press, 1994).

[28] Walter Canon, *The Wisdom of the Body* (New York: Norton, 1939).

sixty-five degrees). But without reference to some other system or level of organization, the feedback mechanism is incompletely explained. The function of the thermostat is to keep the temperature of the house within a certain range; but once we consider the function of anything, we are really considering how it relates to some other system. In this case, there is a relation between room temperature and the needs of the human body for its own temperature control and perhaps also a connection with higher-level economic and political systems involved in energy pricing. How the thermostat works is a question for analysis of its parts; why it does what it does is a question requiring a top-down or systems approach. The choice of a systems-organizational concept such as the feedback loop automatically directs attention to the factors that relate the event or entity to its environment.

The systems approach and the concept of the feedback loop are turning out to be quite fruitful for an understanding of illness. Let us assume that health is the normal state of the organism and that it is ordinarily maintained by means of the operation of numerous interlocking feedback processes. By means of these processes, variables at all levels of the hierarchy of the sciences are interrelated: biochemical, organic (including brain function), emotional, cognitive, interpersonal, sociocultural. Illness will then be regarded as a condition produced by the malfunction or breakdown of one or more of these health-maintaining feedback systems. Such a system may break down for two reasons: there may be a malfunction within the system itself, or the condition to which it attempts to adjust simply exceeds the capabilities for adjustment of the system. The air conditioner may be broken, or if the house is on fire, the air conditioner's cooling capabilities may be exceeded.

The study of any illness would require detailed knowledge of all the systems that are usually involved in its prevention or cure. Diagnosis and treatment of individual cases would require the determination of what factors resulted in this person's breakdown and a decision regarding the most effective means of intervention to return the systems to proper functioning. This approach to the study of illness does not prejudice the researcher or the therapist in favor of either biochemical or environmental factors. Rather, this approach encourages an openness to investigating all possibilities and an openness to correcting the malfunction in whatever manner is most likely to be effective.

The placebo response is not anomalous for a model developed along these lines since the primary assumption of such a model is that the organism is a system of self-correcting (feedback) systems. The only question that needs investigation is how the expectation of recovery enhances these self-healing systems. To use Lakatos's terminology, a natural part of the positive heuristic of a feedback model would be investigation of the mechanisms involved in the placebo response.

Allow me to illustrate the possibilities for feedback models of mental illness by quoting at length from David H. Barlow and V. Mark Durand on the etiology of depression:

Basically it seems that depression and anxiety may share a common, genetically determined biological vulnerability in many cases. . . . This vulnerability would be best described as an overactive neurobiological response to stressful life events. Once again, this vulnerability is simply a general tendency to develop depression (or anxiety) rather than a specific vulnerability for depression or anxiety itself.

A second important factor is the role of stressful life events. There is good evidence that these events precede the onset of depression in most cases. How do these two factors interact? The best current thinking is that stressful life events activate our stress hormones which, in turn, have wide-ranging effects on our neurotransmitter systems, particularly those involving serotonin and norepinephrine. There is also evidence that activation of these stress hormones over the long term may actually "turn on" certain genes producing long-term structural and chemical changes in the brain. For example, processes triggered by long-term stress may actually lead to atrophy of neurons in parts of the brain such as the hippocampus that contribute to the regulation of emotions. This kind of structural change might have ongoing implications for the regulation of neurotransmitter activity. The extended effects of stress may also disrupt the circadian rhythms in certain individuals, who then become susceptible to the recurrent cycling that seems so uniquely characteristic of the mood disorders. . . .

Those of us who develop mood disorders also possess psychological vulnerability experienced as feelings of inadequacy for coping with the difficulties confronting us. As with anxiety, we may develop this sense of control in childhood. It may range on a continuum from feeling totally confident and in control to feeling that events are utterly beyond our ability to cope. When these vulnerabilities are triggered, it is the "giving up" process that is crucial to the development of depression. . . . A variety of evidence indicates that these attitudes and attributions correlate rather strongly with biochemical markers of stress and depression such as by-products of norepinephrine. . . . There is also some evidence that early experience with stress, perhaps years before the onset of mood disorders, may create more enduring cognitive vulnerability that enhances, and makes more severe, the biochemical and cognitive response to stress later in life.

Finally, it seems clear that social and cultural factors such as the number or quality of our interpersonal relationships or our gender . . . may "protect" us from the effects of stress and, ultimately, the development of mood disorders. Alternatively, these factors may at least ensure that we recover from these disorders more quickly.[29]

So here we have an account of mood disorders that involves genetic, neurochemical, environmental, social, and cultural factors and accounts for the disease by means of a negative feedback loop, where one type of factor exacerbates the effects of the others. The interesting thing about such a feedback model is that it explains so easily why two radically different kinds of treatment—pharmacological and cognitive—should be equally effective.

---

[29] Barlow and Durand, *Abnormal Psychology*, 278–279.

Neither the medical nor the psychosocial model could explain why the other sort of treatment should work. The feedback model also explains why a combination of antidepressant medication and cognitive therapy should work better than either alone: the negative cycle is interrupted at two different points.

This example can be no more than a hint of how medical and psychiatric researchers and therapists might be better able to utilize resources of all types as a result of a more adequate model of illness. However, I hope it is suggestive nonetheless. As Kuhn and Feyerabend have pointed out, the crucial factor in the abandonment of a theory (model) faced by serious anomalies is often the availability of an alternative. In this case, most of the contributions of many of the older theories are saved, while some of their more serious difficulties are avoided. The development of a biopsychosocial model seems to be exactly what is needed to advance psychiatry beyond its present schizophrenic state.

6. Conclusion

I have looked at the two most important models in the mental health sciences today. I assessed the progress of the two models using increasing treatment efficacy as a measure. The main question addressed was whether the psychosocial model, despite its own lack of progress, has nonetheless made a significant contribution to the overall development of the field, as the works of Feyerabend and Lakatos would suggest that it might. The answer is that thanks to the limited success the model's practitioners have had in the clinic, we can see that illness is a much more complex phenomenon than the medical model would lead us to suspect, and the reinterpretation of the effects of psychotherapy as placebo response highlights this anomaly as an important clue to the direction medical research of the future must take. This provides one instance in support of the claim that the limited relativism, the theoretical proliferation that Anglo-American postmodern epistemologists expect us to have to live with, will be not detrimental to the progress of science but a significant help.

Finally, the recent development of a biopsychosocial model of mental illness not only is very promising for the field of mental health but also serves as a fine illustration of the benefits to be derived from abandonment of modern reductionist thinking.

PART II

Philosophy of Religion

5 • • •

Beyond Modern Liberalism and Fundamentalism

1. Introduction

American Protestant Christianity is often described as a "two-party system." The division between "liberals" and "conservatives" (the latter including both fundamentalists and evangelicals) is a deep one and is often marked by acrimony and stereotypes.[1] I leave it to the sociologists and historians to account for the acrimony.[2] My goal in this chapter is to help clarify the differences between the intellectual positions of these two groups and to advance the thesis that the *philosophy* of the modern period is largely responsible for the bifurcation of Protestant Christian thought. (A similar argument could be made for the Catholic church, but the Catholic scene is complicated by the issue of the teaching authority of the church.)

Modern theologians have inevitably shared with their culture the assumptions of modernity. I have argued previously that three of the most important sets of assumptions have to do with the nature of knowledge, of language, and of causation. However, Ludwig Wittgenstein has claimed that it is *pictures*, rather than propositions, *metaphors*, rather than statements, that determine our philosophical convictions. Thus, in each case the philosophical assumptions of modernity have been caught up by means of pictures or

---

[1] See Roger E. Olson, "Whales and Elephants: Both God's Creatures but Can They Meet? Evangelicals and Liberals in Dialogue," *Pro Ecclesia* 4, no. 2 (Spring 1995):165–189.

[2] See, for example, Robert Wuthnow, *The Restructuring of American Religion, Society, and Faith Since World War II* (Princeton: Princeton University Press, 1988); George Marsden, *Understanding Fundamentalism and Evangelicalism* (Grand Rapids, Mich.: Eerdmans, 1991); and Martin E. Marty, *Modern American Religion, Volume 2: The Noise and the Conflict, 1919–1941* (Chicago: University of Chicago Press, 1991).

metaphors that have turned out to provide very limited options to theologians for making sense of their discipline. Limited, in fact, to two. This, I claim, is the reason that there are *two* strands of modern Protestantism, not the spectrum of positions that one might have expected. It is not possible in one chapter to present a historical survey of these two theological traditions. I restrict myself to describing two *ideal types*, but I illustrate each type by referring to a few prominent historical examples.[3]

Historian Claude Welch characterizes the liberal tradition as emphasizing

> divine immanence as a corrective to the Latin overemphasis on transcendence ... [and] thus a different view of God's relation to the natural and historical process and an evolutionary perspective; the understanding of revelation not as an intrusion but as correlative to human discovery, as a process of God disclosing himself through genuine human means in a never-ending process of criticism and experiment; religious experience as a verifiable datum comparable to scientific data; the Bible as a document of religious experience and thus a different sort of authority.[4]

If we take the foregoing as an account of the liberal type of theology, we can construct a parallel account of conservative theology, both fundamentalist and conservative evangelical. First, in place of an emphasis on God's immanence is a focus on God's power to intervene in natural and human affairs. Second, revelation itself is an intervention into human life, conveying information about God and God's relation to the universe. The Bible's authority derives from God's direct revelation. So it is the Bible, not experience, that functions as the data for theology. Finally, the emphasis on revelation as a source of information about divine realities hints at the conservatives' representative or propositionalist theory of religious language.

In brief, my explanation for the existence of these two types is as follows: The 'building' metaphor governing modern epistemology required theologians to find an indubitable foundation for theology; the two options turned out to be Scripture or a special sort of religious experience. Modern theories of language allowed religious language to be understood as either representative or expressive. The reductionist-determinist worldview of modern science allowed for only two accounts of divine action: either God intervenes in the clockwork universe, or God works immanently within all of its processes. The conservative type of theology is characterized by scriptural

---

[3] For a more extensive treatment, see Nancey Murphy, *Beyond Liberalism and Fundamentalism: How Modern and Postmodern Philosophy Set the Theological Agenda* (Valley Forge, Penn.: Trinity Press International, 1996).

[4] Claude Welch, *Protestant Thought in the Nineteenth Century*, 2 vols. (New Haven: Yale University Press, 1972, 1985), 2:232.

foundationalism, a representational (propositional) theory of religious language, and an interventionist view of divine action. The liberal type is experiential, expressivist, and immanentist.

I hope also to make clear in this chapter that these central structures of modern thought have had a destructive influence on theology. However, it has been the thesis of this book that the assumptions of modernity are being called into question. In the following two chapters, I try to indicate where theology may be going next.

2. Foundationalism and Theological Method

Foundationalism has had a powerful influence on the development of modern theology. Theologians have been captivated by the picture of their theology as a building needing a solid foundation. But what is that foundation to be? The short answer is that there have turned out to be only two options: Scripture or experience. Conservative theologians have chosen to build on Scripture;[5] liberals are distinguished by their preference for experience. This forced option has been a major cause of the split between liberals and conservatives.

2.1. Foundationalism in Early Modern Philosophy of Religion

Let us first see how foundationalism shows up in early modern philosophy of religion since this will have an important influence on conservative theology. A significant epistemological change from René Descartes to John Locke concerns the question of whether religious knowledge is part of one great structure, which includes knowledge of the empirical world as well, or whether it is a separate edifice. Descartes argued from the "clear and distinct" ideas in his mind to the existence of God and from there to knowledge of the external world. So he envisioned the whole of knowledge as one great edifice, founded on special, indubitable ideas and with theological knowledge as a necessary middle story between the foundation and the top floor of science.

In contrast, Locke distinguished three kinds of knowledge. A first kind was empirical science, founded on ideas from sensory experience. A second kind was indubitable knowledge, similar to Descartes's, based on "relations of ideas" and constructed by means of deductive reasoning; geometry is one instance of this, and another is Locke's argument for the existence of God.[6] A third kind of knowledge was based on revelation—that is, on God's "extraordinary way of

---

[5] See Ronald Thiemann's account of foundationalist uses of Scripture in *Revelation and Theology: The Gospel as Narrated Promise* (Notre Dame, Ind.: University of Notre Dame Press, 1985).

[6] John Locke, *An Essay Concerning Human Understanding* (1690; reprint, New York: Dover, 1959), 4.10.

communication." In *The Reasonableness of Christianity* (1695), Locke presented his conclusions regarding the theological doctrines that could be certified on the basis of Scripture: the Messiahship of Jesus was essential; but some doctrines, such as the Trinity and predestination, he judged unfounded.

So we may imagine the epistemological scene as envisioned by Locke to include the great edifice of science, a separate structure of theology founded on Scripture, and additional deductive structures founded on "the relations of ideas." But the theological structure is not entirely independent of the deductive argument for the existence of God: God's existence makes the whole idea of revelation intelligible, so, pursuing the architectural imagery, we might say that these two structures are connected by an arch or a buttress.

The problem Locke faced, and one that has plagued scriptural foundationalists ever since, is how to know that *this* book, the Christian Bible, is in fact the expected revelation. The very fact that this question can be asked creates problems for a *foundationalist* use of Scripture—it undermines it. Conservative apologetics from Locke's day to the present have attempted to shore up the basement. Locke argued that miracles served as outward signs to convince "the holy men of old" that God was indeed the author of their purported revelations.[7]

2.2. Foundationalism in Conservative American Theology

Locke's theological structure has continued to influence conservative theologians, especially in America. A great impetus came from the work of Thomas Reid, founder of commonsense realism. Reid influenced Princeton theologians such as Charles Hodge and Charles's son, Archibald Alexander Hodge, whose work, in turn, greatly influenced the American fundamentalist movement. Reid's role was to call into question the philosophical arguments that had been taken by liberals to undermine Locke's apologetic structure.

A clear example of the repetition of Locke's theological architecture can be found in the writings of Baptist theologian Augustus H. Strong.[8] For Strong, theology is the science of God and of the relation between God and the universe (1). Its aim is to ascertain the facts respecting God and to exhibit these facts in an organic system of truth. The possibility of theology is grounded in the existence of God and in God's self-revelation. Revelation presents "objective facts," which serve as "the ground of theology" (13). Systematic theology "takes the material furnished by Biblical and Historical Theology and with this material seeks to build up into an organic and consistent whole all our knowledge of God and of the relations between God and the universe" (41).

---

[7] Ibid., 4.19.

[8] Augustus H. Strong, *Systematic Theology: A Compendium and Commonplace Book,* 12th ed. (1907; Philadelphia: Judson Press, 1949).

Note the foundationalist metaphors: facts from Scripture as ground, theology as building. Later sections of his *Systematic Theology* offer Cartesian- and Lockean-style proofs for the existence of God (71–89), "reasons *a priori* for expecting a revelation from God" (111–114), and "positive proofs that the Scriptures are a divine revelation" (145–195).

The special foundational status of Scripture in conservative theology is well represented in the following quotation from Charles Hodge, in which he claims that even if there are other sources of theological knowledge, each must be tested against the biblical norm:

> The duty of the Christian theologian is to ascertain, collect, and combine all the facts which God has revealed in the Bible. . . . It may be admitted that the truths which the theologian has to reduce to a science, or, to speak more humbly, which he has to arrange and harmonize, are revealed partly in the external works of God, partly in the constitution of our nature, and partly in the religious experience of believers; yet lest we should err in our inferences from the works of God, we have a clearer revelation of all that nature reveals, in his word; and lest we should misinterpret our own consciousness and the laws of our nature, everything that can be legitimately learned from that source will be found recognized and authenticated in the Scriptures; and lest we should attribute to the teaching of the Spirit the operations of our own natural affections, we find in the Bible the norm and standard of all genuine religious experience.[9]

From the perspective of the epistemologist, an interesting feature of fundamentalist and conservative evangelical theology is the sort of claims that are made about Scripture. One of the central tenets of fundamentalism is the verbal inspiration of Scripture and its complete *inerrancy*. It is often pointed out that strict doctrines of inerrancy did not appear in Christian history until the modern period.[10] Notice that the demands of foundationalist epistemology explain why conservatives would want to be able to make such radical claims about the truth of Scripture: if Scripture is to provide an *indubitable* foundation for theological construction, then all of its teachings must be free from error, lest the theologian make erroneous judgments in distinguishing true teachings from false ones or essential teachings from incidental cultural assumptions. Not all conservative theologians are infallibilists or inerrantists, but we can see that the ideal type of scriptural foundationalist theology would be expected to have such a doctrine.

Conservative theologians vary in their accounts of the means of construction from Scripture to theology. Some speak rather indiscriminately of induction, of

---

[9] Charles Hodge, *Systematic Theology*, 3 vols. (New York: Scribner's Sons, 1871), 1:11.

[10] A. A. Hodge made explicit the Princeton doctrine of plenary verbal inspiration, claiming that the Bible is inerrant in its original autographs and infallible in what it teaches. See A. A. Hodge, *Outlines of Theology* (1878); and A. A. Hodge and Benjamin B. Warfield, "Inspiration," *Presbyterian Review* (1881).

deduction, and of theology as mere organization of the facts of Scripture. But in all cases, the assumed direction of reasoning is what the foundationalist theory would lead us to expect: from the scriptural foundation to the higher levels of doctrine and theology; never from doctrine to the truth or meaning of the texts.

Elisabeth Schüssler Fiorenza provides a good summary of the early and most extreme versions of this approach to Scripture and theology. This type

> understands the Bible in terms of divine revelation and canonical authority. . . . In its most consistent forms it insists on the verbal inspiration and literal-historical inerrancy of the Bible. The biblical text is not simply a historical expression of revelation but revelation itself. It does not just communicate God's word but *is* the Word of God. As such it functions as *norma normans non normata* or first principle. Its mode of procedure is to provide through proof texts the ultimate theological authority . . . for a [theological] position. . . . The general formula is: Scripture says, therefore. . . . The Bible teaches, therefore. . . . As Holy Scripture the Bible functions as an absolute oracle revealing timeless truth and definite answers to the questions and problems of all times.[11]

Recent theologians of this type, however, tend to have more nuanced views of religious language and theological reasoning, and many recognize the need for critical methods to ascertain the meaning and application of scriptural texts. One example is Donald Bloesch, who is explicitly foundationalist in his understanding of the justification of theological claims: "As evangelical Christians we can and must speak of *foundations* of the faith. These are not, however, a priori principles or self-evident truths but the mighty deeds of God in the history of biblical Israel, the significance of which is veiled to us until our inner eyes are opened by the working of the Spirit."[12]

So in contrast to views such as A. A. Hodge's, it is not the words of Scripture themselves that undergird theology but rather the acts of God that are recorded therein. Furthermore, Bloesch distinguishes between purely historical events and their "revelational meaning" (19). To illustrate: one can believe that Jesus' tomb was empty and even that he rose from the dead without grasping the revelation that Jesus is the divine savior of the world.

Bloesch would like to be able to say that Scripture is inerrant, but he believes the term has been co-opted by "a rationalistic, empiricistic mentality that reduces faith to facticity" (27). Instead, he speaks of the abiding truthfulness and normativeness of the biblical witness (27). "What makes the

---

[11] Elisabeth Schüssler Fiorenza, *In Memory of Her: A Feminist Theological Reconstruction of Christian Origins* (New York: Crossroad, 1984), 4–5.

[12] Donald G. Bloesch, *Holy Scripture: Revelation, Inspiration, and Interpretation* (Downers Grove, Ill.: InterVarsity Press, 1994), 20.

Bible significant is not that it contains self-evident truth—truth that is universally recognizable—but that it conveys particular truth that is at the same time self-authenticating" (28).

So we see here a softening of the original foundationalist demand for *universally* accessible truth based on *indubitable* foundations.[13] Yet despite the hesitancy regarding inerrancy (and the absolute certitude such a doctrine provides), it is still the case that the authority of Scripture is *unchallengeable*. There is no other norm by which it can be called into question, not religious experience, church teaching, or culture.[14]

2.3. Undermining Locke

Let us now back up historically and look at the factors that drove liberal theologians to abandon the structure of religious knowledge first set out by Locke. Recall that I described Locke's view of religious knowledge rather whimsically as two structures connected by a buttress: theology is founded on Scripture, but Scripture's authority derives from the fact that it is revealed by God. The claim for revelation is *buttressed* by means of a rational argument for the existence of God and the further inference that something like the Christian revelation was to be expected from such a God.

Two factors conspired to demolish confidence in the Lockean structure. One was the work of philosophers such as David Hume and Immanuel Kant, showing that traditional arguments for the existence of God were invalid. The other factor had to do with shifting views of the proper relation between reason and revelation. For Locke, if reason could show that a book was the product of divine revelation, then it was reasonable to accept *all* of its contents even if the contents themselves could not be certified as true on the basis of reason. But the eighteenth-century British deists granted reason a more significant role, saying that only those tenets of traditional theology that could be established independently of revelation ought to be accepted.[15] Thus, reasonableness became a criterion for what is or is not to be accepted *within* the scriptural accounts.

In eighteenth-century Germany there had been a move similar to Locke's to shore up orthodox forms of belief by seeking rational support for the

---

[13] This raises the question of what is left of foundationalism if one gives up on the indubitability of the foundations. I suggest two criteria: the assumption that knowledge systems must include a class of beliefs that are somehow *immune from challenge* (if not indubitable) and the assumption that all reasoning within the system proceeds in one direction only—from that set of special beliefs to others, but not the reverse.

[14] See Donald G. Bloesch, *Essentials of Evangelical Theology, Volume 1: God, Authority, and Salvation* (San Francisco: Harper and Row, 1978), chap. 4.

[15] See Jeffrey Stout, *The Flight from Authority: Religion, Morality, and the Quest for Autonomy* (Notre Dame, Ind.: University of Notre Dame Press, 1981), 117.

claims of revelation. They were followed by the "neologists," who, in a manner exactly parallel to the deists, restricted the content of divine revelation to what can be known independently by natural reason.[16] Thus, reason was unleashed to sift Scripture for truth, and in many cases what remained after the sifting turned out to be too little to support the structure of orthodox Christian theology.

One variety of test applied to Scripture was historical-critical method. Albert Schweitzer well expresses the liberals' conclusion that what historical reason leaves standing is too meager a foundation for Christianity. In the following passage he describes the crucial shift from Scripture construed as a source of historical knowledge to Scripture construed as the source of an ongoing religious experience, which is then foundational for Christianity:

> The historical foundation of Christianity as built up by rationalistic, by liberal, and by modern theology no longer exists; but that does not mean that Christianity has lost its historical foundation. The work which historical theology thought itself bound to carry out, and which fell to pieces just as it was nearing completion, was only the brick facing of the real immovable historical foundation which is independent of any historical confirmation or justification.
>
> Jesus means something to our world because a mighty spiritual force streams forth from Him and flows through our time also. This fact can neither be shaken nor confirmed by any historical discovery. It is the solid foundation of Christianity.[17]

So reason, once the buttress supporting a theology founded on scriptural revelation, has now undermined the structure. If Scripture is to serve at all, it must be a repository of something more basic and less prone to rationalist attack. That more basic something—for Schweitzer, the mighty spiritual force streaming from Jesus through our own time—can be categorized more broadly as religious experience.

2.4. Foundationalism in Modern Liberal Theology

With Schweitzer, writing in 1906, we are again ahead of our story. Let us go back now to the beginning of modern liberal theology. In 1799 Friedrich Schleiermacher published his famous *Speeches*, in which he proposed that the essence of religion (of all religion, not just Christianity) is a certain sort of feeling or awareness. He described this feeling differently over the years of his theological career: as intuition of the infinite, as immediate perception of

---

[16] See Richard Crouter, Introduction to Friedrich Schleiermacher, *On Religion: Speeches to Its Cultured Despisers* (Cambridge: Cambridge University Press, 1988), 6–7.

[17] Albert Schweitzer, *The Quest of the Historical Jesus* (1906; reprint, New York: Macmillan, 1950), 399.

the universe and of the existence of all finite things in and through the infinite, as immediate consciousness of the deity, and, in his mature work, as "awareness of absolute dependence," or, what he took to be the same, as "God-consciousness."[18]

Schleiermacher's achievement in his systematic theology was to show how all (legitimate) doctrines were derivable from this foundational experience. But they were derivable not in a logical sense but in the sense that they were apt or adequate *expressions* of that core experience. So, for example, the source of the doctrine of creation is the awareness not only of humankind's dependence upon God but also of the absolute dependence of everything else. The doctrines of grace and sin derive from the Christian's experience of the waxing and waning of God-consciousness. The divinity of Christ consists in his uninterrupted and perfect God-consciousness.

Now in what sense is this a *foundationalist* use of experience for theology? First, Schleiermacher described the relevant experience as universal and unmediated. It is universal in the sense that, although this experience is colored differently in different cultures, and for Christians by the influence of Jesus, it is the common source of *all* religions. It is a kind of experience that is available in principle to all, not just to Christians. When Schleiermacher claimed that the awareness of absolute dependence is unmediated, he meant that it does not depend on inference or interpretation. Thus, it is the true *source* or *origin* of religion, not a product of anything prior. In other words, there is no deeper foundation. Second, doctrine is to be evaluated in light of experience, never the reverse. So God-consciousness is the origin of all religion; first-order religious language (prayer, preaching, etc.) as an expression of that consciousness is foundational for all doctrine and theology.

Liberal theologians since Schleiermacher have followed him in taking human religious experience as a starting point for theology. For example, in America, William Newton Clarke began his systematic theology as follows:[19] "Theology is preceded by religion—religion is the reality of which theology is the study. Religion is the life of man in his superhuman relations" (1). "As the science of religion, [theology] seeks to discover and make known the true, rational, abiding foundation of real and eternal religious life" (5); "it is the unfolding and exposition of the concepts that enter into religion" (4).

Notice that liberals do not deny a role for Scripture in theology; they merely deny that it is foundational for theology. That is, the use of Scripture itself is undergirded by a theory of universal religious experience.

---

[18] Friedrich Schleiermacher, *The Christian Faith,* ed. H. R. Mackintosh and J. S. Stewart (1821–1822; reprint, Edinburgh: T. & T. Clark, 1960), § 4.

[19] William Newton Clarke, *An Outline of Christian Theology,* 12th ed. (1894; Edinburgh: T. & T. Clark, 1913).

There are two closely related features of liberal theology that may strike the uninitiated as peculiar. The first is an emphasis on Christianity as one of a class of world religions, in contrast to the more traditional and conservative attempts to explain other religions in light of Christian convictions. The second is the peculiar nature of the experiences cited as foundational for Christian theology. There is Schleiermacher's feeling of absolute dependence. "Feeling" here translates the German word *Gefühl,* but it is not an adequate translation. In attempting to convey the sort of experience that is meant, Claude Welch writes:

> *Gefühl* is not a "faculty" parallel to the faculties of thinking and willing. . . . Feeling was equated with immediate self-consciousness. The feeling of utter dependence belonged to the highest level of human self-consciousness, in which the antithesis between the self and other which characterizes the sensuous self-consciousness disappears again. . . . It is thus the deepest (or highest) level of self-existence, not an isolable "religious experience," but an "original relation of intuition and feeling."[20]

Other liberal theologians provide equally abstruse accounts of foundational religious experience. For example, Karl Rahner, the great twentieth-century Catholic theologian, traces theology to the experience of self-transcendence; the midcentury Protestant Paul Tillich characterizes the primordial religious experience as being grasped by ultimate concern. Ordinary Christians might well wonder if they have ever had such experiences and why plain old Christian experience, say of conversion or prayer or conviction of sin, should not be the focus instead. The foundationalist theory answers this question. Foundations must be universally accessible and indubitable. Therefore, the requisite experiences must not be specifically Christian in character or subject to mistake or misinterpretation—there are spurious conversions, imagined voices masquerading as answers in prayer.

So a thoroughgoing experiential foundationalist must base the system on a kind of experience that is available to all people, regardless of culture and religious training, and it must be immediate, independent of interpretation, and such that if one has it, one is unable to doubt that one has it or to be mistaken about its character. Not all theologians who count themselves in the liberal tradition will fit this ideal type, of course, but one can see here an explanation for seeking an experiential foundation that moves as far in this direction as possible.

Let me sum up so far. I have claimed that foundationalist epistemology, characteristic of modern thought in general, has had a dramatic effect on

---

[20] Welch, *Protestant Thought,* 1:66.

conceptions of the nature of theology. If theology must have an indubitable foundation, a natural direction to turn was to Scripture, and here, ideally, one will want an inerrantist account of its truth. I have also described some of the factors that led liberal theologians to seek a deeper level of support in religious experience, and I have claimed that the foundationalist theory led them to seek a peculiar *sort* of experience, universal and unmediated.

Thus, we see that there are two distinct strategies for satisfying the demand for indubitable foundations for theology. Scripture itself is understood differently by proponents of the two strategies. Conservatives emphasize that these books are the result of acts of God, not of human discovery, and emphasize the factual character of their contents. Scripture provides precise and true accounts of supernatural realities. Liberals see Christian Scripture as belonging to a class of writings that express, with different degrees of aptness, insights regarding God and human life that arise from religious experience. So according to the liberals, Christian Scripture may be especially authoritative for Christians, but it differs from other religious writings in degree, not in kind.

3. Modern Theories of Language

Notice, in the foregoing contrast between liberal and conservative theologies, the different ways in which each must speak about religious language. Conservatives emphasize factuality, truth, precise representation. Liberals see the aptness or adequacy of theological language for religious expression to be a matter of degree.

There is a correlation between these two understandings of religious language and theories developed by philosophers of language in the late modern period. I claimed in Chapter 1 that the predominant modern philosophical theory can be described as referential or representative—words get their meaning by referring to objects; the purpose of language is to represent states of affairs. This referential approach to language had to be supplemented by the expressivist theory to account for realms of discourse such as ethics and aesthetics. In general, this is the thesis that language that is not factually meaningful, if significant at all, merely expresses the attitudes, intentions, or emotions of the speaker. In 1955 R. B. Braithwaite proposed an expressivist theory of religious language: when Christians say "God is love," they are really expressing their own intention to lead 'agapeistic' lives, an intention they fortify by telling inspirational stories about Jesus—which need not be true.[21]

---

[21] R. B. Braithwaite, *An Empiricist's View of the Nature of Religious Belief* (Cambridge: Cambridge University Press, 1955). For an account of Braithwaite's views, see James Wm. McClendon Jr. and James M. Smith, *Understanding Religious Convictions* (Notre Dame, Ind.: University of Notre Dame Press, 1974), 23–29.

It would be anachronistic to claim that these two twentieth-century philosophical theories contributed to the split between liberal and conservative theology since the two theological traditions were well developed long before that. However, it is often the case that philosophy serves to uncover and formalize assumptions already implicit in a worldview. In this case, it is plausible to suppose that another picture or metaphor—the image of language itself as a picture or mirror of reality—has permeated modern thinking, influencing theologians and philosophers alike.

Many Christians, I imagine, would dismiss Braithwaite's theory out of hand, but its emphasis on expression is closer to Schleiermacher's understanding of religious language than is the representative theory. Schleiermacher defined Christian doctrines as "accounts of Christian religious affections set forth in speech"; the Christian symbols were therefore to be evaluated in terms of their adequacy for expressing the Christian's inner awareness.[22]

We find a contemporary expressivist account of religious language in the works of feminist theologian Patricia Wilson-Kastner:

Theology and religious faith are not the same. Religious faith constitutes a fundamental personal relationship to the sacred. Faith may be expressed in a variety of physical, emotional, or intellectual ways, but they all spring from a primary, suprarational acceptance of the divine, rooted in a sense of the presence of the Ultimate to the self. Theology is the rational spelling-out and explaining of one's faith. There are many possible explanations, even for the same individual, and therefore many possible theologies. These theologies are influenced by point of view, questions raised by the individual and the culture of which the person is a part, the intellectual framework of the person formulating the theology, and so forth. Theology is a superstructure which arises from a faith, and expresses it on one significant but limited level. . . .

If one were to search among other human acts for a comparison to the activity of faith, the best would be, I think, aesthetic experience. Insight, intuition, creativity, and appreciation—each has its analogue in a faith which both apprehends and feels itself grasped by the divine, reaches new depths of itself and others, and enjoys the beauty of all in light of the Ultimate. Theology, in this case, is most comparable to activities like aesthetics, or art, or literary criticism. It is a limited, modest, always inadequate, but absolutely essential endeavor to explain intellectually what beauty is, how it is present in and to us, and how we realize it. At the same time, to claim that any faith is perfect or any theology the final or full answer is as absurd as the notion that any artist has perfectly apprehended or expressed all beauty.[23]

---

[22] Schleiermacher, *The Christian Faith*, § 15.

[23] Patricia Wilson-Kastner, *Faith, Feminism, and the Christ* (Philadelphia: Fortress Press, 1983), 6.

Note both the expressivist language and the building metaphor in her description of theology as a "superstructure."

In more conservative branches of the Christian tradition, referential views of religious language abound. Here, however, the referents are supernatural, rather than natural, realities. Doctrines, if they are true, accurately represent these (largely) invisible states of affairs. Notice how the representational theory of language depends on scriptural foundationalism. The problem for the representational theory is epistemological: how is one to *know* that sentences accurately represent *invisible,* supernatural realities? The only plausible answer is by means of divine revelation.

The expressivist theory of religious language coheres with and reinforces experiential foundationalism. If the essence of religion is feeling, an inner awareness, then expressivist language is really the only sort possible for first-order religious language—what is there to say about a feeling other than to express it? But religious perceptions do not come with precise descriptions attached. The human race must grope for adequate ways to communicate an awareness that is of a different order from awareness of the physical universe. The appropriate kind of language is symbolic or metaphorical. It is not, in any straightforward sense, a representation of objective external realities.[24]

4. Science, Causation, and Divine Action

If the foundationalist image of knowledge and the 'picture' picture of language have dominated modern theology, no less has another picture held modern theologians in thrall. In the years following Isaac Newton's formulation of the laws of mechanics, modern philosophers and scientists came to think of the universe as a gigantic machine. The most striking proponent of this view was Pierre Simon de Laplace, who envisioned every atom in the universe as a component in an unfailingly precise cosmic clockwork mechanism. He was not unaware of the theological implications. There is a famous story in which Napoleon is said to have asked Laplace about the role of God in his system. Laplace's reply: "I have no need of that hypothesis."

In less picturesque terms, the atomism, reductionism, and determinism of modern thought constituted a worldview in which it became difficult or impossible to give an account of divine action. That is, if science gives a complete and adequate account of the causes of all events, where, if at all, is there room for God to act?

---

[24] For a comparable account, see George Lindbeck's distinction between the cognitive-propositional and experiential-expressivist models of religion and doctrine in *The Nature of Doctrine: Religion and Theology in a Postliberal Age* (Philadelphia: Westminster Press, 1984).

There is irony here. The notion of a law of nature began as a metaphorical extension of the idea of a divinely sanctioned moral code.[25] For early modern scientists, as well as for medieval theologians, the notion of a law of nature served as an account of how God managed the physical universe. In fact, René Descartes took the laws of motion to follow from a more basic principle, explicitly theological: "God is the First Cause of movement and . . . He always preserves an equal amount of movement in the universe."[26]

However, within a century or so, the metaphorical character of the term 'law of nature' had been forgotten, and the laws were granted some form of real existence independent of God. Some philosophers and theologians argued that if God were to violate such a law, it would show God to be inconsistent—first willing the law and then willing its contrary. Thus, the 'laws' that were once expressions of the will of God came to be seen as obstacles to divine purposes.

The simplest solution for reconciling divine action with the modern conception of the clockwork universe was deism, a very popular option in the eighteenth century. Many deists concluded that, even though God was the creator of the universe and author of the laws of nature, God was not at all involved in ongoing natural processes or in human affairs. They maintained a notion of God as the source of moral principles but rejected all the rest of positive religion, including the notion of revelation.

My thesis is that modern theologians who would stay within the Christian fold have found only two strategies—interventionism and immanentism—for reconciling their accounts of divine action with the Newtonian-Laplacian worldview. Liberals and conservatives, as before, divide rather neatly into two camps. Conservatives take an interventionist approach to divine action—God is sovereign over the laws of nature and is thus able to overrule them to produce special divine acts. Liberals take an immanentist approach, emphasizing God's action in and through all natural processes.

There may be no other single factor that has such thoroughgoing consequences for theology; thus, the divide between liberals and conservatives on this issue opens a veritable chasm between their theological outlooks. This issue is of fundamental importance in determining one's views on theological method and Scripture: immanentism requires an experiential foundation for theology since scriptural foundationalism is dependent upon an interventionist view of revelation.

4.1. Interventionism

Interventionism has generally been the doctrine of choice for conservative theologians. These theologians hold that in addition to God's creative activity,

---

[25] See Bas C. van Fraassen, *Laws and Symmetry* (Oxford: Clarendon Press, 1989), 1–14.

[26] René Descartes, "Principles of Philosophy," part 2, xxxvi, in *Philosophical Works of Descartes,* trans. E. S. Haldane and R. T. Ross (Cambridge: Cambridge University Press, 1985).

which includes ordaining the laws of nature, God occasionally violates those very laws in order to bring about extraordinary events. God makes something happen that would not have happened in the ordinary course of nature. According to Charles Hodge, there are three classes of events in regard to divine action:

> In the first place, there are events . . . due to the ordinary operations of second causes, as upheld and guided by God. To this class belong the common processes of nature; the growth of plants and animals, the orderly movements of the heavenly bodies; and the more unusual occurrences, earthquakes, volcanic eruptions, and violent agitations and revolutions in human societies. In the second place, there are events due to the influences of the Holy Spirit upon the hearts of men, such as regeneration, sanctification, spiritual illumination, etc. Thirdly, there are events which belong to neither of these classes, and whose distinguishing characteristics are, First, that they take place in the external world, *i.e.,* in the sphere of the observation of the senses; and Secondly, that they are produced or caused by the simple volition of God, without the intervention of any subordinate cause. To this class belongs the original act of creation, in which all coöperation of second causes was impossible. To the same class belong all events truly miraculous. A miracle, therefore, may be defined to be an event, in the external world, brought about by the immediate efficiency, or simple volition of God.[27]

In response to the question of how God relates to the laws of nature, Hodge writes:

> The answer to that question, as drawn from the Bible is, First, that He is their author. He endowed matter with these forces, and ordained that they should be uniform. Secondly, He is independent of them. He can change, annihilate, or suspend them at pleasure. He can operate with them or without them. "The Reign of Law" must not be made to extend over Him who made the laws. Thirdly, as the stability of the universe, and the welfare, and even the existence of organized creatures, depend on the uniformity of the laws of nature, God never does disregard them except for the accomplishment of some high purpose. He, in the ordinary operations of his Providence, operates with and through the laws which He has ordained. He governs the material, as well as the moral world by law. (1:607)

So it is a mistake to think that the laws, once 'created,' are immutable; they merely reflect God's ordinary way of working, and they can be suspended on occasion for some higher purpose.

Note that an assumption held by some contemporary Christians, that an event is an act of God only if it cannot be explained by natural laws, is a

---

[27] Hodge, *Systematic Theology,* 1:618.

degenerate view of divine action by Hodge's standards. God works in regular processes just as much as in miraculous interventions.

Millard Erickson is a contemporary example of this type. He defines miracles as "those special supernatural works of God's providence which are not explicable on the basis of the usual patterns of nature." However, he says, "one of the important issues regarding miracles involves their relationship to natural laws or the laws of nature."[28] Erickson considers several proposed answers, including the view that miracles require the laws of nature to be broken. His preferred position is the following:

> A third conception is the idea that when miracles occur, natural forces are countered by supernatural force. In this view, the laws of nature are not suspended. They continue to operate, but supernatural force is introduced, negating the effect of the natural law. [Here Erickson refers to C. S. Lewis's book *Miracles*.] In the case of the [floating] axhead [recorded in 2 Kings 6:6], for instance, the law of gravity continued to function in the vicinity of the axhead, but the unseen hand of God was underneath it, bearing it up, just as if a human hand were lifting it. This view has the advantage of regarding miracles as being genuinely supernatural or extranatural, but without being antinatural, as the second view makes them to be. To be sure, in the case of the [great catch of] fish, it may have been the conditions in the water which caused the fish to be there, but those conditions would not have been present if God had not influenced such factors as the water flow and temperature. And at times there may have been acts of creation as well, as in the case of the feeding of the five thousand. (408)

The image of the unseen hand of God at work in the world is ideal for representing this view of the nature of divine action.

4.2. Immanentism

The liberals' immanentist view of divine action was a reaction both against deism, with its view that God is not active at all within the created world, and against the conservative theologians' view that God performs special, miraculous acts. The liberal view emphasizes the universal presence of God in the world and God's continual, creative, and purposive activity in and through all the processes of nature and history.[29] This view made it possible to understand progress, both evolutionary progress in the natural world and human progress in society as manifestations of God's purposes.

A primary motive for emphasizing God's action *within* natural processes was the acceptance of the modern scientific view of the world as a closed

---

[28] Millard Erickson, *Christian Theology* (Grand Rapids, Mich.: Baker, 1990), 406.

[29] See Owen Thomas, ed., *God's Activity in the World: The Contemporary Problem* (Chico, Calif.: Scholars Press, 1983), 3.

system of natural causes, along with the judgment that a view of divine activity as intervention reflected an inferior grasp of God's intelligence and power. That is, this view suggested that God was unable to achieve all of the divine purposes though an original ordering and also that God was inconsistent in willing laws and then also willing their violation. In short, the higher view of divine action was thought to be one in which God did not need to intervene. Thus, the interpretation of divine activity in terms of miracles tended to disappear in the liberal tradition.

We find variations on these themes from Schleiermacher up through the present. Schleiermacher claimed that divine providence and the operation of causal laws entirely coincide; the word 'miracle' is just the religious word for 'event.' Furthermore, he argued that it can never be in the best interests of religion to interpret an event as a special act of God in opposition to its being a part of the system of nature since to so interpret it works against the sense of the absolute dependence of the *whole* upon God.[30]

The mid-twentieth-century New Testament scholar Rudolf Bultmann argued for the "demythologization" of Christianity. Views of divine action as intervention in the chain of finite events are mythological, he claimed, in that they make God a cause among causes. A nonmythological account of divine action requires that we think of God as acting not between events in the chain of natural causes but within them. Bultmann says:

> Faith acknowledges that the world-view given by science is a necessary means for doing our work in the world. Indeed, I need to see the worldly events as linked by cause and effect not only as a scientific observer, but also in my daily living. In doing so there remains no room for God's working. This is the paradox of faith, that faith "nevertheless" understands as God's action here and now an event which is completely intelligible in the natural or historical connection of events. This "nevertheless" is inseparable from faith.[31]

Faith, by which Bultmann means a person's existential orientation, is the essence of religion. From this it follows that

> first, only such statements about God are legitimate as expressions of the existential relation between God and man. Statements which speak of God's actions as cosmic events are illegitimate. The affirmation that God is creator cannot be a theoretical statement about God as *creator mundi* in a general sense. The affirmation can only be a personal confession that I understand myself to be a creature which owes its existence to God. It cannot be made as a neutral statement, but only as thanksgiving and surrender. (66)

---

[30] Schleiermacher, *The Christian Faith*, §§ 46, 47.
[31] Rudolf Bultmann, "The Meaning of God as Acting," in Thomas, ed., *God's Activity*, 64.

For a more recent example: Maurice Wiles claims that removal of the need for God's correction of the irregularities in Newton's model of planetary motion has been the removal of a problematic concept of a "God of the gaps." "This process has not meant, however, that it has become impossible to speak in any way at all of God in relation to the natural world. Rather . . . "it has made possible the reaffirmation of a more profound concept of God as the transcendent ground of there being a world at all."[32] Wiles argues that to speak of God acting *in history*, then, is in fact to speak of the varying human response that is elicited by the unvarying divine presence in historical events. Some events more than others elicit the response of faith—especially the events surrounding Jesus Christ. Thus, the distinction between general and special acts of God pertains not to a difference in God but to a difference in human perception.

To sum up so far: when modern science led to the belief that all events are determined by the operation of natural laws, the question arose as to whether and how God could still be said to act. Deists denied that God still acts. For Christian theologians, there have appeared to be only two options: to say that God must occasionally break the laws of nature in order to accomplish divine purposes or to say that God's purposes are completely achieved in and through the lawful operations of nature and history.

5. The Pervasive Consequences of Theories of Divine Action

5.1. Doctrine

Brian Hebblethwaite and Edward Henderson have written that "whatever theological question is raised, some conception of God's action in the world will turn out to be involved in any answer proposed."[33] To see how the topic of divine action pervades the entire theological enterprise, consider again this quotation from Bultmann:

> First, only such statements about God are legitimate as expressions of the existential relation between God and man. Statements which speak of God's actions as cosmic events are illegitimate. The affirmation that God is creator cannot be a theoretical statement about God as *creator mundi* in a general sense. The affirmation can only be a personal confession that I understand myself to be a

---

[32] Maurice Wiles, "Religious Authority and Divine Action," in Thomas, ed., *God's Activity*, 183.

[33] Brian Hebblethwaite and Edward Henderson, eds., *Divine Action: Studies Inspired by the Philosophical Theology of Austin Farrer* (Edinburgh: T. & T. Clark, 1990), 1.

[34] Bultmann, "The Meaning of God," 66.

creature which owes its existence to God. It cannot be made as a neutral statement, but only as thanksgiving and surrender.[34]

Bultmann then goes on to say:

> Moreover, statements which describe God's action as cultic action, for example, that He offered His Son as a sacrificial victim, are not legitimate, unless they are understood in a purely symbolic sense. Second, the so-called images which describe God as acting are legitimate only if they mean that God is a personal being acting on persons. Therefore, political and juridical conceptions are not permissible, unless they are understood purely as symbols. (66)

This is a clear example of the way a theory about how God acts influences the very meaning of doctrinal statements. The doctrine of the atonement cannot be an objective statement about a cultic or juridical act of God in the past if it is the case that God only acts upon individual persons in the immediacy of a personal relationship.

5.2. Commensurability Versus Incommensurability with Science

It will already be apparent that one's theory of divine action has consequences for how one regards religious language. Bultmann reasons that if the doctrine of atonement could not refer to an objective past act of God, then any language that gives this impression must be purely symbolic. This factor has conspired with another to result in a typical liberal understanding of religious language as separate from and incommensurable with the language of science. The other factor, of course, is that all events are assumed to be both natural events and divine acts. Thus, any event can be described in scientific terms, which link it to antecedent conditions and natural laws, or it can be described as it fits into God's purposes. But great confusion arises if these two separate linguistic frameworks are mixed. The religious description must be kept in a compartment separate from the scientific description.

This linguistic compartmentalization is but the more recent version of a strategy that goes back to Kant, whose work greatly influenced the rise of liberal theology. One of Kant's goals was to provide an account of knowledge that would protect both religion and the concept of human freedom from the determinism of Newtonian science. He did this by distinguishing between the phenomenal realm and the noumenal realm. Causal determinism pertains only to the phenomenal realm of sensory experience, not to noumena such as God and morally free selves. His theory entailed that it is absolutely illegitimate to apply categories from the phenomenal realm to God. Whatever we can know about God is a product of practical reason—reasoning about moral duties. I borrow a term from the philosophy of science and call any view that similarly compartmentalizes religion and science an incommensurabilist thesis.

The contrary position held by conservatives, which I call the commensurabilist thesis, is that science and theology are similar enough epistemologically and linguistically to interact. The positive side of this thesis is that it allows for a coherent view of reality. Some knowledge comes from scientific observation and reason, some comes from revelation, and there are some truths that can be known by either route. Scientific and theological knowledge can be described in the same epistemological terms. Both begin with facts, whether these be the facts of empirical observation or the facts of Scripture. Scientists and theologians alike proceed in their reasoning from facts to theories, interpretations, systematic summaries.

However, if it is possible for scientific and religious knowledge to overlap and to be related by logical implication, then it is also possible for them to conflict. Here we find the root of liberal and conservative differences on the evolution controversy. Liberals not only reject the claim that creation and evolution are in conflict; they also reject the very possibility of conflict. The appearance of conflict results from an improper juxtaposition of incommensurable languages.

Some proponents of the commensurabilist approach to religion and science have overly simple views of both scientific and theological reasoning. However, Nicholas Wolterstorff has worked out a sophisticated account of how Christian convictions bear on scientific theorizing. A crucial term in his work is that of a "control belief." Wolterstorff notes that scientific theories are never determined solely by the facts; this logical gap between theory and data indicates that the evaluation of theories must involve other considerations. Wolterstorff suggests that one of these other considerations is beliefs as to what constitutes an acceptable *sort* of theory on the matter being investigated. These control beliefs can be derived either from theology or from philosophy. Sometimes they lead to the rejection of certain sorts of theories. One example was Cartesian physicists rejection of Newton's theory of gravity because of their philosophical control belief that there can be no action at a distance. In other cases, control beliefs lead to the pursuit of theories of certain sorts, such as Albert Einstein's continued search for hidden variables in quantum theory on the basis of this theological control belief that "God does not play at dice." History shows that some control beliefs have furthered scientific advance, whereas others have interfered with its progress.

To complete the account of the proper relation between Christianity and science, Wolterstorff develops the notion of "authentic Christian commitment." This refers to that complex of beliefs and actions to which Christians, after careful consideration, believe they must be committed in order to be followers of Jesus Christ. Once a Christian scholar has come to a decision about the content of authentic Christian commitment, that commitment should function as a source of control beliefs for evaluating theories in the scholar's field.

The title of Wolterstorff's book is *Reason Within the Bounds of Religion*,[35] a play on Kant's *Religion Within the Limits of Reason Alone*. The title makes it clear that Wolterstorff is deliberately reversing the direction set by Kant's philosophy. In particular, he is rejecting the incommensurability thesis, as well as the priority Kant gave to reason over revelation.

In sum, an immanentist view requires an incommensurabilist position on the relation between religion and science in order to avoid the confusions that arise from mixing two different kinds of descriptions of the same event. An interventionist view of divine action permits a commensurabilist view of science and religion since it takes revelation to provide information for the completion of a single, true view of reality by means of supernatural communication.

5.3. Theological Epistemology and Divine Action

I argued previously that modern theologians have found only two sources for theological foundations: Scripture or a peculiar sort of universal religious experience. A theory of religious language correlates with each of these starting points. Representationalism or propositionalism is supported by the view that God has revealed in Scripture information about unseen realities. The expressivist view, that religious language at its most basic is a symbolic expression of the believer's religious awareness, is a correlative of experiential foundationalism since both assume that the essence of religion is an inward awareness of God.

The connections with the topic of divine action are as follows: if one holds an interventionist view of divine action, then it is perfectly reasonable to expect God to intervene in the world of human thought. In other words, the revelation contained in Scripture is but one instance among many of direct, providential action by God on behalf of the human race.

A. A. Hodge makes this connection clear. To the question "What are the necessary presuppositions . . . which must be admitted before the possibility of inspiration . . . can be affirmed?" he answers: first, "the existence of a personal God, possessing the attributes of power, intelligence, and moral excellence in absolute perfection," and, second, "that in his relation to the universe he is at once immanent and transcendent. Above all, and freely acting upon all from without. Within all, and acting through the whole and every part from within, in the exercise of all his perfections, and according to the laws and modes of action he has established for his creatures, sustaining and

---

[35] Nicholas Wolterstorff, *Reason Within the Bounds of Religion,* enl. ed. (Grand Rapids, Mich.: Eerdmans, 1984).

governing them, and all their actions."[36] So Hodge is claiming that God's immanent action must be supplemented by action from without if there is to be a revelation. Strong puts it more simply: "Religious ideas do not spring up wholly from within. External revelation can impart them. Man can reveal himself to man by external communication, and, if God has equal power with man, God can reveal himself to man in like manner."[37]

Hodge goes on to assert that the divine influence by which God's self-revelation is accomplished extends even to the choice of words, so that the thoughts God intended to convey are communicated with infallible accuracy.[38] So here we see Hodge's foundationalism wedded to an extreme form of the representationalist theory of language and both grounded in his interventionist view of God's action. With such a source of theological knowledge, who would want to turn to the nebulous realm of religious experience as a source for theology?

Maurice Wiles, on the liberal side, also recognizes the connection between theories of divine action and the proper use of Scripture in theology:

> If we agree that the acceptance of some authority . . . [such as the Bible] . . . is a part of the tradition within which a Christian theologian works, we shall have to acknowledge that when we take up the question of divine action, of what we can properly mean by speaking of God acting, we appear to be deeply committed already on the subject of our investigation. . . . For whatever may be our precise conception of the inspiration of the prophets or biblical writers, . . . it has normally been understood to involve some kind of special divine action. . . . Unless God acts in a special way in special events it is difficult to see how we could have religious authorities from within history and with the degree of specialness which Christians do in fact ascribe to their authorities.[39]

The point of Wiles's article, however, is to argue that one can in fact attribute authority to Scripture *without* an interventionist account of divine action. His strategy is to claim that, even though God acts uniformly in all events, some people respond more fully to God's presence, and their words provide authoritative guidance for others. Wiles puts it as follows:

> Now it is an inevitable feature of the variety to be found within human history that some people by virtue of their personality and of their situation are more fully responsive to the divine action than others. Their words and actions in turn will provide a particularly important focus for calling out such responses from others who follow them. And since that quality of life in them to which others

---

[36] A. A. Hodge, *Outlines of Theology*, enl. ed. (Grand Rapids, Mich.: Eerdmans, 1949), 65.
[37] Strong, *Systematic Theology*, 12.
[38] Hodge, *Outlines of Theology*, 66–67.
[39] Wiles, "Religious Authority," 181–182.

will respond was itself grounded in responsiveness to the divine action, we may rightly speak of the events of their lives as acts of God in a special sense towards those of us who are influenced by them. In calling them special acts of God we would not be implying that there was any fundamental difference in the relation of the divine action to the particular worldly occurrences of their situation; we would be referring to the depth of response and the creative potential for eliciting further response from others embodied in those particular lives or those particular events. (188)

The most important such life, for Christians, is that of Jesus Christ. Thus, Wiles continues,

if certain events [such as the life of Jesus] can be given such special importance without implying a different kind of activity on God's part in relation to the worldly occurrences concerned, then clearly the records which partly record and partly constitute such events can properly be regarded as having religious authority without that fact implying any special interventionist activity as responsible either for their composition or for their recognition as authoritative. (191–192)

So Wiles is confident that an immanentist account of divine action is compatible with granting Scripture the status of "a religious authority of the utmost importance" (193). However, such a view allows one to ascribe some measure of religious authority to the scriptures of other faiths as well. Furthermore, Wiles claims that some teachings in Christian Scripture can be rejected on the grounds that they conflict with more important scriptural doctrines. So it is clear that, even though Wiles is able to justify a special place for Scripture on the basis of his immanentist account of divine action, he is not able to justify a *foundationalist* use of Scripture. And religious experience, understood as greater responsiveness to God's action within the world, is the more basic category.

Strong's previously quoted phrase about religious ideas springing up from within the person is an apt account of the liberal view of inspiration. Since God does not directly impart knowledge of religious realities, this knowledge must arise within human consciousness by natural means—by perception of the divine dimension within or under surface realities. A common way of putting the matter in contemporary language is to say that religion involves the perception of *meaning* as opposed to mere knowledge of the facts.

6. Conclusion

6.1. Overview

I have claimed, first, that the modern foundationalist theory of knowledge presented theologians with only two options: to use either Scripture or religious experience as the foundation for theology. Second, modern philosophical theories of language have presented theologians with only two options: language that is descriptive, representational, and propositional or language that is merely expressive of the inner awareness, attitudes, and existential orientation of the speaker. Third, the modern scientific and philosophical conception of the material universe as a closed causal system has presented theologians with two options: to suppose that God occasionally violates the laws of nature in order to bring about special events or to suppose that all of God's purposes are accomplished in and through the operations of natural laws. Finally, Kant provided a model for insulating religion from science, and modern theologians since then have had to take a stand on the commensurability or incommensurability of theological and scientific ways of apprehending reality.

The choice of any one of these options tends to determine the choice of options from each of the other three pairs. This gives us two quite distinct types of theology, one associated with the conservative wing of the church, the other with the liberal. Conservative theology tends to be scriptural, propositional, interventionist, and commensurabilist. Liberal theology tends to be experiential, expressivist, immanentist, and incommensurabilist.

6.2. Problems with Each Type

So here we stand at the end of the modern period. Theologians have had two hundred years to try the various permutations on each of these positions. They have written theology in rationalist settings and romantic settings; in terms of Continental thought and Anglo-American thought; in times of cultural optimism and dark despair. Have we reached a point in history when it is fair to say that neither of these two theological strategies will work? I cannot prove that a theological genius will not come along in the next generation to solve problems her predecessors failed to solve. But I can point out that each of the theological types just described has problems that appear at this point to be insoluble.

The problem with the foundationalist use of Scripture is the question that always arises about how one can know, with the requisite certitude, that the Christian Bible is, in fact, the revealed word of God. Conservative theologians provide arguments, but none of them is strong enough to serve as the *foundation* for a system of religion.[40]

---

[40] Cf. David Hume: "We may establish it as a maxim, that no human testimony can have such force as to prove a miracle and make it a just foundation for any such system of religion." David Hume, "Of Miracles," in *An Inquiry Concerning Human Understanding,* ed. Charles W. Hendel (1748; reprint, Indianapolis: Bobbs-Merrill, 1955), 137.

There is a different but equally perplexing problem for those who attempt to use religious experience as the foundation for theology. Wallace Matson in his history of philosophy describes most modern theories of knowledge as "inside-out"; that is, the usual modern approach to the understanding of knowledge was to begin with the contents of one's experience—inside one's mind—and then argue from those ideas or experiences to knowledge about objective realities outside the mind. The arguments have always turned out to be problematic. The liberal use of religious experience as a foundation for theology is another instance of inside-out reasoning, and the question always arises of how to know that one's religious experience is experience of a real, objective divinity. That is, how can one ever know that religion is anything more than a symbolic expression of humankind's highest aspirations or basic life attitudes, as Ludwig Feuerbach suggested already in Schleiermacher's day?[41]

The problem with an interventionist account of divine action, especially as expressed by Erickson, is that it neglects the qualitative difference between God and ordinary created causes. To make God a force that moves physical objects is to make God a part of the system of physical forces. And if God is such a force, we ought to be able to measure divine action just as we do the forces of nature. The problem with an immanentist view of divine action is that it either removes the aspect of intention from God's acts or else makes every event equally intentional: earthquakes and the Holocaust as well as the growth of crops and the birth of Jesus.

The representative or propositional view of religious language has been criticized for its neglect of the self-involving character of religious discourse. It also fails to take account of the fact that human language has been developed to describe mundane realities and may not provide fitting categories for describing divine realities. (This criticism applies to early propositionalists but not their more recent followers, such as Donald Bloesch.) Furthermore, if the epistemological problems with scriptural foundationalism cannot be solved, then the issue must be faced of how one is ever to know that theological propositions accurately represent a reality beyond human experience.

The expressivist account of religious language seems to require a sharper separation between the cognitive and the expressive functions of language than can really be maintained. Suppose we say that the doctrine of creation is not a description of something God did at the beginning of time but rather an expression of one's sense of dependence upon God. But what good is it to have such a sense of dependence if one is not *actually* dependent upon God? Traditional accounts of dependence have focused on the fact that God created everything in the beginning and that God now keeps all things in

---

[41] Ludwig Feuerbach, *The Essence of Christianity* (1841).

existence. But if theology is not capable of making either of these statements about what God does, and of understanding them in a fairly straightforward propositional way, then what meaning does the expressivist account of the doctrine of creation have apart from describing an inner state of the believer? And should that inner state be of interest to anyone else?

The incommensurabilist view of the relation between theology and science seems to disregard the point just made, that we cannot detach values and meaning from the way things are. However, the commensurabilist view seems to disregard some important differences between the purposes of religion and of science; it disregards some important differences in the kinds of language that are used in each.

This is a grim assessment of the achievements of modern theology. But I want to stress that the problem is not with theology but rather with modernity. It may be only a slight exaggeration to say that it has simply been impossible to do theology in an intellectually respectable way using the resources of modern thought.

The next three chapters consider some of the new moves that are possible for theologians making use of the resources of Anglo-American postmodern philosophy. Chapters 9 and 10 provide an account of the relations between theology and science that supersedes the modern options.

6 • • •

Philosophical Resources for Postmodern Conservative Theology

1. Introduction

The title of this chapter is not an oxymoron; it was inspired by George Lindbeck, who claims to have provided a philosophical basis for "postliberal" theology. In *The Nature of Doctrine*, he presents an account of the nature of religion, doctrine, and theological method intended to supplant the views of the liberal tradition; he has done so by making use of some of the recent philosophical developments that are here called "postmodern."[1]

However, a flaw in his account is the assumption that the liberal tradition (his "experiential-expressivist" type) has superseded what he calls the cognitive or propositional view of religion and doctrine. It is this latter view that characterizes conservative theology, both fundamentalist and evangelical. In other words, he is assuming a three-stage development, from propositionalist, to experiential-expressivist, to his own cultural-linguistic view, or from preliberal, to liberal, to postliberal.

However, if we think about the main philosophical influences on the liberal and American fundamentalist traditions, the picture we get of their relations is not that liberalism supersedes fundamentalism but rather that they are parallel developments. Each of these branches of Christian thought was deeply influenced by a philosopher whose work was a reaction to Humean skepticism: Immanuel Kant for the liberals, Thomas Reid for the fundamentalists. The fact that Reid and Kant were almost exact contemporaries makes it appealing to represent the history as in Figure 6.1.

---

[1] George Lindbeck, *The Nature of Doctrine: Religion and Theology in a Postliberal Age* (Philadelphia: Westminster Press, 1984).

FIGURE 6.1   Philosophical antecedents of the liberal and conservative traditions

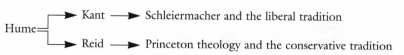

If this is the case, then it is worthwhile to ask, What does or should succeed modern *conservative* theology in a postmodern era? By 'conservative,' I mean to refer to both fundamentalist and conservative evangelical theology. (See Chapter 5 for a characterization of the views of fundamentalist and conservative evangelical theologians.) The latter is often referred to as post- or neofundamentalist, so there is a historical progression from modern fundamentalism to modern evangelicalism and thence, I suggest, to postmodern evangelicalism.

In the previous chapter, I set out to show how each of three modern philosophical positions has created limited options—usually only two—for theologians. Liberalism, I argued, represents the taking of one option from each pair; American fundamentalism and its heirs represent the taking of the other set of options. In other words, the modern philosophical climate forced a split between liberals and conservatives by providing two distinct 'channels' for the development of theological thought. Perhaps there always has been and always will be a range of views and tendencies within Christianity, from left to right, from liberal to conservative. Philosophy does not cause this variation; my claim, rather, was that philosophical options caused a decisive split and made two quite distinct traditions in place of a spectrum of variation.

In this chapter, I first look at the use postliberal theologians are making of the new postmodern philosophical resources. However, I focus on conservative theology here, and on resources for its reformulation in a postmodern framework, since less has been written on this subject so far. In particular, I describe resources provided by Alasdair MacIntyre for the justification of truth claims. However, if it is the case, as I claim, that modern philosophy served to bifurcate Christian theology into two discrete traditions, we might expect the differences among postmodern theologians to be less stark than those between their modern liberal and conservative predecessors. In fact, we may find theologians ranging along a continuum rather than divided into two camps. It is far too soon, however, to tell whether this will be the case.[2]

---

[2] However, see Roger E. Olson, "Whales and Elephants: Both God's Creatures but Can They Meet? Evangelicals and Liberals in Dialogue," *Pro Ecclesia* 4, no. 2 (Spring 1995):165–189. Olson traces significant parallels between postliberals such as Lindbeck and Hans Frei and postmodern evangelicals (which he calls postconservative evangelicals) such as Clark Pinnock, Mark Ellingson, and Stanley Grenz. "I believe that one crucial reason why evangelical-liberal dialogue happens so seldom and is so unfruitful (in terms of reaching accord) when it does take place is that both sides tend to be obsessed with *modernity* and that *postmodernity* may provide a new and better framework for such encounter" (169).

2. Postliberal Theology

It seems fair at this point in theological history to attribute the development of postliberal theology to the 'Yale School.' Here I include Paul Holmer, with his Wittgensteinian thesis that theology is the *grammar* of faith;[3] Hans Frei's identification of the historical critical approach to Scripture as a modern *referential* theory and his rejection of it in favor of a narrative approach;[4] Ronald Thiemann's critique of foundationalist doctrines of revelation and his development of a holist theological method;[5] and the contributions of George Lindbeck.

2.1. George Lindbeck

Lindbeck's recommendation for postliberal theology (which he says might be called postmodern as well) grows out of a cultural-linguistic understanding of religion borrowed from the social sciences. This view emphasizes the respects in which religions resemble cultures or languages together with their correlative forms of life. Religions are idioms for the construing of reality and the living of life. In such a scheme, doctrines are best understood as second-order discourse—as rules to guide practice and the use of first-order religious language (praise, preaching, exhortation, and the like).

Lindbeck's cultural-linguistic view does not ignore the cognitive and experiential dimensions of religions; he claims that the linguistic categories and grammar provided by religion are necessary *conditions* for both cognition and experience. A religion is a communal phenomenon that shapes the subjectivities of individuals rather than being primarily a manifestation of those subjectivities. It is a linguistic medium that *makes possible* the description of realities and the formation of beliefs rather than being a catalog of those beliefs.

The question of truth arises in two ways in a cultural-linguistic approach. One involves the consistency or coherence of each part of the system with the rest—first-order community practices and beliefs must be consistent with second-order theological and doctrinal statements and vice versa. Such consistency measurements are intrasystemic or "intratextual." The second is a question about the 'truth' of the religion itself, but this is better expressed as a question about the *adequacy* of the system as a whole to conform its

---

[3] Paul Holmer, *The Grammar of Faith* (San Francisco: Harper and Row, 1978).

[4] Hans Frei, *The Eclipse of Biblical Narrative* (New Haven: Yale University Press, 1974); and Hans Frei, *The Identity of Jesus Christ: The Hermeneutic Basis of Dogmatic Theology* (Philadelphia: Fortress Press, 1975).

[5] Ronald Thiemann, *Revelation and Theology: The Gospel as Narrated Promise* (Notre Dame, Ind.: University of Notre Dame Press, 1985).

adherents in the various dimensions of their existence to what is "Ultimately Real."[6]

Lindbeck's position is obviously indebted to postmodern philosophy as herein defined. He has combined a holist epistemology with a Wittgensteinian appreciation for the intrinsic relations between language and practice. A Wittgensteinian emphasis on the variety of uses of language shows up in his thesis that doctrines are rules for the use of first-order religious language. In addressing epistemological questions, Lindbeck compares religions to comprehensive scientific theories (paradigms) and explicitly rejects foundationalism. Finally, a communitarian emphasis is built into the postmodern philosophy of language and epistemology that Lindbeck employs.

2.2. Ronald Thiemann

In *Revelation and Theology*, Thiemann has shown how modern theology pressed the doctrine of revelation into the service of foundationalist epistemology. The foundationalist model when applied to theology called for a source of indubitable knowledge of God. Modern doctrines of revelation attempted to meet this demand. Thiemann considers three examples—John Locke, Friedrich Schleiermacher, and Thomas Torrance—showing that all three theologians followed Descartes in construing claims to knowledge of God as in need of justification and showing how all three adopted foundational epistemological theories to justify such claims. Modern philosophical theologians such as Locke often adopted a dual strategy, on the one hand showing that the contents of revelation are not contrary to reason and on the other hand claiming that 'revelation' designates a special category of truths undergirded by a unique mode of knowing and therefore not knowable by ordinary uses of reason. This strategy unfortunately requires an "impossibly fine balance" between the distinctiveness of revelation and its similarity to ordinary reason, and this, Thiemann claims, leads to incoherence in foundationalist doctrines of revelation.

In his account of an alternative, nonfoundationalist approach to theology and revelation, Thiemann uses W.V.O. Quine's model of knowledge as a net or web, where there is no foundation or starting point and where justification of a problematic belief involves showing its connections with beliefs held to be unproblematic. Thiemann conceives of nonfoundationalist theology as primarily *descriptive* of Christian belief and practice (in contrast to explanation or theoretical defense). This theology attempts to show the intelligibility, aptness, and warranted assertibility of Christian beliefs. It requires close attention to the patterns inherent in particular beliefs and practices rather

---

[6] Lindbeck, *The Nature of Doctrine,* 64–66.

than to a general theory of rationality. As judge and critic of practice and belief, it seeks its criteria of judgment within the first-order language of church practice, evaluating and criticizing according to criteria internal to the Christian faith.

Thiemann sees the following as characteristics of a nonfoundational theology: (1) justification of any particular belief is specific to Christian faith, community, and tradition; (2) the second-order language of theology is closely tied to the first-order expressions of the community's faith; and (3) nonfoundational theology employs holist justification, which seeks the relation between a disputed belief and the web of interrelated beliefs within which it rests—it is a process of rational persuasion. Notice that Thiemann's account lacks Lindbeck's concern with evaluation of the religion as a whole—why be Christian rather than Buddhist or Marxist?[7]

The main purpose of Thiemann's book is to show that the doctrine of God's prevenient grace—and thus a limited notion of revelation—can be defended despite difficulties due to its long involvement in foundationalist doctrines of revelation. He argues for the doctrine of prevenience by showing that it is separable from "incoherent" modern doctrines of revelation and that it turns out to be presupposed by practices and beliefs that, within the community, are both uncontroversial and constitutive of Christian identity—namely, practices such as the Eucharist and beliefs about God's identity and reality.

In Thiemann's work we see once more a thoroughly postmodern conception of theology. His indebtedness to postmodern epistemology, with its entailed rejection of individualism, is explicit. Furthermore, his requirement that the language of theology be closely tied to the first-order language of Christian life and to Christian practice shows his dependence on the postmodern linguistic tradition.

3. Postmodern Conservative Theology

Despite the fact that Lindbeck has provided penetrating criticism of the experiential expressivism of the modern liberal tradition, there are important assumptions that he shares with his predecessors, which justify calling his work post*liberal.* The first is his concern with providing a theory of religion generally, not a theory of Christianity. That is, he follows his liberal predecessors in assuming that Christianity is but one of a class of phenomena, all

---

[7] His account is weak here because, to put the matter in terms of Chapter 3, his epistemological resources come from the earliest stages of the development of an Anglo-American postmodern epistemological tradition rather than from the later stages represented by Imre Lakatos, Theo Meyering, and Alasdair MacIntyre.

instances of 'religion.' Second, he treats religions as, in the first instance, human phenomena—religions are like languages or cultures.

There are aspects of Lindbeck's theological program, however, that would seem to be much more appealing to conservative Christians than to liberals, especially his view of the role of Scripture in church life and theology. Yet at other points, Lindbeck's program is likely to appear inadequate to conservatives. The most significant of these is his construal of religious truth. His *definitions* of truth are likely to appear problematic; even more problematic is the lack of adequate *criteria* in Lindbeck's theological program for assessing the truth of religions and thus too little protection against religious relativism.

The purpose of this section is to inquire about what might be the distinguishing features of a conservative theology if pursued within a postmodern framework. If we ask what has distinguished conservative from liberal theology in the modern period and then ask further how we might express those distinctions without presupposing modern philosophical categories, we arrive at something like the following: first, postmodern conservative theology must maintain some special role for Scripture over against experience as authority for theology; second, it must provide for special acts of God; and, third, it must provide for the possibility of making truth claims for Christianity. This latter requirement involves both a definition of truth that is compatible with postmodern philosophy and criteria for judging the truth of a religion.

A second purpose of this section is to substantiate my claim that we should expect convergence between theologies of the right and the left during the postmodern era. I do this by mentioning as I go along the resources for maintaining each of these three conservative distinctions that can already be found within the developing postliberal tradition.

3.1. Divine Action

In the postmodern era, we should expect some convergence between theologians from left and right on the issue of divine action since the scientific worldview that led to divergent positions has been thoroughly discredited. In fact, a variety of scholars from all over the theological map are working toward new conceptions of divine action that allow for special divine acts but at the same time recognize the integrity of the created order.[8] Many of these scholars are attempting to do their work in light of changes in accounts of

---

[8] See, for instance, Brian Hebblethwaite and Edward Henderson, eds., *Divine Action: Studies Inspired by the Philosophical Theology of Austin Farrer* (Edinburgh: Clark, 1990); and Thomas F. Tracy, ed., *The God Who Acts: Philosophical and Theological Explorations* (University Park, Penn.: University of Pennsylvania Press, 1994).

natural causation called for by specific developments in science.[9] One of the most significant contributions here is Arthur Peacocke's work on divine action understood analogously to top-down causation within the created order.[10]

Additional evidence for convergence is the fact that postliberal theologians themselves have made some small contributions toward a more robust understanding of divine action. One factor is Lindbeck's insistence that the Bible is to be used to interpret scientific reality rather than the reverse. This is easier said than done, of course, but it certainly represents a refreshing new attitude toward the proper relations between theology and science compared with the predominant attitudes in the modern period.

Another resource is Thiemann's work on the doctrine of revelation.[11] In line with his holist methodology, he argues that the concept of revelation is integrally tied to that of the *prevenience* of God—the recognition that God has acted first in the divine-human relationship, eliciting human response. This concept of God's prevenient action cannot itself be rejected without at the same time rejecting nearly the whole of Christian belief and practice. So here we see a strong argument for reconsidering the problem of divine action in Christian theology, even if Thiemann has not presented his own account of how God's action should be construed. However, a thorough response to the modern problem of divine action will require a great deal more than this, not the least of which is a review of the entire metaphysics of causation.[12]

3.2. A Special Role for Scripture

I believe it is the role accorded to Scripture in Lindbeck's program for "intratextual theology" that will be most appealing to conservatives. Following Frei, Lindbeck criticizes the modern tendency to 'translate' the Bible into categories that are intelligible and relevant to contemporary readers. Many conservatives would agree with Lindbeck's claim that this strategy has often

---

[9] See, especially, Robert J. Russell, Nancey Murphy, and C. J. Isham, eds., *Quantum Cosmology and the Laws of Nature: Scientific Perspectives on Divine Action* (Vatican City State and Berkeley, Calif.: Vatican Observatory and Center for Theology and the Natural Sciences, 1993); and Robert J. Russell, Nancey Murphy, and Arthur Peacocke, eds., *Chaos and Complexity: Scientific Perspectives on Divine Action* (Vatican City State and Berkeley, Calif.: Vatican Observatory and Center for Theology and the Natural Sciences, 1995). These volumes are the first in a projected series of five books resulting from a study of divine action in light of a variety of recent scientific advances. Topics to come are recent developments in evolutionary biology, neuroscience, and quantum theory.

[10] See Arthur Peacocke, *Theology for a Scientific Age*, 2d, enl. ed. (Minneapolis: Fortress Press, 1993).

[11] Thiemann, *Revelation and Theology.*

[12] See my "Divine Action in the Natural Order: Buridan's Ass and Schrödinger's Cat," in Russell et al., eds., *Chaos and Complexity*, 325–357.

resulted in a reduction of biblical thought to whatever is acceptable by modern standards. Lindbeck's program calls for reversing the direction of interpretation: it is the contemporary world that needs to be interpreted in biblical categories, not the other way around. The biblical narratives create a world, and it is within this world that believers are to live their lives and understand reality. This is in some respects a return to traditional styles of interpretation, which assumed that Scripture creates its own domain of meaning.

Alasdair MacIntyre's recent writings, especially in *Whose Justice? Which Rationality?* provide valuable supplement and support for Lindbeck's view of the role of Scripture in Christianity. Whereas Lindbeck's concern is with the role of scriptures in religions, MacIntyre's concern is with any sort of large-scale tradition. All traditions, he maintains, begin with authorities of some sort, most often texts. In fact, a tradition can be understood as an ongoing argument about how best to interpret and apply a set of formative texts. David Kelsey (another member of the Yale School) has argued that the statement 'Scripture is authoritative for theology' is analytic.[13] On the basis of MacIntyre's account of the role of texts in all traditions, we could generalize Kelsey's claim, saying that 'formative texts are authoritative for traditions' is analytic. Thus, no special pleading is necessary to justify the authority of Christian Scripture for Christian practices and Christian theology.

I find it helpful to represent MacIntyre's contribution visually as follows: Lindbeck and Thiemann are both using Quine's web model for their accounts of theological knowledge. Quine's web is bounded by experience, and this suggests a picture as in Figure 6.2.

FIGURE 6.2 A Quinean web of beliefs

---

[13] David H. Kelsey, *The Uses of Scripture in Recent Theology* (Philadelphia: Fortress Press, 1975), 99.

FIGURE 6.3   A MacIntyrean tradition

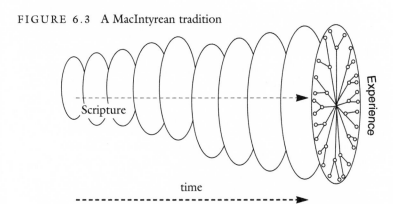

The problem in adopting this model for theology is that there is no 'place' for Scripture. However, MacIntyre's description of a tradition suggests a more complex picture with three dimensions, allowing us to represent the historical dimension, as in Figure 6.3. Here, current experience (and practice) provides the context for interpretation and application of the formative texts (the earliest formulations of the web), which have an ineliminable place in the tradition.

3.3. A Postmodern Account of Truth

It is with regard to the meaning of and criteria for truth that I believe postliberal and postevangelical theologians are likely to have the most disagreements. In this section, I first describe Lindbeck's proposals and then those of MacIntyre. I believe that from a conservative point of view, MacIntyre provides resources for a more satisfactory account of the truth of Christianity than does Lindbeck.

3.3.1. Lindbeck on Truth   Lindbeck correctly points out that propositionalists and experiential expressivists will have different conceptions of truth and that his own cultural-linguistic view requires yet a third conception. The word 'true' is used in three different ways in Lindbeck's system. I have already mentioned intrasystematic truth, which is a coherence theory amended to take account of the need for coherence not only among beliefs but also between belief and practice. This is an account of what it means to say that a particular belief is true *within* the context of a given religious framework. It can also be applied to the religious system itself: to say that a religion is intrasystematically true is to say that it is consistent and coherent.

However, intrasystematic truth by itself is inadequate. The same problem arises here for Lindbeck as for any holist epistemologist: the problem of competing, equally coherent systems (see Chapter 3, section 2). Thus, Lindbeck defines two further senses of 'true': categorial truth and ontological truth. A religion is categorially true if its categories are adequate "for construing reality, expressing experience, and ordering life" (47–48). Finally, a religion taken as a whole is ontologically true insofar as it serves to conform those who practice it "to the ultimate reality and goodness that lies at the heart of things" (51). That is, correspondence to reality of religious utterances is not an attribute that utterances have in and of themselves, but only in their role in "constituting a form of life, a way of being in the world, which itself corresponds to the Most Important, the Ultimately Real" (65).

These conceptions of truth are related to one another as follows:

> Intrasystematic truth or falsity is fundamental in the sense that it is a necessary though not sufficient condition for the second kind of truth: that of ontological correspondence. A statement, in other words, cannot be ontologically true unless it is intrasystematically true, but intrasystematic truth is quite possible without ontological truth. An intrasystematically true statement is ontologically false—or, more accurately, meaningless—if it is part of a system that lacks the concepts or categories to refer to the relevant realities, but it is ontologically true if it is part of a system that is itself categorially true (adequate). (64–65)

Lindbeck's attention to the issue of categorial adequacy is quite important for the assessment of religious claims. However, I think he would be better advised to speak simply of categorial adequacy rather than categorial truth. 'Adequacy' is used comparatively, whereas 'truth' is not; and it is certainly the case that the aptness of categories for the description of religious realities is a matter of degree.[14]

Lindbeck's conception of ontological truth is unusual, to say the least. It is actually closer to pragmatic theories of religious truth, such as John Hick's,[15] than to the modern propositionalists' correspondence theory. I believe it will be an unsuitable replacement for the modern correspondence theory in the eyes of conservatives not because it is different but because (as far as I can tell) there are no *criteria* for the assessment of such truth claims.[16]

---

[14] Richard Rorty contends that categorial adequacy or correspondence is as empty as the notion of correspondence of propositions to the world. Richard Rorty, *Objectivism, Relativism, and Truth* (Cambridge: Cambridge University Press, 1991), 151–161. If one takes categorial adequacy to mean that a category system "cuts the world at its joints," or accurately reflects the extant "natural kinds," then I agree. But others, such as C. I. Lewis and Rudolf Carnap, have taken a pragmatic approach to categorial adequacy, and this avoids the problems of a correspondence view.

[15] John Hick, *An Interpretation of Religion: Human Responses to the Transcendent* (New Haven: Yale University Press, 1989).

[16] This is true of Lindbeck's proposal but not of Hick's. For Hick, transformation of believers from ego-centeredness to reality-centeredness is a criterion for mythological truth. However, Hick argues that all the world religions are (probably equally) true in this sense—a conclusion conservatives, at this point at least, will not accept.

3.3.2. MacIntyre on Truth   Alasdair MacIntyre also recognizes the need for a revised concept of truth. His proposal is much more suitable than Lindbeck's for postmodern conservative theology.[17] MacIntyre's account is thoroughly *post*modern despite its indebtedness to Aristotle and Thomas Aquinas. MacIntyre claims that the modern theory of sentence-to-fact correspondence has been as conclusively refuted as any theory can be.[18] In contrast to modern correspondence accounts, he takes truth to be *adequatio intellectus ad rem*. The intellect must be understood here not as a Cartesian mind but as intelligence embodied and engaged in the world. Judgments are true in a secondary sense—judgments made by an intellect that possesses adequate conceptual resources and methods of enquiry. Having an adequate grasp of reality means being able to say how things are rather than how they seem to be from some particular, partial, and limited standpoint; adequacy is known by contrast with inadequacy. Enquiry aims at transcending distortions and limitations; truth is the *telos* of enquiry.

There are interesting parallels between MacIntyre's account of truth and Lindbeck's notion of ontological truth (although one must keep in mind that MacIntyre's is intended to apply to moral standpoints, Lindbeck's to religious standpoints). Lindbeck calls a religion ontologically true if it serves to conform the adherents in the various dimensions of their lives to what is ultimately real. So both Lindbeck and MacIntyre are realists of a sort. Furthermore, when the intellect as MacIntyre understands it is adequate to reality, in effect a variety of dimensions of one's life are conformed to what is real. Both emphasize the intimate relation between knowing and engaging in social practices.

The important difference between Lindbeck and MacIntyre is that when we raise the question of how one is to know which religion or moral standpoint is (ontologically) true, Lindbeck has no answer, whereas MacIntyre has developed an impressively nuanced account (see Chapter 3, section 3.3). For members of a community to claim that they have an adequate grasp of reality is to claim that their account, at least in its central contentions

> does not suffer from the limitations, partialities and one-sidedness of a merely local point of view, while any rival and incompatible account must suffer to some significant extent from such limitations, partialities, one-sidedness. For only if

---

[17] Alasdair MacIntyre deals with truth in *Whose Justice? Which Rationality?* (Notre Dame, Ind.: University of Notre Dame Press, 1988); Alasdair MacIntyre, *First Principles, Final Ends, and Contemporary Philosophical Issues* (Milwaukee: Marquette University Press, 1990); and Alasdair MacIntyre, "Moral Relativism, Truth, and Justification," in Luke Gormally, ed., *Moral Truth and Moral Tradition: Essays in Honour of Peter Geach and Elizabeth Anscombe* (Blackrock, Ireland: Four Courts Press, 1994), 6–24.

[18] MacIntyre, *Whose Justice?* 358. MacIntyre refers his readers to P. F. Strawson, "Truth," in *Logico-Linguistic Papers* (London: Methuen, 1971), 190–213.

this is the case are they entitled to assert that their account is one of how things are, rather than merely of how they appear to be from some particular standpoint or in one particular perspective. And this assertion is what gives content to the claim that this particular account is true and its rivals false.[19]

Part of knowing how things *are* is being able to say how, in consequence, they must appear from a range of different, limited, local points of view. So claims to truth are to be vindicated, in part at least, by being able to explain why things appear as they do from a rival point of view. I distinguished in Chapter 3 between diachronic and synchronic elements in MacIntyre's account of justification. Diachronic justification involves being able to show that one's current understanding solves problems its predecessor could not solve and to explain why the predecessor could not solve them. In *Whose Justice?* MacIntyre says: "The original and most elementary version of the correspondence theory of truth is one in which it is applied retrospectively in the form of a correspondence theory of falsity" (356). In the development of a tradition, crises arise and new sets of shared beliefs develop. Thus, between the older beliefs and the world as it is now understood to be, there is a radical discrepancy. "It is this lack of correspondence, between what the mind then judged and believed and reality as now perceived, classified, and understood, which is ascribed when those earlier judgments and beliefs are called *false*" (356). Thus, "to claim truth for one's present mind-set and the judgments which are its expression is to claim that this kind of inadequacy, this kind of discrepancy, will never appear in any possible future situation . . . no matter what developments in rational enquiry may occur" (358).

Synchronic justification of one's own standpoint or tradition over against its rivals involves showing that one's tradition has the resources for overcoming its own intellectual crises, while the rivals meet with persistent and intractable problems on their own terms. The claim to truth of one's own standpoint is vindicated if it also has the resources to explain why the competitors had to fail on their own terms.

> The test for truth in the present, therefore, is always to summon up as many questions and as many objections of the greatest strength as possible; what can be justifiably claimed as true is what has sufficiently withstood such dialectical questioning and framing of objections. In what does such sufficiency consist? That too is a question to which answers have to be produced and to which rival and competing answers may well appear. And those answers will compete rationally, just insofar as they are tested dialectically, in order to discover which is the best answer to be proposed so far. (358)

---

[19] MacIntyre, "Moral Relativism," 12.

In short, a tradition is to be called true if it has proved itself better than its live competitors in terms of its ability to overcome its own problems and even, in some cases, the problems of rivals that cannot be solved using the rivals' own resources and, furthermore, is able to explain why things must have appeared as they did to its predecessors and contemporary rivals from their more limited or defective perspectives.

I want to distinguish now, as MacIntyre would not, between his accounts of the meaning of truth and of the criteria for vindicating truth claims. I am not sure I want to advocate MacIntyre's account of the *meaning* of truth as *adequatio intellectus ad rem* mainly because, excerpted from the corpus of his work, it is sure to be misunderstood; it may be seen as an attempt simply to turn back the philosophical clock, or it may be translated into a modern correspondence theory with an associated modern realism. However, I believe his account of the *criteria* for vindicating the truth claims of traditions or rival moral standpoints can be readily appropriated and applied to the problem of adjudicating between rival theological or religious traditions. I propose, then, that when we claim for a religious standpoint that it is true, we *mean* to say that in its central contentions it will never be shown to be inadequate in any future situation, no matter what developments in rational enquiry may occur. Borrowing a term from Lindbeck, we might define truth as "unsurpassability." The *criterion* for making such a bold claim is survival of the sort of dialectical questioning of the standpoint in relation to its rivals that MacIntyre has so eloquently described.

3.3.3. Replies to Objections MacIntyre's account of truth offers little by way of justification to those who are committed to the correspondence theory of truth (as I presume most conservative theologians are). I attempt to set out *some* of the steps that might lead one to reject the correspondence theory in favor of my MacIntyrean unsurpassability theory. Such a short account is not likely to be convincing; however, my purpose is not to convert readers from a modern to a postmodern perspective, only to show how some postmodern philosophy (for which there is considerable argument elsewhere) bears on the theological task.[20]

To have some criteria for success in formulating a theory of truth, we must ask what are the uses for which we need the words 'true' and 'truth.' Richard Rorty provides a list of three:

---

[20] For critiques of the correspondence theory of truth, see Nicholas Rescher, *The Coherence Theory of Truth* (Washington, D.C.: University Press of America, 1982); Richard Rorty, *The Consequences of Pragmatism* (Minneapolis: University of Minnesota Press, 1982); and Rorty, *Objectivism*.

(a) an endorsing use
(b) a cautionary use, in such remarks as 'Your belief that S is perfectly justified, but perhaps not true'—reminding ourselves that justification is relative to, and no better than, the beliefs cited as grounds for S, . . .
(c) a disquotational use: to say metalinguistic things of the form "S" is true *iff* _____.'[21]

David Bloor also provides a list of three uses, the first two of which match Rorty's.

> First, there is what may be called the discriminatory function. We are under the necessity to order and sort our beliefs. We must distinguish those which work from those which do not. "True" and "false" are the labels typically used. . . .
>
> Second is the rhetorical function. . . . Truth is involved precisely as an idea of something potentially different from any received opinion. It is thought of as something that transcends mere belief. It has this form because it is our way of putting a question mark against whatever we wish to doubt or change or consolidate. . . .
>
> The third function . . . is what may be called the materialist function. All our thinking instinctively assumes that we exist within a common external environment that has a determinate structure. The precise degree of its stability is not known, but it is stable enough for many practical purposes. The details of its working are obscure, but despite this, much about it is taken for granted. Opinions vary about its responsiveness to our thoughts and actions, but in practice the existence of an external world-order is never doubted. It is assumed to be the cause of our experience, and the common reference of our discourse. I shall lump all this under the name of "materialism." Often when we use the word "truth" we mean just this: how the world stands. By this word we convey and affirm this ultimate schema with which we think. Of course this schema is filled out in many different ways. The world may be peopled with invisible spirits in one culture and hard, indivisible (but equally invisible) atomic particles in another.[22]

The foregoing give us a total of four uses: to distinguish between beliefs we endorse and those we do not; to enable us to say that what seems true may not in fact be true; to use in formulas where the sentences are not specified; and to refer to our general understanding about the nature of reality.

I distinguished earlier between definitions of the meaning of truth and truth criteria. The very notion of a *criterion* is contested, but the best understanding seems to be as follows: X is a criterion for Y if X is the best possible evidence

---

[21] Rorty, *Objectivism*, 128.
[22] David Bloor, *Knowledge and Social Imagery*, 2d ed. (Chicago: University of Chicago Press, 1991), 40–41.

for Y, short of a necessary and sufficient condition, and $X's$ being evidence for Y is a matter of definition rather than a matter of experience.[23] For example, having a high IQ is definitionally related to achieving high scores on IQ tests but is not identical with any particular test outcome (since the tests have limited reliability), so a high test score is a criterion for a high IQ.

To see the value of a MacIntyrean account, consider the alternative; let us assume that the correspondence theory gives an account of the meaning of truth. The next question is, What are the criteria for truth? For simple sentences about observable states of affairs, we might be satisfied with saying that the sentence in some way pictures or represents the way things are. 'The cat is on the mat' is true *iff* the cat to which we refer is indeed on (not under or beside) the mat to which we refer. But when we ask for criteria for truth claims regarding entire traditions, we need an account something like MacIntyre's. For here we are not concerned with individual sentences in a context where language and epistemology can be taken for granted. Rather, we are concerned with the whole system of concepts, epistemological and metaphysical theories, and even 'local' theories of truth!

For the sake of argument, let us grant that something like MacIntyre's account of the justification of traditions is both necessary and adequate. The question now arises as to what grounds we could have for assuming that passing MacIntyre's tests ensures that a tradition's beliefs and concepts adequately correspond to reality or correspond better than the rejected rivals (i.e., are true in the correspondence sense). The answer is that we *cannot* have any such grounds. There is certainly no definitional connection between such justification and correspondence. Nor could there be a weaker experiential connection; such grounds would require some sort of direct insight into the nature of reality, putting us in a position to compare reality itself with our favored way of conceiving and talking about it.

The impossibility of making an argument for our best method of justification as a reliable criterion for truth-as-correspondence has led some philosophers simply to drop the concept of truth. This has been a common strategy in recent philosophy of science.[24] Others choose to *define* truth as warranted assertability. This has the advantage of closing the gap between meaning and criteria, but it has the disadvantage of making 'truth' useless for Rorty's and Bloor's second function; it becomes self-contradictory to say, "This is our best-supported theory, but nonetheless it may be false."[25]

---

[23] Anthony Kenny, "Criterion," in Paul Edwards, ed., *The Encyclopedia of Philosophy* (New York: Macmillan, 1967), 2:258–261.

[24] The recent discussion of realism in philosophy of science is an attempt to smuggle the correspondence theory of truth in the back door. I see this as an unfortunate muddle of positions germane to philosophy of language, metaphysics, and epistemology. See Chapter 2.

[25] A major purpose of MacIntyre's "Moral Relativism" is to argue against such a reduction of truth to justification.

At this point, we can see the wisdom of my MacIntyrean definition. The criterion (unsurpassed so far) provides the best *possible* evidence for truth (will remain unsurpassed), and furthermore, the criterion has a reasonable (conceptual) connection with the meaning of truth. The criterion falls short of a necessary and sufficient condition for truth—truth claims are fallible, as are all other claims. However, this is just what we should have expected: it should not be possible to have a higher degree of certainty regarding the truth of 'S is true' than of S itself.

The suitability of a MacIntyrean approach is further supported by our reflecting on what would lead us in the future to conclude that we had been mistaken about a truth claim. As MacIntyre points out, it will be the result of developing better concepts or theories in light of which the present system appears inadequate—it will not be a result of a comparison of any sort between the old conceptions and 'reality' itself. This does not, of course, rule out the discovery of new information; new information is likely to have played a role in the development of the successor position.

Let us now test this account by seeing if 'true' as so conceived still performs all necessary functions. Bloor's third use, to affirm the general worldview our community assumes, is exactly what this definition is designed for; to say that our tradition is true is exactly to affirm that "this is how things stand." Also, within a tradition, the usual testing and endorsing or denying of individual statements will be possible (Rorty's and Bloor's first function). Finally, we are able to say that our tradition has all the marks of truth, yet we are still able to raise questions about its ultimacy since truth claims are fallible.

MacIntyre's is far from an absolutist account of knowledge and truth. In the best of cases, one can claim only that a given tradition at a given stage of its development is the best so far. "No one at any stage can ever rule out the future possibility of their present beliefs and judgments being shown to be inadequate in a variety of ways."[26] So whereas the meaning of 'truth' is unsurpassability, *claims* to truth are always fallible. Those conservative theologians who are used to making absolute truth claims may be put off by this feature of MacIntyre's theory and claim that it is in fact relativistic. However, this objection can be met by pointing out that absolutism and relativism are not dichotomous positions; rather, they serve as *limits* on a scale or range of possible positions regarding the decidability of truth claims. Neither absolutism (this side of the Eschaton) nor 'absolute' relativism is a real option, so we need to consider theorists' relative positions on the scale of possibilities in between. Among theorists who take adequate account of the complexities of judgments regarding the truth of traditions, I believe, MacIntyre is further from relativism than anyone else (see Chapter 3). So for theologians

---

[26] MacIntyre, *Whose Justice?* 361.

who are concerned about the cognitive content of Christian beliefs and who intend to make truth claims for Christianity vis-à-vis other religions and worldviews, MacIntyre provides crucially important resources.

4. Conclusion

I suggested in this chapter that if we project conservative theological concerns into a postmodern philosophical framework, there are at least three requirements for success. First, a special place must be maintained for Scripture as authority for theology. I claim that the postliberals have gone some way in spelling out a suitable position but that MacIntyre's concept of the role of formative texts in traditions is a valuable clarification and supplement. Second, conservative theology will need an account of truth that is philosophically respectable and also applicable to theology. MacIntyre's epistemological work is exceedingly important in this regard. His account of truth, at least with my modifications, seems to be intelligible, consistent with other (usable) postmodern philosophical developments, and applicable to religious, as well as other traditions. What is most important about his work, however, is that he presents what I believe to be the most thorough and precise account to date of *how* judgments can be made concerning the truth claims of rival large-scale traditions. As such, his account provides the best *available* antidote to relativism. Third, there is need for a more robust account of divine action than that developed by modern liberal theologians, but I have not addressed that problem here.

But in each of these areas, I have suggested, conservative positions ought to be expected to differ only in degree from postliberal positions. So in the case of truth, because epistemological positions on the decidability of truth claims fall along a spectrum bounded by but not including absolutism and relativism, theologians ought to be expected to vary by degrees from pluralist toward exclusivist positions.

There should be a similar spectrum of positions regarding the balance between divine action and creaturely causation, whose limits are occasionalism (God does all things) and deism (God does nothing apart from creation). A third continuum emerges from the interplay between text and experience in the interpretation and application of the Bible. This last issue is taken up in the following chapter.

7 • • •

Postmodern Philosophy of Language and Textual Relativism

1. Introduction

In Chapter 5, I claimed that modern theories of language provided only two options for understanding theological discourse, neither of which was adequate: either religious language must be counted as factual language, but with its own sorts of referents, or else it must be (in the first instance, at least) an expression of the subject's inner religious awareness.

I also claimed, in Chapter 1, that J. L. Austin has been one of the major contributors to Anglo-American postmodern philosophy. In this chapter, I consider the use of Austin's speech-act theory by James Wm. McClendon Jr. and James M. Smith to address problems concerning religious language.[1] I argue that a principal value of this Austinian understanding of religious language is that it overcomes the dichotomy between the referential and expressivist functions of language, thus offering a way ahead beyond the modern liberal and conservative positions.

In addition, I highlight a new problem for philosophers of religion that arises from misunderstandings about language—and one that will be at least as devastating to Christian self-understanding if not answered. This is the problem of the instability of textual meaning—that is, relativism with regard to textual interpretation. These relativistic views have arisen as but one aspect

---

[1] See James Wm. McClendon Jr. and James M. Smith, *Understanding Religious Convictions* (Notre Dame, Ind.: University of Notre Dame Press, 1975); and James Wm. McClendon Jr. and James M. Smith, *Convictions: Defusing Religious Relativism* (Valley Forge, Penn.: Trinity Press International, 1994) (the latter book is a revision of the former).

of a general skeptical reaction to the demise of foundationalism in epistemology. I argue that a solution is already at hand in the works of none other
than J. L. Austin and James McClendon.

2. McClendon and Smith's Use of Austin

Austin rejected the Fregean predilection for artificial languages, as well as
the linguistic atomism of his predecessors: for Austin, the meaning of an
utterance is as much a function of the context in which it is used as it is of
the words that make up the utterance (see Chapter 1, section 3.3 for a discussion of this type of holistic account of language). Most important, however, was his move to shift attention from meaning as reference to meaning as use.[2] Or to put the matter more accurately, if language is used for
more complex purposes than simply to describe facts, then we have to ask
more complex questions about it than the question that had so long pre-
occupied philosophers—namely, how does language *mean*? Now it is necessary to ask more broadly how language functions and what counts as success in using it.

McClendon and Smith summarized Austin's criteria for a "happy" speech
act under four headings. (1) Preconditions—speaker and hearer must share
a common language and be free from relevant impediments to communication. (2) Primary conditions—the speaker must issue a sentence in the common language that is a conventional way of performing that kind of speech
act. (3) Representative or descriptive conditions—the sentence must bear a
relation to a state of affairs that is appropriate to that sort of speech act. (4)
Affective or psychological conditions—the speaker must intend to perform
the speech act by means of the sentence and have the relevant attitudes or
affects; the hearer must take the speaker to have the requisite intentions and
affects (uptake).[3]

To use an example from McClendon and Smith's *Understanding Religious
Convictions*, for a speaker happily to *confess* that "God led Israel across the
Sea of Reeds," the following conditions must be satisfied: (1) This sentence
must be an understandable sentence in a shared language, and (2) this sentence must be of a recognized 'confessional' form. (3) There must have been
a suitable state of affairs involving the people Israel, a sea, and an act of God.
(4) The speaker must have intended the utterance as a confession of faith and

---

[2] Ludwig Wittgenstein, in his later work, made a similar move. He focused on the use of language to make moves in a "language game." See, especially, Ludwig Wittgenstein, *Philosophical
Investigations*, trans. G.E.M. Anscombe (New York: Macmillan, 1953).

[3] For Austin's own account, see J. L. Austin, *How to Do Things with Words* (Cambridge,
Mass.: Harvard University Press, 1962).

must have a suitable attitude toward this event such as awed gratitude; the hearers must have taken the speech act as a confession of faith.[4]

According to this account, both the expressivist and referential theories of language can be seen to express partial truths, yet neither alone provides an adequate account of religious (or any other) language. To "state the facts" about God without an appropriate attitude toward God (fourth condition) is surely to have failed to get the point of what one is saying. Yet to confess religious attitudes detached from any factual content (third condition) is to confess nothing. Notice that different kinds of speech acts will require different kinds of relation to the real world: happily to confess that Jesus has come in the flesh requires a different state of affairs than happily to pray that he will come again. Here, *use* is the primary category for the analysis of language; *appropriate reference and appropriate expression are subordinate factors, in that use determines what counts as appropriate reference and appropriate affect.*

2.1. Recent Developments

Since the publication of *Understanding Religious Convictions,* the most important advance in the understanding of religious language has come from the Yale School. These authors, apparently unaware of the contributions of McClendon and Smith, have reached comparable conclusions about religious language as a result of common influences of both Austin and Ludwig Wittgenstein. For example, George Lindbeck has argued that to understand doctrinal change, we must ask what *use* is made of doctrines by Christians. Lindbeck emphasizes their regulative function: they prescribe and proscribe forms of first-order religious language and regulate its relation to communal practices.[5] Ronald Thiemann has argued that to understand the doctrine of revelation, we must ask what Scripture, taken as revelation, *does.* He answers that its primary force is to narrate promises.[6] Neither Lindbeck's nor Thiemann's work presents a full-fledged account of religious language, but both, happily, reflect an awareness of the need for a theory of religious language that goes beyond both the referential and expressivist theories. Both also reflect a recognition of the embeddedness of religious language in the shared life of a community and the impossibility of understanding language without understanding the conventions and practices of that community—a Wittgensteinian point.

---

[4] McClendon and Smith, *Understanding Religious Convictions,* 65–66; McClendon and Smith, *Convictions,* 62–63.

[5] George Lindbeck, *The Nature of Doctrine: Religion and Theology in a Postliberal Age* (Philadelphia: Westminster Press, 1984).

[6] Ronald Thiemann, *Revelation and Theology: The Gospel as Narrated Promise* (Notre Dame, Ind.: University of Notre Dame Press, 1985).

3. The Relativity of Textual Interpretation

If the issue of expressivism versus referentialism has created a gulf between liberal and conservative theologians, it has done so quietly—it has created failures
to understand but little direct conflict.[7] However, I suspect that the issue of
relativism with regard to textual interpretation will be more explosive. For
years there has been a widespread recognition of interpretive relativity: recognition of various forms of historicism, of the hermeneutic circle, of contextual
interpretations. None of this is new. What *is* new is a different attitude: whereas
earlier thinkers saw these sources of relativity as something one ideally would
want to overcome, some current literary theorists see it as neither possible *nor*
desirable to attribute stable meanings to texts. Literary-critical terms with origins in poststructuralism are becoming more and more prevalent in the vocab-
ularies of both theologians and biblical scholars. But can the Christian intellectual world survive if deconstructionist and reader-response theses are taken
with full seriousness? David Lehman presents an extreme view, describing
deconstructionism as "not merely postmodernist but preapocalyptic. It is a catastrophe theory inasmuch as it proceeds from the perception of an extreme linguistic instability that undermines the coherence of any statement—a breakdown in our collective confidence in the power of words to communicate ideas
and represent experience. It announces or implies that a rupture has occurred,
an irreparable break with the past, and that nothing can ever be the same
again."[8] In this section, I first trace some of the philosophical and literary roots
of reader-response criticism and deconstructionism and then argue on the basis
of an Austinian theory of language that extremely relativistic conclusions
regarding the meaning of texts are unwarranted.

3.1. Sources of Deconstructionism and
Reader-Response Criticism

To analyze developments in literary theory, it will be helpful to have before
us the dimensions or conditions for the successful use of language as we have
come to know them from the works of Austin and Wittgenstein and
McClendon and Smith. Let us begin by distinguishing between linguistic

---

[7] One exception here has to do with conflict between feminists and conservatives over gen-
dered language for God. Margo Houts argues that mutual failure to understand the different
theories of language assumed by conservatives and liberal feminists (with their associated differences in theological method—see Chapter 5) deepens the controversy. See Margo Houts,
"Language, Gender, and God: How Traditionalists and Feminists Play the Inclusive Language
Game" (Ph.D. diss., Fuller Theological Seminary, 1993).

[8] David Lehman, *Signs of the Times: Deconstruction and the Fall of Paul de Man* (New York:
Poseidon Press, 1992), 41. Notice the modern assumptions implicit in Lehman's comment: language *describes* experience or communicates (expresses?) ideas.

and social conventions. The former include grammar, in the most basic sense of the word, and proper word usage. Social conventions include proper forms for various speech acts such as requests, prayers, promises. In Wittgensteinian terms, these conventions arise within *language games* and the *forms of life* with which they are associated—'grammar' in Wittgenstein's specialized sense. There is, again, the referential dimension—the relation between language and world. In addition, it is helpful to distinguish within McClendon and Smith's affective dimension two categories, which I call expressivist conditions and uptake. Expressivist conditions include both the speaker's (writer's) intentions and appropriate accompanying attitudes and emotions. Uptake, as for Austin, is the hearer getting the point of what is being said (written).

This gives us a list of five dimensions or kinds of conditions for successful use of language:

1. Linguistic conventions
2. Social conventions
3. Reference
4. Expressivist conditions
5. Uptake

The writings of Ferdinand de Saussure, the founder of modern linguistics, are essential for an understanding of the works of contemporary literary theorists such as Jacques Derrida, Paul de Man, and Stanley Fish. Saussure distinguished between *langue,* the linguistic system, and *parole,* particular speech acts, and insisted that the linguist must study *langue. Langue* stands over against individual speakers, who can choose to use the system on specific occasions but cannot choose the system; the system limits what can be said.

A second Saussurian distinction is between diachronic and synchronic linguistics. Diachronic linguistics studies the changes in language over time and is of less interest than synchronic linguistics, which studies the relations among signs at a given point in history. Saussure's synchronic linguistics involved a nonreferential theory of signs wherein signs point only to other signs. The crucial way in which signs relate to one another is by means of difference: they are defined not positively by their content but negatively by the simultaneous presence of other signs in the system. That is, human sound capacities form a continuum; we break up the continuum in order to identify sounds as words: 'bat' versus 'cat' versus 'cot.' Thought, too, is a continuum, and the development of distinct ideas is dependent upon the making of linguistic distinctions. So, for example, 'red' is not to be understood by reference to red things but by the limiting presence in the language of 'orange' and 'violet' and 'pink.'

In the 1960s, Saussure's study of synchronic systems of difference was generalized to other fields, producing "structuralist" approaches in anthropology, psychology, philosophy. Structuralism views all cultural phenomena as products of systems of signification, wherein it is the relations among the elements of the system, rather than the relations between the elements and 'reality,' that produce meaning. All such systems are arbitrary, and there is no way of apprehending reality independently of them.

Similarly, structuralist literary critics reject the idea that a literary text reflects a reality that is already given. They focus their attention on the text itself, as opposed to either the author's intent ("the intentional fallacy") or the effect on the reader ("the affective fallacy"). The key to a text is form: structures of sound, rhythm, rhyme, sequences of images, even ratios of passive to active verbs.

3.1.1. Deconstructionism Both reader-response criticism and deconstructionism are reactions against structuralist theories. Deconstructionists such as Paul de Man and Jacques Derrida reject the claim that structures are given in the texts. "'Form' itself turns out to be more an operative fiction, a product of the interpreter's rage for order, than anything vested in the literary work itself."[9]

Deconstructionists accept the Saussurian and structuralist rejection of a referent external to the text: "The word doesn't reflect or represent the world; the word contains the world and not the other way around. Therefore, texts are self-referential—they refer only to themselves, not to anything outside themselves. There is no such thing as the real world. . . . All that's left is a succession of misleading signs, a parade of words beyond the power of humanity to control them."[10] Deconstructionism also accepts (but intensifies) the structuralist distinction between textual meaning and authorial intention. This was already suggested at the end of the preceding quotation: words are beyond the power of humanity to control them. Thus, "the author is dead." As Michel Foucault says: the existentialist 'I' has been destroyed, translated into a 'one.' "It is not man who takes the place of God, but anonymous thinking, thinking without a subject."[11] Authors are unwitting mouthpieces for reigning ideologies. In fact, says Paul de Man, a text is as likely to conceal as to reveal the intentions of the author: literary criticism allows for two incompatible, mutually self-destructive points of view and

---

[9] Christopher Norris, *Deconstruction: Theory and Practice* (London: Methuen, 1982), 22.

[10] Lehman, *Signs of the Times,* 41–42.

[11] Quoted without citation in John Passmore, *Recent Philosophers* (La Salle, Ill.: Open Court, 1985), 27.

therefore puts an insurmountable obstacle in the way of any reading or understanding.[12]

The central preoccupation of deconstructionism is a reaction to Saussurian assumptions about the role of difference in language. To 'deconstruct' is to blur the distinction between two terms—binary opposites—especially in cases where one member of the pair is more highly valued than the other: primary/derivative, necessary/possible, present/absent. The point of this can be seen if we recall that it is just such differences, in Saussure's linguistics, that account for the meaning of terms. By blurring distinctions between terms, the deconstructionists aim to show that linguistic conventions, as understood in the Saussurian tradition, are inadequate to fix the meaning of a text. Furthermore, the very practice of deconstructionism, as well as some of the actions of its adherents, is meant to show that social conventions can be flouted.

So external reference is denied; the author's intentions are concealed; conventions are ignored. By negating one by one the conditions for successful communication, the deconstructionists are able to argue that any and every text inevitably undermines its own claims to a determinate meaning. As a consequence, the role of the reader must be emphasized in the production of meaning.

3.1.2. Reader-Response Criticism   Reader-response criticism rejects the structuralists' rejection of the "affective fallacy" and agrees with deconstructionists in claiming that structure is in the eye of the beholder. Michael Vander Weele distinguishes three categories of reader-response critics: psychological, social, and intersubjective. The first, including Norman Holland and David Bleich, emphasizes the variety of interpretations produced by different individual readers and denies that meaning is tied to conventions. The social model (Stanley Fish and Jonathan Culler) emphasizes the literary competence that comes from participation in and understanding of a cultural tradition of reading. Intersubjective theorists (Wolfgang Iser, Louise Marie Rosenblatt) stand between the other two types and emphasize the transaction between unique individuals and social conventions.[13]

Although Vander Weele categorizes Fish as a member of the social type, I believe a survey of his earlier and later works will illustrate both poles of the

---

[12] Quoted without citation in Lehman, *Signs of the Times,* 129. It strikes me as odd to have two footnotes in a row indicating that an author is named by another but the source is not given. In an account of deconstructionism, it would be much more appropriate to cite the text without naming the author!

[13] Michael Vander Weele, "Reader-Response Theories," in Clarence Walhout and Leland Rykern, eds., *Contemporary Literary Theory: A Christian Appraisal* (Grand Rapids, Mich.: Eerdmans, 1991), 125–148.

spectrum of reader-response theories. The early Fish is an ally of decon-structionism, but the later Fish will turn out to be an ally of Austin and McClendon and Smith in their postmodern understandings of language.

Fish began by focusing on the question "What does this word (sentence, poem, play) do?" He emphasized that in the sequence from writer to text to reader, meaning 'happens' only when the text has an effect on the reader: "There is no direct relation between the meaning of a sentence (paragraph, novel, poem) and what its words mean. . . . It is the experience of an utter-ance . . . that *is* the meaning."[14]

The sort of effect the early Fish sought to understand can be illustrated by his analysis of the following sentence: "That Judas perished by hanging him-self, there is no certainty in Scripture: though in one place it seems to affirm it, and by a doubtful word hath given occasion to translate it; yet in another place, in a more punctual description, it maketh it improbable, and seems to overthrow it" (71). Fish points out that the first clause is understood to be shorthand for "the *fact* that Judas perished by hanging himself." Thus, the reader is set up to expect that the rest of the sentence will follow from this positive assertion, and thus "there is no" ought to be followed by "doubt" rather than "certainty." The rest of the sentence, step by step, frustrates the expectation set up in the first clause, progressively disorienting the reader. So the sort of response with which Fish is concerned here is psychological: frus-tration, confusion, and the like.

However, the later Fish is concerned with genuine Austinian uptake. In "Is There a Text in This Class?" he concentrates on *understanding* texts and emphasizes the shared *conventions* that make it possible for reader or listener to "get it."[15] Here his illustration is an anecdote:

> On the first day of the new semester a colleague at Johns Hopkins University was approached by a student who, as it turned out, had just taken a course from me. She put to him what I think you would agree is a perfectly straightforward question. "Is there a text in this class?" Responding with a confidence so per-fect that he was unaware of it, . . . my colleague said, "Yes; it's the *Norton Anthology of Literature*," whereupon the trap (set not by the student but by the infinite capacity of language for being appropriated) was sprung: "No, no," she said, "I mean in this class do we believe in poems and things, or is it just us?" (305)

---

[14] Stanley Fish, "Literature in the Reader: Affective Stylistics," in Jane P. Tompkins, ed., *Reader-Response Criticism: From Formalism to Post-Structuralism* (Baltimore: Johns Hopkins University Press, 1980), 77–78.

[15] Stanley Fish, *Is There a Text in This Class?* (Cambridge, Mass.: Harvard University Press, 1980), 303–321.

Even though Fish uses the anecdote to illustrate his claims regarding the "instability of the text" and the "unavailability of determinate meanings," he argues here, against the supposed implication that texts can mean anything we want, that the possibilities for different interpretations are in fact sharply limited by the practices and assumptions that make up the text's social context. In this case, it is the general rubric "first day of class" that makes the first meaning available; the second becomes available only within the narrower context of "Fish's victims." Both interpretations were a function of public and constituting norms of language and understanding.

So the later Fish still maintains that reader response is what constitutes the meaning of the text, but he argues for the necessity of *social conventions* to enable uptake. He also recognizes that these same conventions enable the reader or listener to reach correct understanding of the writer's or speaker's *intention* and of the intended *reference*. We could say that the later Fish's point is that neither linguistic conventions nor referent nor intention alone is sufficient to establish meaning. Social conventions must be considered as well.

3.2. Consequences of Poststructuralism for Biblical Criticism

It will have been obvious all along that deconstructionist and psychological-type reader-response theories are fatal for any community that intends to take the Bible as authority for thought and practice, but it is worth noting how directly and explicitly these arguments cut against the most widely held understandings of the goals of biblical interpretation. First, word studies had already been called into question by the structuralists on the grounds of Saussure's rejection of diachronic semantics: meanings of words change over time and cannot be known by means of their etymologies. But deconstruction pushes the point to the extreme by flouting synchronic conventions— by demolishing conventional associations and distinctions and creating new, idiosyncratic meanings. Recall, also, the early Fish's denial of a direct relation between the meaning of a sentence and what its words mean.

Second, some hermeneutic theories, beginning at least as early as the work of Friedrich Schleiermacher, have sought the meaning of the text in the mind of the author. For Schleiermacher, the goal of interpretation was to enter imaginatively and sympathetically into the author's religious consciousness, reliving and rethinking the author's thoughts and feelings (although Schleiermacher did not see this as the sole hermeneutic task). More recently, E. D. Hirsch Jr. has argued that the meaning of the text is to be understood *primarily* in terms of the author's will or intention.[16]

---

[16] E. D. Hirsch Jr., *The Aims of Interpretation* (Chicago: University of Chicago Press, 1978).

Yet many today would deny the possibility of recovering the author's intentions. The deconstructionists and early reader-response theorists join the New Critics and other poststructuralists in asserting that the author's intentions are not available to the interpreter; deconstructionists would add that these intentions would be of no interest even if they were. So these critics would deny that the discovery of authorial intent should be or could be the goal of biblical criticism.

Hans Frei has claimed that historical-critical approaches to the Bible assume that the meaning of a text is to be identified with the history behind the text.[17] Notice that this is a species of *referential* theory of language—the primary sense in which the texts have meaning is by virtue of their historical referents. But deconstructionists close off this avenue also with their claim that texts refer only to other texts. There is at least some truth here. Our access to the history behind the text is primarily by means of the text itself, and the critic's reconstruction is, after all, nothing but another text. There is no objective, independent reality against which the original text can be compared. So the deconstructionists are right—we have not a text and a fixed historical referent but two sets of texts, the biblical passages and the critics' interpretations.

So it appears that if these poststructuralist claims are true (or even if they are not true but nonetheless come to dominate academia), then study of the Bible will have no practical import, however interesting it may be to play with a variety of interpretations.

To many readers, deconstructionist claims will appear willfully perverse and deserve only to be ignored. But as I have indicated, there are at least partial truths here that present serious challenges to Bible readers; and because of these partial truths, a frontal attack on deconstructionism may not be successful. I suggest an indirect strategy: namely, to unmask the *modern* assumptions upon which the deconstructionists' negative conclusions are based. I then shift to a ('postmodern') Austinian understanding of language and show that, despite the fact that many deconstructionist criticisms of traditional theories of hermeneutics are valid, we are not thereby compelled to accept textual relativism. In doing so, we find ourselves retracing the steps from the early to the later Fish.

3.3. Modern Assumptions Behind Deconstructionism

I noted in the Introduction to this volume that the term 'postmodern' is so closely associated with deconstructionism that I hesitate to use it to describe philosophers such as Austin. The irony is that deconstructionist arguments against stability of meaning all trade on modern assumptions about the

---

[17] Hans Frei, *The Eclipse of Biblical Narrative* (New Haven: Yale University Press, 1974).

nature of language; furthermore, to provide a refutation of this 'avant-garde' literary movement we need only *return* to the work Austin did nearly a half century ago. Modern assumptions are clearly evident in two of the positions just described. (1) Texts have no external referent; if reference is the basis of all meaning, then texts have no fixed meaning. (2) Texts conceal the author's intention; if (nonreferential) language is significant in that it expresses the inner state of the speaker or writer, then, again, the texts must have no fixed meaning.

The deconstruction of Saussurian differences also betrays a modern mindset in that it is parallel to a mistake made by some modern epistemologists. Deconstructionists argue that the conventional meanings of any pair of terms can be deconstructed. In fact, all meaning is based on convention; any convention can be violated, as they show by producing thoroughly unconventional readings of texts. The point they seem to be missing, however, is that their unconventional interpretations are intelligible only against a background of conventions that they are not violating in a given instance.

The parallel argument from epistemology is an argument for skepticism based on the fact that any belief can be called into question. However, it is now widely recognized that total skepticism does not follow from this fact since one needs to assume the truth of many beliefs in order meaningfully to call other beliefs into question. Descartes and his more skeptical followers were able to make this mistake because of their foundationalist model of knowledge. If the acceptability of one's entire system of beliefs depends on a relatively small set of foundational beliefs, then the criticism of these few supposedly indubitable beliefs brings down the whole system.

The lesson to be learned from this episode in the history of epistemology is that negative conclusions regarding the part (dubitability of specific individual beliefs, indeterminacy of meaning in particular instances) cannot automatically be generalized to the entire system. The argument by analogy from epistemology to theory of meaning goes through because in both cases there is something about the context that must be assumed in order to arrive at the negative conclusions in the first place; and this something blocks the generalization from part to whole. So in epistemology, one must assume the truth of some beliefs in order to generate reasonable doubts (e.g., Descartes must assume that there is such a thing as dreaming to get his skeptical argument off the ground); deconstructionist arguments for total indeterminacy of meaning make use of linguistic conventions that cannot simultaneously be called into question without defeating those very arguments. Thus, total indeterminacy of meaning does not follow from the fact that particular conventions can be ignored at particular times.

4. An Austinian Answer to Textual Indeterminacy

Let us now abandon the modern supposition that biblical texts must be understood in the first instance either as descriptions of historical events or as expressions of mental states of the authors and consider them instead to be speech acts (or collections of speech acts). It has already been suggested by others that Austin's speech-act theory has valuable implications for hermeneutics.[18] My purpose here is more specific: I intend to use Austin's theory to demonstrate the fallacies in arguments based on deconstructionism or early reader-response theories for the claim that biblical texts have no fixed meaning.[19]

At this point we need to make a distinction. It is common to analyze the hermeneutic problem into two aspects: the first is the question of what the text meant in its original setting; the second is how to appropriate that meaning in our own very different historical setting. If the deconstructionists' arguments are valid, then the problem for biblical studies is not merely that of historical distance; it is the more radical problem that texts have no stable meaning even in their original setting. The focus of the present section is to answer this radical claim; the problem of historical distance is taken up in section 5.

4.1. An Argument for Stability of Meaning

My argument here might be characterized as a transcendental argument.[20] I begin with the assumption that the biblical texts (often, sometimes) served in the context of the early church to perform felicitous speech acts. If this was the case, then we can argue that the necessary conditions for happy speech acts (as described by Austin) *must have been* fulfilled. Then we see what can be said about the deconstructionists' three attacks on the determinacy of meaning.

It is not unreasonable to assume the success or effectiveness or happiness of the New Testament texts (at least much of the time) in their original settings. In fact, one might describe the canonization process as that of choosing from among early Christian writings those that had been found useful, effective, in a variety of Christian communities—canonicity as universal (or nearly universal) uptake.[21] What criteria, then, would these texts need to have satisfied in those settings, and what are the consequences of their having done so for deconstructionist claims?

---

[18] See, especially, the works of Anthony Thiselton: "The Parables as Language-Event: Some Comments on Fuchs's Hermeneutics in the Light of Linguistic Philosophy," *Scottish Journal of Theology* 23 (1970):437–468; *The Two Horizons: New Testament Hermeneutics and Philosophical Description* (Grand Rapids, Mich.: Eerdmans, 1980); and *New Horizons in Hermeneutics: The Theory and Practice of Transforming Biblical Reading* (Grand Rapids, Mich.: Zondervan, 1992).

[19] For a parallel, Wittgensteinian critique, see Thiselton, *New Horizons*, 126–128.

[20] Thiselton, in ibid., 205, points out that Schleiermacher was the first to raise transcendental questions about the possibility of hermeneutics.

[21] "Indeed, constant copying and circulation could almost be described as a prerequisite to final inclusion in the New Testament, for books not found generally useful, and hence not copied and circulated, would not have found their way into the canon." Norman Perrin and Dennis Duling, *The New Testament: An Introduction* (New York: Harcourt Brace Jovanovich, 1982), 450.

4.1.1. Conventional and Expressive Conditions   To presuppose the felicity of the speech act (or set of acts) that a text is meant to perform is to suppose that the author was successful in employing linguistic conventions in order to enact his intentions. Notice, first, that to assume that an author succeeded in expressing or enacting her intention by means of linguistic conventions is to assume that there *were* linguistic conventions. To note that a set of texts were preserved and circulated to a variety of communities over a span of years shows that those conventions were somewhat widespread and invariate over time.

Second, if we know what an author *did* through or by means of a text, and if we have no reason to suppose that the author was dishonest or incompetent in using the language, then we have public access to what the author intended. There is no hidden mental component—the intention or the meaning—to be sought beyond the speech act itself (a Wittgensteinian point). So it is true *in a sense* that we can never recover the mind of the author—it is true in the trivial sense that we never have immediate access to anyone's thoughts but our own. But it is obviously false in another sense since in the normal, "happy" state of affairs, people's speech acts are public enactments of their intentions.

So if the deconstructionist lament over the disappearance of the author is meant to point out that we have no access to the inner awareness of the author, it is true but uninteresting. It is only interesting if one believes that knowing the meaning requires access to private intentions and that texts generally or always fail to enact the writer's intentions. But this latter claim amounts to saying that all texts fail to perform happy speech acts, and it is obviously false.

Now it may appear that my argument here is circular—that is, to claim that the texts performed happy speech acts is simply to state in different words that the texts had stable meaning in their own day. To put it another way: does not the deconstructionist (and early reader-response) challenge raise exactly the suspicion that to everyone in the New Testament communities, the texts may have meant something different—and I am simply assuming the contrary?

To see why the argument is not circular, we need to emphasize that getting the meaning—uptake—is no more a private matter than it is to have an intention. If uptake were a private "I get it!"[22] then it would be entirely

---

[22] As it is for Fish (and here he parts company with Austin): "If everyone is continually executing interpretive strategies and in that act constituting texts, intentions, speakers, and authors, how can any one of us know whether or not he is a member of the same interpretive community as any other of us? The answer is that he can't, since any evidence brought forward to support the claim would itself be an interpretation (especially if the 'other' were an author long dead). The only 'proof' of membership is fellowship, the nod of recognition from someone in the same community, someone who says to you what neither of us could ever prove to a third party: 'we know.'" Fish, *Is There a Text?* 183–184.

possible for a whole church full of readers to 'get' something different. But on the account of language here presented, getting the meaning is 'operationalized' as a communal (shared, intersubjective) response to the text—a living of its import rather than a mere hearing of it. The intrinsic relation between language and action, emphasized by both Austin and Wittgenstein, is crucially important here.[23] So conceived, it would have been a public matter whether the texts 'meant' the same to everyone. And in some cases, as shown in Paul's letters, the author could *and did* object when his writings had been taken wrongly.

The fact that there was controversy over the meaning of texts in New Testament times is no rebuttal of my claim; in fact, it supports the claim. The mistake made by deconstructionists, I have argued, is to ignore the conventional aspect of language. The result is that no adequate criteria are left for judging any interpretation to be a *mistake*. If this *were* the case, then we would have an analog to Wittgenstein's "private language," and he has argued persuasively that such a thing is inconceivable.[24] So the fact that there were controversies, and that when looking back, we can recognize some interpretations as mistakes, provides grounds for a reductio ad absurdum of the deconstructionist position.

4.1.2. Referential Conditions

To presuppose the felicity of speech acts performed by New Testament texts is to suppose that appropriate referential or representative conditions obtained. Note that what constitutes *appropriate* referential conditions will depend on the kind of speech act in question. For example, consider Hans Frei's suggestions about the purpose of the gospel narratives. Frei claimed that the *force* of the gospel narratives is to provide identity descriptions—stories to render a character. Their purpose is to say: this risen Christ whom you know as present to you in worship is in fact Jesus of Nazareth, who was born . . . taught . . . suffered and died.[25]

The referential conditions for a speech act of this sort include the background condition (1) that the readers must in fact know the presence of the risen Christ. The more immediate conditions that must be fulfilled for the success of the gospel stories as speech acts are (2) the narrative must serve to identify one specific individual, and for this purpose certain historical facts

---

[23] Dennis M. Patterson has made the same point: "What Fish's account leaves out is the constitutive role of action in the constitution of meaning. Meanings do not spring from interpretations but from action—ways of *using* signs." Dennis M. Patterson, "The Poverty of Interpretive Universalism and the Reconstruction of Legal Theory," *Texas Law Review* 72, no. 1 (August 1993):49.

[24] See Wittgenstein, *Philosophical Investigations,* esp. §§ 269, 275.

[25] Hans Frei, *The Identity of Jesus Christ: The Hermeneutic Basis of Dogmatic Theology* (Philadelphia: Fortress Press, 1975).

needed to be true—enough facts to distinguish Jesus from any other similar characters. We might include here the identity of his parents, his hometown, the outlines of his public ministry, and the circumstances of his death. (3) The stories of his teaching and actions must be truly *characteristic* of him—that is, they must present an accurate portrait of his character. Notice that truth*likeness* is at least as important here as objective historical accuracy. In fact, we can sometimes render a character more accurately by means of stories about what the person might have done than by the recounting of specific incidents.

Contrast the force of the Gospels with Paul's preaching of the resurrection. Here Paul was addressing communities in which some still lived who had known Jesus. The force of Paul's speech acts is to proclaim that this well-known historical figure has been raised. The representative conditions here are reordered. As a background condition, there must have been a historical Jesus known to those present by acquaintance or testimony, and this condition we can easily assume to have been fulfilled. The more immediate and interesting condition is that there must have been some peculiar event involving the body of that well-known figure that could reasonably have been described by the metaphorical term 'resurrection.' But since this event was not directly observable, the most that could be asked was that a sufficient number of hearers had access to enough evidence to be able reasonably to accept Paul's testimony.

So it is indeed true that today we have no access to the historical events 'behind the texts,' but in some cases the original hearers or readers did have such access, and we can infer a good deal about that history from their endorsement of the texts. But it is worth reiterating that the history is not to be equated with the meaning; nor is the reconstructed history in any sense *foundational* for the meaning of the text. The order must be the reverse—first to understand what the text was *doing* in its original setting, then to ask what historical knowledge (some of) its readers must have had in order for it to succeed.

To sum up, if we assume that something like Austin's speech-act theory is an adequate account of language, then insofar as we have reason to believe that biblical texts performed happy speech acts in their original settings, exactly to that extent do we have reason to believe that the *conditions* for happiness were met. These conditions include (relatively) stable linguistic conventions, (approximate) fulfillment of a variety of relevant historical conditions, and close (enough) correspondence between what the authors intended to say and what they actually said.

The qualifications in parentheses provoke us to ask how stable the conventions must be, how close the correspondences. The only general answer that can be given is: close enough to work. The necessary degree of precision will depend on the particularities of each speech act. So although it may not be possible to argue for an absolute fixity of meaning, it is indeed possible to argue for the degree of stability required for practical purposes, and with a theory of meaning as *use*, practical purposes are exactly the ones that matter.

5. Historical Distance and the baptist Vision

I mentioned previously that only half of the hermeneutic problem is solved if we can show that the texts had a (relatively) determinate meaning in their original contexts. The other half is to show that readers today have access to that meaning. Volumes have been written on how this historical distance is to be overcome—how our contemporary 'horizon' is to be fused with that of the text—in order to permit understanding in our own day. Yet a prior question is, What do we mean by 'understanding'?

In keeping with earlier proposals in this chapter, I suggest that we consider the issue as a matter of uptake. This entails that the first requirement for a community today to get the point of biblical speech acts is that it understand itself to be addressed by the texts. The second requirement is that the community now be in some sense *the same interpretive community* as that of the writer. Here the later Fish is helpful in his analysis of the relations between reading strategies and interpretive communities.

> Why should two or more readers ever agree . . . ? The answer . . . is to be found in a notion that has been implicit in my argument, the notion of *interpretive communities*. Interpretive communities are made up of those who share interpretive strategies. . . . This, then, is the explanation both for the stability of interpretation among different readers (they belong to the same community) and for the regularity with which a single reader will employ different interpretive strategies and thus make different texts (he belongs to different communities). It also explains why there are disagreements and why they can be debated in a principled way. . . . The notion of interpretive communities thus stands between an impossible ideal and the fear which leads so many to maintain it. The ideal is of perfect agreement and it would require texts to have a status independent of interpretation. The fear is of interpretive anarchy, but it would only be realized if interpretation (text making) were completely random.[26]

Thus, the community today must share interpretive strategies with the author and the original readers. How is this possible? Wittgenstein's account of the relation between interpretation of language and shared *forms of life* is relevant here; it suggests the importance of common activities and social

---

[26] Fish, *Is There a Text?* 182.

conventions. The reading strategy (and related understanding of church life) described by McClendon as the "baptist vision" is peculiarly well suited to meet these two requirements for uptake: that the church today understand itself to be addressed by the texts and that it share interpretive strategies with the biblical authors.

5.1. The baptist Vision

McClendon, in his systematic theology,[27] set out to capture the defining features of the tradition stemming from and similar to the anabaptist (or radical) reformation movement of the sixteenth century. This tradition includes a varied collection of church bodies, including Baptists (to the extent that they have not adopted Reformed ecclesiology and theology), Mennonites, Brethren, and some Pentecostals, Disciples, intentional communities. Earlier writers had attempted to characterize this form of church life as 'biblicist,' but all churches would claim their own way as the (or a) biblical way. Consequently, McClendon saw the need for an account of the particular relation in which baptists (translation of the German *Täufer*) stand to the texts.[28] It was for this purpose that he developed his notion of the baptist vision. Such a vision should be "the guiding stimulus by which a people . . . shape their life and thought. . . . Once acknowledged for what it is, it should serve as the touchstone by which authentic baptist life is discovered and described, and also as the organizing principle around which a genuine baptist theology can take shape."[29]

McClendon's proposal can be expressed, he says, as a "hermeneutical motto," which is shared awareness of "*the present Christian community as the primitive community and the eschatological community.*" In other words, "the church now is the primitive church and the church on the day of judgment is the church now; the obedience and liberty of the followers of Jesus of Nazareth is *our* liberty, our obedience" (31).

McClendon claims that this is the common reading strategy found *within* Scripture. When Peter, on Pentecost, says, "This is that which has been spoken through the prophet Joel" (Acts 2:16), he is applying language about one set of events, addressed to one community, to another set of events, speaking it to another community in a later set of circumstances. McClendon quotes Davie Napier, who says: "We have in the Old Testament no past

---

[27] James Wm. McClendon Jr., *Ethics: Systematic Theology, Volume I* (Nashville, Tenn.: Abingdon Press, 1986); James Wm. McClendon Jr., *Doctrine: Systematic Theology, Volume II* (Nashville, Tenn.: Abingdon, 1994).

[28] The lowercase 'b' in 'baptist vision' is meant to indicate that it pertains to this broad movement originating with the *Täufer*, in distinction from denominational Baptists.

[29] McClendon, *Ethics*, 27–28.

which has not already been appropriated in the present, and so appropriated as to *be* in the present, to *live* in the present. [The past] *was* past, but now *is*. . . . As such it is not so much . . . merely memorialized as reexperienced—created and lived again" (33).

So we have here a reading strategy that satisfies the first requirement for Austinian uptake at this end of the historical process. We might describe it as the present church's *determination* to take the texts to be addressed to itself, despite awareness of historical distance, so that the illocutionary force *then* is to be the illocutionary force *now*.

5.2. The Church Now as the Primitive Church

The second requirement for uptake is that the church now be, in some sense, the same interpretive community as the primitive church, and McClendon's baptist vision makes provision for this requirement as well. However, the baptist vision is no naive denial of history. There are inevitable differences between then and now: different customs, different cultures, even different worldviews, categorial frameworks. What we must see, then, is the sense in which *relevant* circumstances can be similar enough to allow for uptake. We can investigate this requirement by considering, again, several of the additional dimensions within which the conditions fall for a happy speech act: linguistic and social conventions, reference, and expressivist conditions, in addition to uptake.

5.2.1. Linguistic and Social Conventions   From a speech-act perspective, translators and exegetes have the same role to play as they do under the guidance of any hermeneutic theory. Their job is to enable the author and reader to share a common language and to clue the contemporary reader in on the linguistic conventions of the author's day.

But to learn a language—that is, to learn its 'grammar' in the philosophical sense—is to learn a worldview. Here we can see the relevance of Lindbeck's claim that texts *create a world*. To understand biblical language is to enter sympathetically into that world, just as one becomes *absorbed* in a good novel.[30] This reading strategy is the opposite of that of modern interpreters, for whom the goal was to bring the Bible into the modern world, to understand it by the lights of modern thought.

At least as important for entering the world of the Bible, however, is taking up the *practices* of the primitive church. "I bid three hearts" cannot succeed as a speech act if there is no bridge game in progress. Likewise, "Do this in

---

[30] George Lindbeck, "The Church's Mission to a Postmodern Culture," in Frederic Burnham, ed., *Postmodern Theology: Christian Faith in a Pluralistic World* (New York: Harper and Row, 1989), 37–55.

remembrance of me" cannot succeed apart from the eucharistic context; Paul's pleas for orderly worship cannot succeed where there is no worship. So we can conclude that in general the speech acts of the Bible cannot succeed if the present church is not actively engaged in an attempt to carry on the practices, the forms of life, of the primitive church.

This may raise a question: does not engagement in the practices of primitive Christianity presuppose that one already knows the meaning of New Testament texts? Here we find a baptist version of the hermeneutical circle. Historical criticism helps to recover the practices of the early church in their own setting; attempting to live out those practices in the contemporary setting sensitizes readers to new meanings in the texts. The New Testament churches were not perfect—they were struggling to become the church. Insofar as contemporary Christian communities, too, are struggling to become the church, they will be better able to hear what the texts are saying and as a consequence better able in the future to 'perform the Scriptures.'

5.2.2. Referential Conditions Another of the conditions for understanding the speech acts of the Bible is knowledge of the original historical context, and here historical methodologies play their usual role. Even with attention to all of these conditions, however, understanding, uptake, will usually not be perfect or complete. The point of this discussion is that current readers can put themselves in better or worse positions to understand the biblical texts. Even though the solitary scholar will still have much to offer—especially for helping to bring about shared linguistic skills—to the extent that she is alienated from the practical life of the church, she will be in a disadvantaged position for uptake. Church bodies that do not insist on discipleship, or that see their forms of life as having legitimately evolved away from the practices of the early church, will likewise be disadvantaged.[31] They will have their own interpretive strategies, which, according to Fish, should be expected to yield different readings—and all the more is this the case for those outside of the Christian tradition altogether.

6. Conclusion

Many take postmodern philosophical moves to be the *cause* of religious skepticism—skepticism with regard to truth claims and now a radical skepticism about whether one can even know the meaning of the biblical texts. However, I believe there is another instance of the irony of intellectual history here. Modern philosophers devised new theories of knowledge and then

---

[31] Postmodern (holist) theologians may find it interesting that philosophy of language can thus be shown to have consequences not only for hermeneutics but also for ecclesiology.

correlative theories of language. As it turns out, foundationalist accounts of knowledge have not worked well for theologians; it has not been possible to reconstruct theological knowledge on the basis of the sort of indubitable foundations, either experiential or scriptural, that modern theories of knowledge seemed to require. The result has been growing skepticism regarding theology's truth claims and finally (for many) the relegation of theology to the expressivist domain, where the categories of truth and falsity do not even apply.

However, since the middle of this century, philosophers have begun calling modern theories of knowledge into question and have devised new accounts of the nature of knowledge, how it is justified, what we mean in calling a belief 'true.' Two factors have driven this change. First, foundationalist theories of knowledge continued to have internal problems, and after three hundred years of trying, philosophers have rightly begun to suspect that the problems are insoluble. Second, it has become more and more obvious that foundationalist theories do not adequately describe the acquisition or justification of our most highly respected bodies of knowledge, namely, the sciences. As Thomas Kuhn has pointed out, if science fails to fit our current theories of rationality, then we have a choice: we can either say that science is irrational, or we can conclude that the theories of rationality need to be changed. More and more, philosophers are opting for the latter.

Those who would claim that the new nonfoundationalist (holist) theories of knowledge are the cause of relativism are making a mistake. Relativism arises for foundationalists when no single set of indubitable foundations can be found. The history of modern epistemology and philosophy of science shows that purported foundations (1) turn out to depend on the supposed nonfoundational knowledge for acceptance, or (2) turn out not to be indubitable, or (3) if they are indubitable turn out to be useless since there is no reliable way to argue from them to any interesting conclusions. So it is the 'facts' of our epistemic predicament, *along with the assumption that there must be foundations,* that produce skepticism and relativism.

To foundationalists, holists sound like relativists because they admit there are no foundations. Now, some holists are relativists, but they need not be. The absence of foundations entails relativism only if foundationalism is true. Holists deny the foundationalist assumption, and as we saw in Chapter 3, some go on to provide nonrelativist accounts of knowledge.

There is a parallel account to be given of developments in philosophy of language. Moderns developed theories of language according to which language is meaningful only if it refers to an external, 'experienceable' reality or, secondarily, if it expresses the intention of the author or speaker. But critics have shown that hermeneutic theories aiming at the recovery of historical referents or authorial intentions run into grave difficulties. One might say that these strategies have turned out not to reveal solid 'foundations' for interpretation of texts. Poststructuralist literary critics have shown that the literal sense of the words is an equally unreliable 'foundation.' But the situation is parallel to that of science and theories of rationality. If modern theories of meaning, combined with the 'epistemic facts' regarding texts, lead to the conclusion that no text has a fixed meaning, there are two options: to stand by modern theories of language (as the deconstructionists do, unwittingly) or to provide more adequate theories of language and meaning. My claim in this chapter is that Austin, McClendon and Smith, and the later Fish have already supplied a more adequate theory of language. All that remains is to exploit it (further) for approaching problems of textual interpretation.

So far I have spoken of theories of knowledge and theories of language as though they merely *describe* our practices of knowledge- and meaning-making. But of course, theory and practice interact: philosophies of science shape scientific research and reporting; theories of hermeneutics shape scholars' approaches to the texts. If, following Austin, we say that meaning is found primarily in what the text *does*, this has consequences for the use of the texts, whether by scholars or by members of churches. *If the texts' ability to perform a definite speech act depends on the existence of a community with shared conventions and proper dispositions, then textual stability is in large measure a function not of theories of interpretation but of how interpretive communities choose to live.* An Austinian theory of language calls upon Christians to adopt the stance toward the texts that McClendon describes as the hermeneutic principle of the baptist vision—"This is that": the illocutionary force then is the illocutionary force for this community here and now; the form of life of the church here and now is to be that of the primitive church. In this motto we find the missing piece of the contemporary hermeneutic puzzle.

This conclusion is consonant with Alasdair MacIntyre's notion of tradition-constituted enquiry. I have concentrated here on the problem of interpreting Christian Scripture, but MacIntyre points out that all traditions, religious and secular alike, are shaped by their interpretation and application of a formative text. He emphasizes that fruitful participation in an intellectual tradition requires prior formation of the character of the participants, the acquisition of virtues that allow them to participate in the practices constitutive of that tradition.[32] This is in sharp contrast to the modern ideal of enquiry in which the solitary knower was required first to rid the mind of all prejudice (tradition) before he could begin.

The foregoing paragraph suggests parallels between the pursuit of theological knowledge and the development of other sorts of intellectual traditions. The following chapter pursues in detail parallels between theology and the natural sciences.

---

[32] See Alasdair MacIntyre, *Three Rival Versions of Moral Enquiry: Encyclopaedia, Genealogy, and Tradition* (Notre Dame, Ind.: University of Notre Dame Press, 1990); and Alasdair MacIntyre, *Whose Justice? Which Rationality?* (Notre Dame, Ind.: University of Notre Dame Press, 1988).

PART III

Science, Religion, and Ethics

8 • • •

Theology and Postmodern Philosophy of Science

1. Introduction

I pointed out in the Introduction that the assumptions of modernity have had a great deal to do with the compartmentalization of science and theology, and I suggested that in the postmodern era it may be time to reassess this long-standing separation. In the Middle Ages, theology was not only *a* science but also the queen of the sciences. A variety of accounts can be given of the queen's deposition. One factor is the general disrepute into which all things religious have fallen in the modern era. But this may not be so much to explain as to restate in more general terms. Jeffrey Stout has provided a brilliant diagnosis of theology's predicament, using Ian Hacking's account of the rise of modern "probable reasoning."[1] Theology was a discipline at home with an epistemology based on authority. When this ancient and medieval account of "probable reasoning" as that which was approvable by the authorities was replaced by the modern notion of probability as proportioning one's beliefs to the strength of the evidence, the epistemological rug was pulled out from under theological reasoning. Stout believes that theology has never recovered.

I have argued elsewhere that theology could not recover so long as its only resources were foundationalist theories of knowledge. However, with the postfoundationalist epistemology represented especially by current philosophy of science, it is once again possible to make theological reasoning

---

[1] Jeffrey Stout, *The Flight from Authority: Religion, Morality, and the Quest for Autonomy* (Notre Dame, Ind.: University of Notre Dame Press, 1981).

respectable.[2] In this chapter, I take up one small part of the debate about the epistemological status of religious or theological knowledge. Within this broader issue of the rational status of religion, there has been a debate regarding the evidential value of religious experience. Do mystics' visions, locutions, and other experiences provide knowledge of God?

I summarize some of the arguments against the evidential value of religious experience, but I then show that such arguments rely on too simple a theory regarding the nature of evidence. Borrowing from philosophy of science, I provide a more adequate account of the relations between theory and evidence, and I then show that in some cases the criteria for sound evidence can be met. Consequently, religious experience can be used legitimately to confirm religious beliefs.

2. The Evidential Value of Religious Experience

One common objection to the claim that religious experience provides evidence for the truth of religious beliefs is that religious experience is essentially private and subjective. It is contrasted with data for science, which are public and replicable and, in that sense, objective. Let us call this the subjectivity problem.

The second problem with religious experience is what I call the circularity problem. It was stated succinctly by Alasdair MacIntyre in a 1955 article titled "Visions." According to MacIntyre, visions are taken by the recipient to convey information about something other than the experience itself—in most traditions, about God. However, we could never know from any such experience that it was a message from God unless we already had knowledge of God and of how messages from God were to be identified. "The decisive evidence for the divine," he says, "would then be anterior to the experience and not derived from it, whereas what we are concerned with here is how far the experience itself can provide such evidence."[3] In other words, to argue from a religious experience to a claim about God is circular since one needed to have knowledge beforehand that God exists, as well as knowledge about how God communicates.

In addition, MacIntyre argues, it may be thought that to treat a vision as a sign of the invisible is to accept in the realm of religious belief a procedure we are accustomed to employ elsewhere. So, for example, we infer unseen

---

[2] See Nancey Murphy, *Theology in the Age of Scientific Reasoning* (Ithaca: Cornell University Press, 1990).

[3] Alasdair MacIntyre, "Visions," in Antony Flew and Alasdair MacIntyre, eds., *New Essays in Philosophical Theology* (London: Macmillan, 1955), 256. MacIntyre's argument is expressed in terms of visions but would apply equally to other kinds of purported experiences from God.

fire from smoke and approaching trains from signals. But the case of religion is not the same; we can infer unseen fires from smoke because we have *seen* fires producing smoke in the past, but we have no experience of the causal connection between God and any visions God might produce.

Here is an example that nicely illustrates MacIntyre's worry. Catherine of Siena, a fourteenth-century mystic, called her book *The Dialogue* because in it she posed questions to God and then wrote (or recorded) long passages that were supposed to be God's replies. One of these is to a question about how to distinguish experiences that come from God from others: "Now, dearest daughter, . . . I will say something about what you asked me concerning the sign I said I give the soul for discerning the visitations she may receive through visions or other consolations. I told you how she could discern whether or not these were from me. The sign is the gladness and hunger for virtue that remain in the soul after the visitation, especially if she is anointed with the virtue of true humility and set ablaze with divine charity."[4] So Catherine would say that she can recognize when a religious experience is from God by these signs: it produces gladness, hunger for virtue, humility, and charity.

Now MacIntyre would ask Catherine, "How do you know that those are reliable signs?"

Catherine would reply, "Because God told me so."

MacIntyre would then enquire, "How do you know it was *God* who told you that?"

Catherine would answer, "Well, the experience produced gladness, humility, charity."

So you see the problem.

The subjectivity and circularity problems reinforce each other. Some authors have pointed out that religious experience is nearly always interpreted in terms of the categories of the religion it is taken to confirm: Catholic Christians have experiences of Christ or the Virgin Mary; Protestants only of Christ; Hindus have experiences of Brahman. Or to put this point more accurately, religious experiences are experienced *as* manifestations of phenomena appropriate to the recipient's belief system. Thus, there is no pure, objective religious experience prior to its interpretation in terms of the adherent's presupposed categories.[5] To state the objection baldly, the subjective biases of the recipient affect the experiences through

---

[4] Suzanne Noffke, trans. and ed., *Catherine of Siena: The Dialogue* (New York: Paulist Press, 1980), 198.

[5] See, for example, Steven T. Katz, "Language, Epistemology, and Mysticism," in Steven T. Katz, ed., *Mysticism and Philosophical Analysis* (New York: Oxford University Press, 1978), 22–74.

and through, and thus they cannot provide any independent confirmation for the presupposed systems of belief. In the following section, I first address the circularity problem, and then I shall be in a position to address subjectivity.

3. Data and Theories of Instrumentation

Scientists, I claim, face a problem analogous to the circularity problem in using their own sort of data to support scientific theories. Here, too, we find arguments from something seen (some measurement or observation) to a theory about something unseen.

Let us look at a very simple example. Most high school chemistry students have had the opportunity to test Boyle's law in the laboratory. For example, one puts a closed container of gas over a bunsen burner. The container has a thermometer and a pressure gauge affixed. The result of the experiment is that as the temperature goes up, the pressure goes up as well—confirmation for the law that the pressure of a gas is directly related to temperature when volume is held constant.

Now generalizations of this sort are an important part of science, but the interesting part is explaining *why* such things occur. Why does the pressure go up? To explain, we need a *theory* about gases, heat, and pressure. Here, in brief, is the theory—called the molecular-kinetic theory. Gases are composed of tiny particles in motion. Pressure is a result of large numbers of particles colliding with the walls of the container. Heat is equivalent to the kinetic energy of the particles—that is, the more heat, the more motion; the more motion, the more heat.

Consider, now, the data involved in the experiment just recounted. How do we take temperature measurements? In this example, we do so with a mercury thermometer. Where does the very idea for a thermometer come from? That is, why should a rising and falling column of mercury in a glass tube mean anything at all? The answer is based in part on the kinetic theory of heat. More heat means more movement of the atoms of mercury; more movement manifests itself as an increase in the volume of the liquid, and the column rises. This theoretical background is an important part of what validates the use of thermometer readings as reliable and useful data in a variety of experimental contexts. In philosophy of science these background theories are called theories of instrumentation because they are used to validate the products of measuring instruments and other parts of an experimental apparatus. Since the 1960s, philosophers of science have been pointing out that scientific data are "theory-laden," and this is part of their reason for saying so.[6]

---

[6] Thomas Kuhn's account in *The Structure of Scientific Revolutions*, first published in 1962 by Princeton University Press, is the most widely known, but he was preceded by N. R. Hanson, *Patterns of Discovery* (Cambridge: Cambridge University Press, 1958).

Notice, now, that MacIntyre could make the same objection to this bit of scientific reasoning as he did in the imagined dialogue with Catherine: "You are claiming that thermometer readings are reliable signs of the temperature of the gas, and you are using those readings as evidence for Boyle's law and ultimately for application of the kinetic theory to gases. But you cannot know that thermometers provide reliable measures of heat unless you already accept the kinetic theory. So the reasoning is circular. The experiment with the gas cannot provide any evidence for the theory."

What reply might we make to MacIntyre? My suggestion is that he is operating here with too simple an account of reasoning. In particular, he is assuming foundationalism in his requirement that one must always argue *from* experience *to* theory. Second, he is assuming too atomistic an account of the justification of theories. So, for example, one experiment supports one theory in science; one vision supports the one simple theory that God exists. But as we have seen in Chapter 3, reasoning in science (and, I argue, in theology as well) is much more complicated: we argue from a variety of experimental results to support a network of scientific theories. Some of those theories, in turn, provide us with grounds for regarding the experimental data as sound.

To illustrate this latter point, consider a more complete account of the relations between experimental measurement and theory regarding the expansion of gases. First, there are a variety of procedures for measuring temperature—the familiar mercury and alcohol thermometers, procedures based on the thermoelectric effect, changes in electrical resistance of materials such as platinum, and others. The confidence that scientists place in each of these measuring techniques is based in part on the consistency of results obtained by the various methods. Second, the operation of each of these instruments is explained by, and thus validated in part by, scientific theory. Thus, an entire network of theory, laws, and experimental results is accepted as a whole because of its consistency and its explanatory power. There is always a degree of circular reasoning involved, but it might be called virtuous, rather than vicious, circularity because it is part of what is involved in showing the consistency of the theoretical network.

Since the time when MacIntyre wrote "Visions," a revolution has taken place in epistemology. The foundationalist assumptions on which MacIntyre's argument is based have been thoroughly criticized by W.V.O. Quine, N. R. Hanson, Thomas Kuhn, and Imre Lakatos, not to mention MacIntyre himself.

4. Theological Equivalents of Theories of Instrumentation

Let us see now whether the foregoing account applies to theological reasoning. I claim that there are striking formal analogies between scientific and theological reasoning. If so, we ought to expect to find vast networks of theological theories where no single theory is supported by any single religious experience but where a variety of experiences support the whole network. Furthermore, we ought to expect there to be something that plays a role equivalent to *theories of instrumentation* in science.

Let us return to the example from Catherine of Siena. Catherine did not have an experience of God speaking to her "out of the blue." She had a whole network of background theories about God, about Jesus Christ, about God's will for human life, and so forth. She also had a long history of previous experiences of relating to God, as well as knowledge of others' experiences.

Of particular interest here is the set of criteria she had for recognizing when she was dealing with God and when not. Recall that her criteria are gladness and hunger for virtue that remain after the experience, growth in humility, and being set ablaze with charity toward others.

To investigate the value of such criteria, let us compare them with a proposal made by Teresa of Avila in her sixteenth-century guide to the spiritual life, *The Interior Castle*.[7] The purpose of Teresa's book was to set out the stages her sisters should expect to go through in their relationship to God. Thus, it was obviously necessary to explain how they were to tell if they were in communion with God, and if so, what God was doing 'in their souls.' Here is a passage in which Teresa explains how to recognize when one has reached the state of union with God in prayer: "This union is above all earthly joys, above all delights, above all consolations, and still more than that. . . . God so places himself in the interior of the soul that when it returns to itself it can in no way doubt that it was in God and God was in it. This truth remains with it so firmly that even though years go by without God's granting that favor again, the soul can neither forget nor doubt that it was in God and God was in it" (2:338, 339).

If Teresa were familiar with modern theology, she might say that such an experience is self-authenticating—an experience such that the one who has it can neither doubt *that* the experience took place nor be mistaken about its character. There have been assorted attempts to ground religious knowledge on self-authenticating experiences (see Chapter 5, section 2.4). Such moves are, rightly, I think, to be regarded with suspicion. The heights of joy and subjective certitude described here surely have value to the recipient but have no *evidential value*, at least not for anyone else.

The difference between Teresa's and Catherine's criteria is that Catherine's judgment is based on the connection between the purported experience of God and other experiences—some at the same time and some later—and,

---

[7] Otilio Rodrigues and Kieran Kavanaugh, eds., *The Collected Works of St. Teresa of Avila* (Washington, D.C.: ICS, 1980), 2:281–500.

most important, to *observable* changes in the recipient's life. The one experience, taken to be an encounter with God, is validated by the way it fits into a network of other experiences or phenomena. Is it *accompanied by* gladness? Is it *followed by* greater humility? Is a felt increase in charity borne out in *action* in the days or weeks or years to come? Because of this last criterion, Catherine is not left to make a judgment on the source of her audition alone; her confessor and her friends will be able to see the changes in her if the experience is valid and will help her to judge its authenticity.

We can see the significance of requiring an interconnected set of experiences, and especially a publicly observable criterion such as growth in charitable action, by considering the most prominent of the competing explanations for religious experiences. Catherine was most concerned that she not be misled by attributing to God experiences that were actually induced by the devil. Teresa was concerned to detect demonic influences but was apparently more worried by the possibility that the experiences were merely the product of the recipient's *imagination.* Modern investigators, similarly, are more concerned by the possibility that religious experiences are merely psychological phenomena with no reference to a transcendent God. In fact, at first glance, such experiences can easily be explained psychologically. Religious people want to have experiences that confirm their beliefs. This desire is the cause of the experiences, whether directly and intentionally or, more likely, through a process of autosuggestion such that the experiences seem to come from an external source. Let us call this the self-inducement theory of religious experience.

That Teresa was aware of and concerned about this possibility is shown in the following passage, where she attempts to explain why some experiences seem as if they could not have been produced by the person's own imagination:

Wonderful effects are left so that the soul may believe; at least there is assurance that the locution doesn't come from the imagination. Furthermore, if the soul is attentive, it can always have assurance for the following reasons: First, there is a difference because of the clarity of the locution. It is so clear that the soul remembers every syllable and whether it is said in one style or another, even if it is a whole sentence. But in a locution fancied by the imagination the words will not be so clear or distinct but like something half-dreamed.

Second, in these locutions one often is not thinking about what is heard (I mean that the locution comes unexpectedly and even sometimes while one is in conversation). . . . It often refers to things about the future that never entered the mind, and so the imagination couldn't have fabricated it. . . .

Third, the one locution comes as in the case of a person who hears, and that of the imagination comes as in the case of a person who gradually composes what he himself wants to be told.

Fourth, the words are very different, and with one of them much is comprehended. Our intellect could not compose them so quickly.

Fifth, together with the words, in a way I wouldn't know how to explain, there is often given much more to understand than is ever dreamed possible without words. (2:376)

So Teresa is arguing that the characteristics of the experience itself can provide adequate evidence against the self-inducement theory. However, it is easy enough to discount this claim. First, we simply do not know the extent of a person's powers to create such an experience without realizing it. Second, Ludwig Wittgenstein's arguments against private language are relevant here. Without external, public criteria, there is no real difference between saying something such as "This locution *is* clearer than that" and saying, "This locution *seems* clearer than that." Thus, the first expression has no real use and is therefore meaningless.[8]

So let us consider whether any of Catherine's criteria are public in the required sense and whether they could possibly serve to distinguish between the two explanatory theories: divine encounter versus self-inducement. The criterion of gladness is public enough—that is, we are often enough able to tell whether people we are close to are happy or not. However, this criterion is likely to be met whichever of the theories is true: if one is strongly motivated to have an experience in conformity with one's religious beliefs, and the experience occurs, then one ought to be expected to be happy as a result.

The criterion of increased humility begins to create problems for the inducement theory. Greater smugness is the reaction more to be expected from a person who has just had his desires met and beliefs confirmed.

Hunger for virtue is a noble sentiment but does not mean much unless it is enacted. This leaves the criterion of increased charity. Can this be taken as a reliable sign of the working of God, or is it compatible with the inducement theory as well? It could certainly be argued that in a setting where good works count as validation of one's status as a spokesperson for God, one could have strong motivation for performing such acts.

Catherine's confessor and biographer, Raymond of Capua, states that he intends to relate "the events which establish the credibility of Catherine's account of her inner life."[9] To this end he notes that she never confessed a serious sin. Furthermore, even if we take due account of tendencies to exaggerate and embellish the biographies of 'saints,' Catherine can be said to have adopted a remarkable pattern of service to the poor and sick in her community, often nursing those whom others found too repulsive.

---

[8] See Ludwig Wittgenstein, *Philosophical Investigations*, trans. G.E.M. Anscombe (New York: Macmillan, 1953), esp. §§ 258–263.

[9] Raymond of Capua, *The Life of Catherine of Siena*, trans. Conleth Kearns (Wilmington, Del.: Michael Glazier, 1980), 85.

Raymond's intention was to show that Catherine's charitable actions go so far beyond the ordinary as to warrant her claim to have been in direct contact with God.

This issue raises a theological question: is there a limit to the extent one can reform one's own character for the purpose of gaining a hearing for one's visionary experiences? This is one instance of a larger question: is moral perfection within the grasp of the human will? Christians have generally answered no, and no one has said it more eloquently than the apostle Paul:

> We know that the law is spiritual; but I am not: I am unspiritual, sold as a slave to sin. . . . For though the will to do good is there, the ability to effect it is not. The good which I want to do, I fail to do; but what I do is the wrong which is against my will. . . .
>
> I discover this principle, then: that when I want to do right, only wrong is within my reach. In my inmost self I delight in the law of God, but I perceive in my outward actions a different law, fighting against the law that my mind approves, and making me a prisoner under the law of sin which controls my conduct. Wretched creature that I am, who is there to rescue me from this state of death: Who but God? (Rom. 7:14–25)

Now Paul is making a straightforward empirical claim about human capacities: we want to do good; we often do evil instead—no matter how strong our motivation. So it is possible to recognize lives that do not fit the pattern, lives that violate our general expectations regarding the natural limits of virtue. This means, in turn, that the self-inducement theory has limits; exceptionally noble lives may justifiably call us to raise the question of whether a higher power is involved after all.

So my claim is that Catherine's criteria have some interest for the religious epistemologist. Given the right circumstances, such as the opportunity to observe changes in the lives of those who claim to receive visions or teachings from God, these signs would have some value for distinguishing between experiences generated by the recipient's own imagination and others that could not be so easily explained away. What, exactly, to make of the latter (unexplained) experiences depends, of course, on the tradition within which they are interpreted.

The Christian tradition contains quite a number of teachings similar to Catherine's on criteria for recognizing the work of God in people's lives. There are some variations from one denomination to another, and some individual variation from one author to another, but overall there is quite a bit of agreement. So we have here a theory, which I call the theory of discernment, that states that it is possible to recognize the activity of God in human life by means of signs or criteria, some of which are public and relatively objective. My claim is that the theory of discernment functions in

Christian theology in exactly the same way as theories of instrumentation do in science.

The criteria for discernment can be grouped conveniently under two headings: consistency and fruit. 'Consistency,' for Protestants, means consistency with Scripture. For Catholics, it also includes consistency with church teaching. The use of the consistency criterion, of course, raises all the problems of interpretation that go along with use of the Bible for any purpose—a set of problems I do not go into here, except to note the following: a wooden application of this criterion would mean that no religious experience could ever challenge traditional teaching since such an experience would automatically be judged inauthentic. However, if this criterion is used in conjunction with others, there will be cases where an experience, attested on the grounds of other signs, conflicts with a traditional *interpretation* of Scripture, and the experience, together with critical reflection on the received interpretation, may result in that interpretation being overturned. So there is room for a dynamic interplay among texts, interpretations, and religious experiences.

If this is the case, there is a clear parallel with science, where an observation or experimental result that conflicts with accepted theory will be regarded with suspicion. The decision either to ignore the datum or to revise the theory can go either way and will be made only after the theory has been reevaluated and additional experimentation has been performed.

The criterion of 'fruit' refers to the various effects of the experience in the life of the recipient and her community. The term is appropriate in that Jesus declared that false prophets could be known by their fruits (Matt. 7:16). The apostle Paul listed the fruit of the Holy Spirit as love, joy, peace, patience, kindness, generosity, faithfulness, gentleness, and self-control (Gal. 5:22–23). Catherine, as we have seen, along with many other spiritual writers, would add humility to the list, and contrition for sin is often added as well.

The one significant difference among Christian views of discernment has to do with *who* does the discerning. In both the Catholic and the Reformed traditions, the assumption appears to be that discernment is exercised by the one receiving the experience or at most by that person and her pastor or confessor. In a third major tradition—the Anabaptist, radical-reformation, or free-church tradition—discernment is a function exercised by the gathered community. That is, it is the job of the church to decide who are the true and false prophets.

The communal nature of discernment among Mennonites, Brethren, Quakers, and other churches from this radical tradition allows for another kind of fruit to be added to the list—the agreement and unity of the congregation. This means in the first instance that all members need to agree that the other criteria are met—consistency with Scripture and production of love and virtue. But in addition, the experience being judged must contribute to the building up of the body of believers—not to discord and dissension. It is important to note that this criterion presupposes a church community in which evidence of conversion is required for membership since, as Jesus himself noted, the presence and activity of God produce conflict between true believers and the world.[10] Yet even among 'true believers,' dissension is so common that the church's being brought to unity of mind and heart can well be taken as a sign of the activity of God in the community's midst.

5. Epistemological Problems in Theology

5.1. The Circularity Problem

I began with two objections to the use of religious experience as evidence for religious beliefs: the subjectivity problem and the circularity problem. I have described a theory of discernment and have claimed that it functions in theology in the same way a theory of instrumentation does in science. Now I want to show that circularity is not a problem after all—in fact, the modest degree of circularity involved in the employment of a theory of discernment is a virtue of the system rather than a vice.

Let us return to the example from science. Temperature readings are accepted as usable data because a theory of instrumentation connects the rising and falling of a column of mercury to a conception of "kinetic energy." The theory posits a regular relation between an observable sign (changes in the column of mercury) and an invisible quantity (kinetic energy). Now, recall MacIntyre's claim that we can infer the presence of the unseen from the visible sign only if we have had *experience* of the connection between the sign and that which it signifies. The example of the thermometer shows this claim to be false: no one has ever seen kinetic energy. How, then, is this particular theory of instrumentation confirmed? It is confirmed by the conjunction of two factors. One is the experienced reliability of the instrument—it produces similar or identical readings again and again under similar circumstances, and these results correlate with results produced by other kinds of measuring devices. The other is that the theory of instrumentation follows from theoretical beliefs that we have no good reason to call into question. In other words, the truth of the theory of instrumentation is supported by its consistency with a network of other statements, some derived rather directly from experience; others of a more theoretical nature.

---

[10] "But when you are arrested, do not worry about what you are to say, for when the time comes, the words you need will be given you; it will not be you speaking, but the Spirit of your Father speaking in you. Brother will hand over brother to death, and a father his child; children will turn against their parents and send them to their death. Everyone will hate you for your allegiance to me" (Matt. 10:19–22; cf. Matt. 10:34–36).

The Christian theory of discernment is likewise supported by its connections to a variety of other statements, some based on experience, others of a theoretical (or theological) nature. For example, Jonathan Edwards, the theologian of the Great Awakening, presents a simple theoretical account of why the fruits of the Spirit *should* be taken to provide valid signs of God at work in a human life. The fruits of the Spirit jointly constitute a particular kind of character—what Edwards calls the "lamb-like, dove-like character" of Christ. In light of Christian theology, this is exactly what is to be expected. The fruits are signs that the Holy Spirit is at work in a person's life because the Holy Spirit is in fact the Spirit of Christ, and Christ's spirit should manifest itself in a Christlike character.

The second kind of support for the theory of discernment is experiential—does it work *reliably?* Reliability means, simply, that a measurement or process results in roughly or exactly the same results under similar circumstances. Reliability is always a matter of degree; different degrees are to be expected, depending on the complexity of the matter under study. Measurements with a ruler are highly reliable; measurement with an IQ test is only moderately reliable. We have no data on the reliability of believers' judgments regarding the presence or absence of God's agency in certain events. Whether or not a particular community's judgments are as reliable as those accepted by psychologists and sociologists for equally complex material is open to investigation. But it is significant that communities that exercise communal judgment do not readily abandon the practice. This suggests that the results tend to be consistent over time since a practice that yielded erratic results would soon lose its appeal.

It might be objected that the variety of beliefs and practices found throughout the Christian movement across denominations and over time argues for the unreliability of discernment. I suggest, however, that it argues instead for the need to make more frequent and determined use of the practice. In fact, much of what goes on in the life of churches has never been subjected to this sort of testing. Greater reliance on discernment would turn churches into 'laboratories' for testing theological formulations.

So far, we have only anecdotal information on the reliability of discernment, but its reliability could be checked in the same way that measuring instruments in the human sciences (tests, instruments, etc.) are validated. The fact that discernment presupposes some aspects of Christian theology is a factor in its favor, not a detriment.

5.2. The Subjectivity Problem

Much of what is needed to address the subjectivity problem has already been said. It is clear that suspicion about believers' ability to delude themselves calls for greater emphasis on discernment criteria that are public and intersubjective.

"Gladness" could be as much a result of effective self-deception as of the presence of God. Humility can be feigned. I have suggested, however, that there are limits to the degree to which growth in charity can be undertaken at will; there are limits as well to the extent that it can be feigned. So the criterion of greatest interest for the philosopher must be fruit of a publicly observable sort such as extraordinary growth in virtue. Although we have no laboratory instruments to measure virtue, it is nonetheless a public phenomenon, there for anyone to see. So the kind of experience that is relevant for the confirmation of religious belief is not so much the immediate experiences of the mystics but rather 'experience' in a different sense: the accumulated observations *made by a discerning community* regarding correlations between reports of private experiences such as visions and other, publicly observable phenomena such as acts of charity.

The repeatability of observations or experiments is important in some sciences. The *sorts* of correlations here described are in fact repeatable. Peter Moore observes that

> a mystic is, precisely, one who has tested through his own experience the claims made by earlier generations of mystics. Finally, there is in mystical writing much evidence for the epistemological stability and hence objective validity of mystical experience: concordance among the reports of different mystics, refinement of observations, development of theory, improvement of technique, and so on. In sum, it could be argued that most if not all of the conditions which are met in the case of experiences known to have objective validity appear, from the accounts given by mystics, to obtain in the case of mystical experience too.[11]

Moore's comment raises the issue of objectivity. 'Objectivity' is a word used rather loosely in many circles—perhaps it is more of a commendation than a description. The most appropriate use of the word for present purposes is that of social scientists, whose difficulties in measurement are almost as great as those of the empirical theologian. Here 'objectivity' can be equated with an observation's or measurement's *reliability, validity,* and *intersubjectivity.*

I have already addressed the reliability of the results of discernment. The validity of a measurement refers to its genuine connection with the thing measured—for example, is IQ a valid measure of intelligence? The value of Edwards's theology is that it provides a rationale for believing the fruits of the Spirit to be *valid* indicators of God's activity, not because there is some accidental connection but because they are elements of the character of the divine presence to which they testify.

---

[11] Peter Moore, "Mystical Experience, Mystical Doctrine, Mystical Technique," in Katz, ed. *Mysticism,* 126.

I have also addressed the issue of intersubjectivity: discernment criteria that involve publicly observable effects will be given greater weight by the philosopher just because they allow for, demand, intersubjective agreement. So Catherine's experience of God in the depths of her soul, in the privacy of her room, is not a suitable datum for theology. The fact that such experiences were coupled with extraordinary acts of charity, known throughout much of the Christian world at the time, may very well be an objective datum for confirming her claims to receive revelation from God and thus also the belief system with which her revelations cohere.

5.3. Further Problems

I now wish to address another epistemological worry that may have arisen. I have been arguing that under proper circumstances some instances of some kinds of religious experiences might provide suitably objective empirical support to confirm religious theories. I have emphasized the consistency or coherence of beliefs drawn from experience with beliefs belonging to the theoretical or theological structure of the system. The new worry that is likely to have been raised by the foregoing arguments is that the system now appears too neat, too pat. To use language from philosophy of science, a genuine empirical theory has to be falsifiable as well as confirmable; we need to be able to specify what experiences would call it into question.[12] If the data of religious experience are theory-laden (interpreted, even in a sense produced, in light of the theories they are taken to confirm), and if one of the criteria for recognizing a relevant experience is its conformity to Scripture or church teaching, have I not then described an essentially unfalsifiable system?

I have already mentioned the possibility that the consistency criterion could be used in such a way as to make the system unfalsifiable—but it need not. For example, consider another passage from Catherine's *Dialogue:*

> I have shown you, dearest daughter, that in this life guilt is not atoned for by any suffering simply as suffering, but rather by suffering borne with desire, love, and contrition of heart. The value is not in the suffering but in the soul's desire. Likewise, neither desire nor any other virtue has value or life except through my only-begotten Son, Christ crucified, since the soul has drawn love from him and in virtue follows his footsteps. In this way and in no other is suffering of value. It satisfies for sin, then, with gentle unitive love born from the sweet knowledge of my goodness and from the bitterness and contrition the heart finds in the knowledge of itself and its own sins. Such knowledge gives birth to hatred and contempt for sin and for the soul's selfish sensuality, whence she considers

---

[12] This is Karl Popper's claim. See Karl Popper, *The Logic of Scientific Discovery* (New York: Harper, 1965).

herself worthy of punishment and unworthy of reward. So you see, *said gentle Truth*, those who have heartfelt contrition, love for true patience, and that true humility which considers oneself worthy of punishment and unworthy of reward suffer with patience and so make atonement. (20)

If it is the case that this locution comes from God, it has definite theological implications. I selected this passage because it touches on a disputed point in Christian theology: does human suffering atone for sin (as some Catholics have taught), or does atonement come only through the suffering of Christ, mediated to sinners by grace (as most Protestants maintain)? On first glance, this passage seems to confirm the Catholic view that human suffering is meritorious. But careful reading shows that the correct understanding is more complicated than either Catholic "works" or Protestant "grace alone." Suffering is of value, but only insofar as one is united by love to Christ, which leads to true contrition and, it can be presumed, opens the penitent to grace.

So here is the record of an experience that Catherine judged to be a communication from God, that her Catholic superiors saw fit to publish as such, and that modifies the Catholic thinking of her day in the direction of a not-yet-enunciated Protestant emphasis on grace. (Catherine was writing nearly two hundred years before the Protestant Reformation.) So it is, indeed, possible for religious experience to clash with and thus correct theological theory.

There are two additional problems that cry out for attention, but I only mention them here. The first is the question of the extent to which cultural factors influence the character and content of the sorts of 'revelations' that have been considered here. A range of views is possible, from the assumption that culture and expectations totally determine the content of religious experience to the view that religious experience, though couched in the language of a particular culture, is totally transparent to the divine realities it represents. I have been assuming a middle position on this issue, but I am not able to argue for it here, except to point out that my treatment of Catherine's "grace theology" in the preceding quotation seems to illustrate the possibility of genuinely new content 'getting through' the cultural presuppositions of the recipient.

A middle position on this issue has consequences for the way visionary literature is to be interpreted. We need a criterion something like the "criterion of difference" used in New Testament studies to distinguish the historical sayings of Jesus from those put in his mouth by the early church. In the New Testament, that which differs from the presuppositions of both the Jews and the church can be presumed to be authentic. Likewise, in visionary literature, what differs from the cultural assumptions of the recipient has *some* warrant to be considered genuinely revelatory.

A second problem that ought to be addressed here is the problem of the plurality of religions. David Hume recognized over two hundred years ago that the claims of one religion, if taken seriously, tend to cancel the claims of the others. If Christian experience confirms Christian beliefs, then is it not also the case that Jewish experience confirms Jewish beliefs; Hindu, Hindu; and so on? The first step in addressing this problem would be to ask whether each of these other religions has a criterion comparable to the Christian theory of discernment to separate authentic encounters with the divine from counterfeits, which are presumably as common in other faiths as they are among Christians. I simply do not know the answer to this question.

I suggest that the problem of religious pluralism be taken as analogous to the problem of competing research programs in science. I have argued elsewhere that it may sometimes be possible to apply Lakatos's criterion of empirical progress to theological programs.[13] So one approach to this issue would be to identify the most coherent accounts of competing religions' theoretical (theological) claims and compare them on this basis.

Even more fitting would be to apply MacIntyre's proposals for rational adjudication between competing large-scale traditions. This would be appropriate rhetorically because MacIntyre's own early argument served as the starting point of this chapter but, more important, because religions (as opposed to the technical theological schools that develop within them) are in fact large-scale traditions in exactly the sense MacIntyre describes.[14] The amount of scholarly work required to carry out such a project is enormous, but at this stage of intellectual history no one should expect questions of this sort to be resolved by means of brief arguments or even single-volume treatments of the issue.

6. Conclusion

We live in a period of history when religious truths have been called radically into question. We have inherited several centuries worth of arguments from critics to the effect that religious beliefs fail to measure up to standards of rationality. Furthermore, within the Christian tradition we stand in the shadows of highly acclaimed theologians who have argued that religion should not have been seen in the first place as a venture within the province of reason. Hence, we are thoroughly predisposed to view religious thought as

---

[13] Murphy, *Theology*. For Lakatos's concept of empirical progress, see Chapter 3, section 3.1.

[14] For a discussion of the differences between theology and religion, and for the appropriate points of comparison with scientific theories and traditions, see my "Ian Barbour on Religion and the Methods of Science: An Assessment," *Zygon: Journal of Religion and Science* 31, no. 1 (March 1996):11–19.

subjective, as projection, as entirely explainable in terms of the psychological or social needs that it fulfills.

In this chapter, I have presented a small challenge to that prevailing view by noting some structural parallels between religious thought and scientific reasoning, and in the process I have demonstrated that at least some of the arguments against the rationality of religious belief tell us more about the limitations of the modern epistemological assumptions of their defenders than about the unacceptability of religious claims. I do not expect to have convinced any skeptics, but I do hope to have shown this to be an important area that requires reevaluation in light of the shift from modern to postmodern epistemology.

9 • • •

Theology and Ethics in the Hierarchy of the Sciences

1. Introduction

No one captures the ironies and tensions in modern thought better than Bruno Latour in *We Have Never Been Modern.*[1] The first modern move, he says, was to distinguish nature from culture. Nature is transcendent, always "out there" to be discovered, not created. Culture or society, however, is what we freely make; thus we know it immanently.

This distinction is too familiar to require much comment. It is the distinction between the objective and the subjective, the natural sciences and the social sciences, facts and values. The double irony is that the laws of nature are known only as they are *fabricated* in the laboratory by the new *social order* of scientists, whereas society turns out to transcend the humans who created it—it has an *objectivity* of its own.

An equally important modern move was "the attempt to free intellectual pursuits from the influence of religion."[2] Latour claims that God had to be removed from "the dual social and natural construction."[3] "No one is truly modern who does not agree to keep God from interfering with Natural Law as well as with the laws of the Republic" (33). This "crossed-out God" is distanced from both nature and society, yet kept presentable and usable nonetheless. Latour says: "Spirituality was reinvented: the all-powerful God could descend into men's heart of hearts without intervening in any way in their external affairs. A wholly individual and wholly spiritual religion made

---

[1] Bruno Latour, *We Have Never Been Modern,* trans. Catherine Porter (Cambridge, Mass.: Harvard University Press, 1993).

[2] Ralph McInerny, Introduction to Ralph McInerny, ed., *Modernity and Religion* (Notre Dame, Ind.: University of Notre Dame Press, 1994), ix.

[3] Latour, *We Have Never Been Modern,* 32.

it possible to criticize both the ascendancy of science and that of society, without needing to bring God into either. The moderns could now be both secular and pious at the same time" (33). Latour's irony again.

To recognize such a state of affairs, to date its historical beginning, is to begin to transcend it.[4] But it is only a beginning. It calls into question the compartmentalization of reality—God, nature, society—but it does not tell us how to reunite them. It does not tell us how to proceed toward a more holistic view of enquiry, relating theology to both the natural and the human sciences.

My goal in this chapter is to present a model for relating theology to the full range of sciences. Some of what I have to offer is not original; I have been much influenced by Arthur Peacocke's hierarchical view of the relations between Christian theology and the sciences.[5] But part of what I present is highly unconventional: I argue that *ethics* needs to be construed as a science and that, as such, it serves as a link between the social sciences and theology.

2. A Bit of History

The logical positivists of the 1920s and 1930s were quintessential moderns. One very influential aspect of their program called for the unification of the sciences: The various sciences were to be organized hierarchically according to the complexity of the entities studied. Thus, physics would be at the bottom, then chemistry, biology, psychology, sociology. In addition, the logical positivists hoped to show that the laws of each science could be reduced to the laws of the next lower discipline, and thus the behavior of all of the entities in the universe could ultimately be shown to be a consequence of the laws of physics.

Peacocke has made use of this hierarchical view of the relations among the sciences, but he has qualified it in two crucial respects. First, although he accepts ontological or metaphysical reductionism, the view that entities at higher levels are composed of entities from lower levels, he rejects the view that the behavior of entities at higher levels is strictly determined by the lower-level entities or laws. There is also top-down causation to be taken into account—the effect of the environment or the larger whole on its constituents.[6] Second, in sharp contrast to the predominant atheism of the logical positivists, Peacocke adds Christian theology to the hierarchy of the

---

[4] Latour focuses on the beginnings found in the works of Robert Boyle and Thomas Hobbes, following Steven Shapin and Simon Schaffer, *Leviathan and the Air Pump: Hobbes, Boyle, and the Experimental Life* (Princeton: Princeton University Press, 1983).

[5] See Arthur R. Peacocke, *Theology for a Scientific Age*, 2d, enl. ed. (Minneapolis: Fortress Press, 1993).

[6] For his most recent account, see Arthur Peacocke, "God's Interaction with the World: The Implications of Deterministic 'Chaos' and of Interconnected and Interdependent Complexity," in Robert J. Russell, Nancey Murphy, and Arthur R. Peacocke, eds., *Chaos and Complexity: Scientific Perspectives on Divine Action* (Vatican City State and Berkeley, Calif.: Vatican Observatory and Center for Theology and the Natural Sciences, 1995), 263–288.

sciences, placing it at the top, since the interaction between God and the whole of created reality must be the most complex or all-encompassing level.

Peacocke's work, I believe, provides a valuable starting point for a reconception of the nature of theology and its relation to the sciences. It provides a critique of both liberal and fundamentalist views of the relation between science and theology (see Chapter 5, section 5.2), while recognizing what is true in each. His work recognizes, with the liberals, that theology represents a different level of analysis than science; it has its own peculiar language and concepts and point of view. The work also recognizes, with the conservatives, that theology and science cannot be isolated from each other. Peacocke's model suggests that theology will relate to a given science in much the same way that any two sciences relate to each other.

3. A Proposal

The hierarchy of the sciences is a model or idealization, and it cannot be used to give a flawless account of all of the sciences and their interrelations. It has no place for the historical sciences, and it fails to represent disciplines, such as genetics, that cut across levels. Most important, it is ambiguous as to whether higher levels pertain to more *encompassing* wholes (such as societies versus individuals or whole organisms versus their organs and tissues) or to more *complex* systems. These two criteria usually overlap, but not in every case. If the hierarchy (apart from theology) is taken to be based on more encompassing wholes, then cosmology, the study of the origin and evolution of the *entire* universe, is the highest possible level. If the hierarchy is based instead on the increasing complexity of the systems studied, then we have to ask whether a social system or the human nervous system is not more complex than the abstract account of the cosmos provided by cosmologists.

There is no good way to choose between these criteria. Therefore, it is helpful to represent the relations among the sciences by means of a branching hierarchy, with the human sciences forming one branch and the natural sciences above biology forming the other. Another advantage of this branching model is that it gives due recognition to the aforementioned distinction between the natural and the social.

3.1. The Relations Among the Sciences

I mentioned earlier the positivists' assumption that for any two neighboring disciplines in the hierarchy, the higher could be reduced to the lower in the sense that the behavior of the higher-level entity could be explained in terms of the behavior of its parts. So there are many questions that arise at, say, level two that can be answered only by means of theories and laws from level one.

However, there is also top-down causation. That is, we also sometimes need to move to level three or higher to answer questions at level two. Evolutionary biology is rife with examples of both bottom-up and top-down explanation. Mutations are explained primarily via physics, whereas survival of an altered life form is largely explained environmentally—that is, in terms of factors germane to the science of ecology. Let us call questions arising at a particular level of the hierarchy that can be answered only from a higher-level perspective *boundary questions*.

3.2. Theology and the Sciences

The plausibility of counting theology (or some kindred discipline, religious or metaphysical) as the topmost science in the hierarchy can be seen when we consider some of the boundary questions that arise in the natural sciences.[7] For example, what happened before the Big Bang? It is not clear whether science can address this issue at all, Stephen Hawking notwithstanding.[8] If cosmologists do produce a scientific account of the cause of the Big Bang, then the boundary question is simply pushed back a step.[9]

Let us consider another example: why are the cosmological constants apparently "fine-tuned" for life? That is, why do the particular laws of nature that we find in operation in the universe, among all of the uncountably many possibilities, happen to be among the very narrow range of those resulting in a life-supporting universe?[10] For that matter, why are there any laws at all? What is their ontological status? What gives them their force?[11]

Although none of these questions strictly requires a theological answer, it is clear enough to Christians and other theists that a traditional conception of God and of God's purposes answers them all rather easily. God is the ultimate

---

[7] Note that placing theology at the top is not an attempt to return theology to its medieval status as queen of the sciences; recall that this was originally the positivists' hierarchy in which physics, at the bottom, was king.

[8] His popular account is Stephen Hawking, *A Brief History of Time* (New York: Bantam Books, 1988). For a good summary of the issues, see C. J. Isham, "Quantum Theories of the Creation of the Universe," in Robert J. Russell, Nancey Murphy, and C. J. Isham, eds., *Quantum Cosmology and the Laws of Nature* (Vatican City State and Berkeley, Calif.: Vatican Observatory and Center for Theology and the Natural Sciences, 1993), 49–89.

[9] For a discussion of the relevance of quantum cosmology to theology, see Robert J. Russell, "Finite Creation Without a Beginning: The Doctrine of Creation in Relation to Big Bang and Quantum Cosmologies," in Russell et al., eds., *Quantum Cosmology*, 293–329.

[10] See, for example, John D. Barrow and Frank J. Tipler, *The Anthropic Cosmological Principle* (Oxford: Oxford University Press, 1988).

[11] See Bas C. van Fraassen, *Laws and Symmetry* (Oxford: Clarendon Press, 1989); and William R. Stoeger, "Contemporary Physics and the Ontological Status of the Laws of Nature," in Russell et al., eds., *Quantum Cosmology*, 209–234.

cause of the universe, whatever that first event may have been (or indeed, whether there was a first event at all). The laws are fine-tuned because God designed the universe with creatures like us in mind. The laws of nature reflect the will of God for ordering the cosmos.[12]

There are arguments about the legitimacy of all of the moves I have just made regarding cosmology and physics, but I have not really said anything new here. It is time to shift to the human-science side of the hierarchy, where I do intend to make claims that go beyond the usual theology-and-science dialogue.

4. Ethics and the Social Sciences

My thesis here is that ethics can be and should be understood as a science. This is, of course, contrary to the usual assumption that ethics is to be distinguished sharply from the empirical disciplines. Furthermore, I argue that ethics is the science needed most directly for answering many of the boundary questions that arise in the social sciences. Yet to be scientific, ethics has to have its own most basic boundary question answered, and this question— what is the ultimate *purpose* of human life?—is most naturally answered by a theological system, although metaphysical systems sometimes provide answers to this question as well.

John Milbank's much-discussed book *Theology and Social Theory*[13] makes similar moves. He argues that Christian theology must recover its role as metadiscourse, with the ability to position, qualify, and criticize other disciplines. The theological critique in which Milbank is most interested is in showing the extent to which modern social science assumes non-Christian (heretical or neopagan) theological and ethical positions. In particular, he says, the supposed value-neutrality of the 'secularized' social sciences "is complicit with an 'ontology of violence,' a reading of the world which assumes the priority of force and tells how this force is best managed and confined by counter-force. Secular reason has continued to make this ontology seem coterminous with the discovery of the human construction of the cultural world. . . . Christianity, however, recognizes no original violence. It construes the infinite . . . as a harmonic peace. . . . Peace . . . is the *sociality* of harmonic difference" (4, 5).

So Milbank is claiming that the social sciences assume a view about the intrinsic nature of humans in social interaction, *an ethical stance*, that can be

---

[12] See Nancey Murphy, "Evidence of Design in the Fine-tuning of the Universe," and George F.R. Ellis, "The Theology of the Anthropic Principle," in Russell et al., eds., *Quantum Cosmology*, 407–435 and 367–405, respectively.

[13] John Milbank, *Theology and Social Theory* (Oxford: Basil Blackwell, 1990).

justified only by a metaphysical or theological doctrine about the character of ultimate reality. Both the ethic and the metaphysic are sharply at variance with Christian orthodoxy.

I leave Milbank and his obscure tome at this point and sketch examples of the unconscious value- or ethics-laden character of contemporary social science. I return later in the chapter to Milbank and the question of the relations between the social sciences and theology.

4.1. Ethics in Economics

To explore the ethical content of economics, let us begin with some of the science's simplest explanatory devices: rational choice theory and game theory. Rational choice theory states that actions are a product of the agent's beliefs and values. When spelled out at greater length, the theory states that for any agent x, if

1. x wants d,
2. x believes that doing a is a means to bring about d, under the circumstances,
3. there is no action believed by x to be a way of bringing about d that under the circumstances is more preferred by x,
4. x has no wants that override d,
5. x knows how to do a,
6. x is able to do a, then
7. x does a.[14]

This "thin" description of human behavior is held to apply across cultures and, in fact, is often taken as a definition of rational behavior. It is called a "thin description" because it is neutral regarding the actual values of those being studied.

However, economists tend to add one substantive assumption regarding human values: egoism. They assume that each economic agent is solely or largely concerned with maximizing his or her own private interests.[15] It turns out that this theory, along with the assumption of egoism, serves to explain or predict a great deal of economic behavior.

Another important tool used by economists is game theory, which is a means for investigating how rational individuals choose strategies for maximizing utility in the face of other individuals with competing aims. A classic

---

[14] Alexander Rosenberg, *Philosophy of Social Science* (Boulder: Westview Press, 1988), 26.

[15] Daniel Little, *Varieties of Social Explanation: An Introduction to the Philosophy of Social Science* (Boulder: Westview Press, 1991).

example is the use of the "prisoner's dilemma" to model social and economic behavior. Here is Alexander Rosenberg's version:

> Suppose you and I set out to rob a bank by night. However, we are caught with our safe-cracking tools even before we can break into the bank. In one another's presence we are . . . offered the following "deal." If neither of us confesses, we shall be charged with possession of safe-cracking tools and imprisoned for two years each. If we both confess to attempted bank robbery, a more serious crime, we will each receive a five-year sentence. If, however, only one confesses and the other remains silent, the confessor will receive a one-year sentence in return for his confession, and the other will receive a ten-year sentence. . . . Before we have any opportunity to communicate with one another, we are separated for further investigation. The question each of us faces is whether to confess or not.
>
> Let's go through my reasoning process. As a rational agent I want to minimize my time in jail. So, if I think you're going to confess, then to minimize my prison sentence, I had better confess too. Otherwise I'll end up with ten years and you'll get just one. But come to think about it, if I confess and you don't, then I'll get the one-year sentence. Now it begins to dawn on me that whatever you do, I had better confess. If you keep quiet, I'll get the shortest jail sentence possible. If you confess, then I'd be crazy not to confess as well, because otherwise I'd get the worst possible outcome, ten years. So, I conclude that the only rational thing for me to do is to confess.
>
> Now, how about your reasoning process? Well, it's exactly the same as mine. . . .
>
> The result is that we both confess and both get five years in the slammer. . . .
>
> [So] rationality, maximizing our utility, led us to a "suboptimal" outcome, one less desirable than another that was "attainable."[16]

The moral of this little story is that one person's behavior will be influenced by predictions about the other person's behavior. If I believe the other will cooperate, it is to my benefit to cooperate; if the other is expected to act egoistically, then I must do likewise to avoid the worst possible outcome for myself.

Game theory and rational choice theory each appears to be ethically neutral by itself. But one of the features of the social sciences is that they are reflexive. That is, the results of the studies affect those who are studied whenever those results affect the subjects' beliefs. Game theory deals with the effects on my behavior of beliefs I hold about others' intentions and motives. Let us put together the rather innocuous assumptions of the two theories and see where they lead.

1. To be rational is to maximize my utility. (Note that this is not entirely neutral: 'rational' is in fact a positively valued term.)

---

[16] Rosenberg, *Philosophy of Social Science*, 149–150.

2. Economic exchange can be modeled by competitive games.
3. I must choose my moves on the basis of expectations of how my opponent will play.
4. I expect all (other) rational agents to act to maximize their own utility.
5. Therefore, I must always adopt the most egoistic strategy rather than the cooperative strategy.

Thus, insofar as economists propose egoism as a theory about human motivation, it easily becomes part of a *justification* for egoism when combined with the other assumptions of game theory and rational choice theory.

4.2. Sociology, Politics, and Power

For another example of the role of ethical assumptions in social theory, consider modern positions on the necessity for violent coercion in society. This assumption can be traced to Thomas Hobbes's social contract theory. Here is how James O'Toole describes Hobbes's view of the "state of nature," and the formation of the "social contract":

> In nature, man "finds no stop in doing what he has the will, desire or inclination to do." To Hobbes the "Natural Right" of every individual in this Edenic state is "the liberty each man has to use his own power for the preservation of his own nature, that is to say his own life . . . and consequently of doing anything which in his own judgment and reason he shall conceive to be the aptest means thereunto." Here, particularly in the concluding phrase, we see a statement of a modern notion of liberty. But in the next breath Hobbes gives it all away! Unhappily, he says, in this free and natural state the condition of life is "solitary, poor, nasty, brutish and short" because there is a perpetual "war . . . of every man against every man." Hence, to procure security, and the progress of civilization, humans reluctantly surrender the liberty of nature, entering into a "social contract to live under the rule of law."[17]

It is revealing that O'Toole uses the phrase "Edenic state" to describe the state of nature, for what we have in social contract theory is a new myth of origins at variance with the account in Genesis. In fact, Hobbes's myth is the antithesis of the biblical story. At least as we receive it through Augustine's interpretation, life for the original inhabitants in the biblical Eden is cooperative, not a state of war; bountiful, not poor; idyllic, not nasty; angelic, not brutish; and everlasting. It represents an aberration, a Fall, when the earth creatures assert their will (against God, not one another) to take that for

---

[17] James O'Toole, *The Executive's Compass: Business and the Good Society* (New York: Oxford University Press, 1993), 35–36.

which they have a desire and inclination. These two myths of origin reveal anti-thetical theories of the nature of the person and two antithetical theologies.

A variety of social theorists since Hobbes have followed him in claiming that coercion is necessary to maintain society and that violence is merely the ultimate form of coercion. Max Weber's classic statement on the relation between politics and violence is found in his essay "Politics as Vocation": "Ultimately, one can define the modern state sociologically only in terms of the specific *means* peculiar to it, as to every political association, namely, the use of physical force. . . . The state is a relation of men dominating men, a relation supported by means of legitimate . . . violence."[18]

Reinhold Niebuhr has affected a generation of policymakers with the the-sis he developed in *Moral Man and Immoral Society:*[19] the needs of an insti-tution for its very survival require the people involved in it to do things they would not do (and would not be morally justified in doing) as individuals. Niebuhr's thesis has been dubbed with the congratulatory title of "Christian realism." In *Moral Man* he says:

> The thesis to be elaborated in these pages is that a sharp distinction must be drawn between the moral and social behavior of individuals and of social groups, national, racial, and economic; and that this distinction justifies and necessitates political policies which a purely individualistic ethic must always find embarrass-ing. . . . In every human group there is less reason to guide and check impulse, less capacity for self-transcendence, less ability to comprehend the needs of oth-ers and therefore more unrestrained egoism than the individuals, who compose the group, reveal in their personal relationships. . . . When collective power, whether in the form of imperialism or class domination, exploits weakness, it can never be dislodged unless power is raised against it. (xi–xii)

More recently, Peter Berger has concurred that there is inevitably an element of coercion required to keep a society from being destroyed by the disrup-tive forces within it. "Violence is the ultimate foundation of any political order."[20]

Now in what sense is this an ethical assumption? Is it not, rather, simply a statement of empirical fact, a law of human behavior? The very fact that one of the theorists I have quoted here, Niebuhr, is known primarily as a Christian ethicist might at least make us suspicious that we are not dealing with pure social fact.

---

[18] Max Weber, *Politics as a Vocation* (Minneapolis: Fortress Press, 1965), 1.

[19] Reinhold Niebuhr, *Moral Man and Immoral Society* (New York: Scribner's Sons, 1932).

[20] Peter Berger, *Invitation to Sociology: A Humanistic Perspective* (Garden City, N.Y.: Doubleday, 1963), 69.

Niebuhr's views on the possibility of noncoercive, nonviolent social structures is dependent on a prior ethical judgment regarding the highest good for humankind. This view of the human good is in turn the consequence of a particular theological doctrine. Niebuhr writes in *Moral Man:* "Justice rather than unselfishness [is society's] highest moral ideal. . . . This realistic social ethic needs to be contrasted with the ethics of religious idealism. . . . Society must strive for justice even if it is forced to use means, such as self-assertion, resistance, coercion and perhaps resentment, which cannot gain the moral sanction of the most sensitive moral spirit" (257–258).

Niebuhr's judgment that justice is the highest good that humans can attain in history is in turn based upon his eschatology, that is, his theological account of the end of time. Salvation, the kingdom of God, the Eschaton, are essentially *beyond* history. The reason Niebuhr takes this stand on eschatology, in contrast to a view of the kingdom as realizable within history, is that he has set up the question in terms of the problem of the temporal and the eternal. Since it is not possible to conceive of the eternal being realized in the temporal, he concludes that the kingdom of God is beyond history, and this in turn means that guilt and moral ambiguity must be permanent features of the interim.

Weber's justification is also overtly ethical: it is based on a distinction between an "ethic of ultimate ends" and an "ethic of responsibility." The ethic of ultimate ends is concerned with pure intent and pure means. The ethic of responsibility is concerned with the politically foreseeable results of one's actions in a political order where imperfection and evil are presupposed. Political realists are committed to achieving their ends even at the expense of morally dubious means. And, as already noted, the decisive means for politics is violence.[21]

4.3. Ethics and Social-Scientific Methodology

The preceding cases can serve only as a sort of inductive argument for the implication of ethics in the social sciences, and the reader may object that, as in the case of any inductive argument, these may be rare exceptions to the norm. A more thoroughgoing argument for the role of ethical judgments in the social sciences, and hence for the need for systematic study of such judgments, comes from the recognition that the very methods of social-scientific research involve ethical judgments.

Rosenberg argues that "taking sides on questions of scientific method may commit us to taking sides in fundamental matters of moral philosophy."[22]

---

[21] Account found in James W. Douglass, *The Non-Violent Cross: A Theology of Revolution and Peace* (Toronto: Macmillan, 1966), 262–263.

[22] Rosenberg, *Philosophy of Social Science*, 177.

Consider the question of whether informed consent ought to be required for all experimentation on human subjects. Deontological ethics is based on the categorical imperative, one of whose formulations is that others must always be treated as ends in themselves, never as mere means. Thus, no one can be used for research purposes without consent. But for utilitarians, the moral criterion is the greatest good for the greatest number. Thus, it is conceivable that, so long as an experiment does little or no harm to the subjects and brings about great good for society as a whole, subjects *ought* to be used without informed consent if informing them would interfere with the experiment. So ethical differences contribute to significant differences in experimental design.

In fact, the relations between ethical systems and social science methodology go even deeper. Rosenberg argues that there is a special affinity between utilitarianism in ethics and naturalism in social science, on the one hand, and between deontological ethics and antinaturalism, on the other. Naturalism is the view that the social sciences can and should emulate the methods of the natural sciences; this is possible because there is no significant difference between humans and the natural world that would prevent human behavior being understood by means of observation and formulation of causal laws. This approach can be said to emphasize bottom-up causation at the human levels of the hierarchy of the sciences. 'Antinaturalism' refers mainly to the hermeneutic approach to social science. On this view, human behavior cannot be understood or predicted without understanding the meaning humans attach to their actions. This intentional character of human behavior rules out any possibility of a causal analysis that ignores the issue of meanings. In the terms of this chapter, this approach emphasizes top-down analyses.

Rosenberg argues that utilitarian ethics needs naturalistic social science because its recommendations for social policy require that it be possible to make predictions about the causal effects of various policy options. Naturalism, in turn, needs the utilitarian's argument that it is in fact morally justifiable to treat other human beings as objects (rather than persons).

There is a similar congruence between the hermeneutic approach and the deontologists' emphasis on the necessity of respect for persons. Rosenberg makes the point as follows:

According to Kant one of the features of an ethics that makes rights and duties paramount and subordinates consequences is that moral assessment must focus on *motives* for actions. . . . And according to Kant, the relation among our beliefs about our duties, or desires to fulfill them, and the actions they explain, could not be understood causally without robbing human action of its moral dimension altogether. . . . It is pretty clear how much this moral theory leans on a social science that takes human action and intentionality seriously. (181–182)

So what we see is that different methodological orientations in the social sciences depend essentially on different conceptions of the nature of the human person, and these conceptions are the very stuff of philosophical ethics.

Charles Taylor has probably argued this thesis most carefully and thoroughly. In the Introduction to his two-volume collection, *Philosophy and the Human Sciences,* he explains that the apparently diverse essays all aim to argue against the understanding of human life and action implicit in naturalist approaches to the human sciences.[23] The problem with naturalism is that it fails to recognize a crucial feature of human agency, namely, the involvement of distinctions of worth. Consequently, the naturalistic approach is doomed to fail: a self who can be understood only against the background of distinctions of worth cannot be captured by a scientific language that essentially aspires to neutrality.

But, Taylor says, if he is correct in holding that agents act on the basis of value-laden motives, then he ought to be able to explain why naturalistic social scientists value the value-neutral conception of their sciences. The reason is that naturalists hold to a particular ideal of selfhood: "I am saying that it is the hold of a particular set of background distinctions of worth, those of the disengaged identity, which leads people to espouse what are ultimately rather implausible epistemological doctrines" (6).

> The ideal of disengagement defines a certain—typically modern—notion of freedom, as the ability to act on one's own without outside interference or subordination to outside authority. It defines its own peculiar notion of human dignity, closely connected to freedom. And these in turn are linked to ideals of efficacy, power, unperturbability, which for all their links with earlier ideals are original with modern culture.
>
> The great attraction of these ideals, all the more powerful in that this understanding of the agent is woven into a host of modern practices—economic, scientific, technological, psychotherapeutic, and so on—lends great weight and credence to the disengaged images of the self. The liberation through objectification wrought by the cosmological revolution of the seventeenth century has become for many the model of the agent's relation to the world and hence sets the very definition of what is to be an agent. (5)

So, contrary to claims for the value-free character of the social sciences, these examples show that it takes but a little scratching to find ethical judgments under the surface. These judgments may be taken for granted within the mainstream of the intellectual world: for instance, who could doubt that

---

[23] Charles Taylor, *Philosophy and the Human Sciences* (Cambridge: Cambridge University Press, 1985).

self-preservation is a good thing, that justice is the highest good at which governments aim?

But these assumptions *are* questionable; there are alternative points of view, and we need to know whether and how such judgments are justifiable. Thus, the social sciences raise questions that they alone are not competent to answer—boundary questions, again. So it would be useful if we could add to the top of the hierarchy of the social sciences the 'science' of ethics. This would be the science whose job it is to compare and evaluate systematic theories of the good for humankind and assist in spelling out the consequences when such theories are embodied in social practices. Is it possible to conceive of ethics in this manner? To address this question, we need to take a slight detour though the writings of Alasdair MacIntyre.

4.4. Excursus on MacIntyre

I am heavily indebted to MacIntyre in a variety of ways for my conception of ethics as (at least potentially) scientific.[24] MacIntyre has argued that the correct form of ethical claims is something like the following, conditional statement: "If you are to achieve your *telos*, then you ought to do *x*." It is a peculiar feature of modern Enlightenment views of ethics that their proper form has been taken to be apodictic: "You ought to do *x*." Moderns have developed competing theories regarding the most basic moral claims: "You ought to act so as to achieve the greatest good for the greatest number" versus "You ought to act so that the maxim of your action can be willed universally." But because morality is taken to be autonomous—that is, unrelated to other knowledge—there is no way to arbitrate between these most basic construals of the moral 'ought.' This impossibility results in the interminability of moral debates in our society. However, the interminability should not, says MacIntyre, be taken as the intrinsic nature of moral discourse but rather ought to be seen as a sign that the entire Enlightenment project has taken a wrong turn.

The wrong turn was the attempt to free morality and ethical reasoning from religious tradition. For it is religious tradition (or metaphysical traditions) that provides the starting point for settling moral disputes. Such traditions provide the resources for answering the question, What is the greatest good for humankind? Is it happiness? Is it living in accord with the dictates of reason? Is it a just heavenly reward? Or is it more complex than any of these?

---

[24] The following account is taken from Alasdair MacIntyre, *After Virtue*, 2d ed. (Notre Dame, Ind.: University of Notre Dame Press, 1984); and Alasdair MacIntyre, *Whose Justice? Which Rationality?* (Notre Dame, Ind.: University of Notre Dame Press, 1988).

So theology or metaphysics provides a concept of the purpose for human life. Ethics is the discipline that works out answers to the question of how we ought to live in order to achieve our highest ends. In addition, MacIntyre argues, such theories of human flourishing can be fully understood only insofar as we know how they have been or could be socially embodied, so the social sciences are the descriptive side of a coin whose reverse, normative side is ethics.

Thus, MacIntyre's contribution here is to argue that the modern view that insulates moral reasoning from knowledge of the nature of reality, *both theological and scientific*, is an aberration. Ethics needs theology, and the social sciences need ethics. Furthermore, I would add, ethics itself can be done scientifically. The same sorts of empirical data and reasoning that go into social scientific studies of means to achieve lesser ends can be applied to the question of how to achieve ultimate ends.

5. The Relation Between Theology and Ethics

More needs to be said both about the scientific nature of ethics and about the role of theology in answering the most pressing boundary question that arises in ethics: what is human life for? To appreciate the possibilities for a science of ethics, we should review briefly the 'logical structure' of science. Scientific theories do not exist in isolation but are linked together logically to form clusters, which may be called research programs, or paradigms. According to Imre Lakatos, research programs are unified by a core theory, a highly abstract, even metaphysical account of the nature of the subject matter under investigation. The core theory is not directly testable but gains its support from the role it plays in the research program as a whole: all lower-level theories follow from the core theory, and it is confirmed insofar as those lower-level theories prove to be acceptable. The lower-level theories, in turn, are supported by empirical data. Science progresses by means of the competition among research programs, each with its own distinctive core theory and its "positive heuristic," a plan for development of the program to increase its range of explanatory power (see Chapter 3, section 3.1).

This brief sketch of the structure of science puts us in a position to consider the possibilities for ethics. In this field there would be a variety of core theories—theories as to the essence of the good life—based on the various religious and metaphysical traditions' accounts of the purpose of human life. The positive heuristic of each program would involve the plan to spell out in increasing detail the consequences (applications) of that vision of the good in concrete circumstances. For example, if the chief goal of life is to "enjoy God forever," then part of what constitutes the good life under the concrete conditions of earthly existence will be to develop the capacity for prayer—the capacity to enjoy the presence of God here and now. Prayer is a practice that must be learned and cultivated and that requires the development of virtues such as perseverance and self-knowledge.

Christian subtraditions differ in their relative emphasis on this-worldly and otherworldly goals. Those who stress earthly transformation might place a lower priority on the discipline of prayer and give greater emphasis to service of God in this life. Theological elaboration will be needed in order to know what sort of service God requires. The life pattern of Jesus suggests that feeding the hungry and caring for the sick are important forms of service. But here social scientific findings are at least as important as theology. How can the hungry best be fed—by means of individual charity, food stamps, or full employment? What is the best system for delivery of health care?[25]

A recent article by Stanley Hauerwas, titled "Murdochian Muddles: Can We Get Through Them If God Does Not Exist?" both supports and illustrates my claim that ethical systems, with their core theories about the telos of human life, depend in turn on a theological or metaphysical account of reality.[26] Here Hauerwas compares his own work in Christian ethics with that of philosopher Iris Murdoch. She claims explicitly that her ethical system follows from a metaphysical theory. Hauerwas examines the contrasting metaphysic that follows from the Christian doctrine of creation and uses these metaphysical differences to explain the differences in their ethical conclusions, despite close agreement on methods of moral reasoning.

Murdoch is an atheist; the modern technological age has demythologized religion and made traditional theological claims unintelligible. Her alternative to traditional religion is a Christianity "without a personal God or a risen Christ, without beliefs in supernatural places and happenings, such as heaven and life after death, but retaining the mystical figure of Christ occupying a place analogous to that of Buddha: a Christ who can console and save, but who is to be found as a living force within each human soul and not in some supernatural elsewhere."[27] The mystic Christ is an image of the Good. As absolute, above all the virtues, the Good is a pure source, "the principle which creatively relates the virtues to each other in our moral lives" (507).

Despite her denial of the existence of a personal God, Murdoch takes prayer to be an essential exercise. But here prayer is meditation: "A withdrawal, through some disciplined quietness, into the great chamber of the soul"

---

[25] See Nancey Murphy and George F.R. Ellis, *On the Moral Nature of the Universe: Theology, Cosmology, and Ethics* (Minneapolis: Fortress Press, 1996), chap. 6. Here we spell out social consequences of the core theory that humankind was created in order to emulate the self-sacrificial life of Jesus.

[26] Stanley Hauerwas, "Murdochian Muddles: Can We Get Through Them If God Does Not Exist?" in Maria Antonaccio and William Schweiker, eds., *Iris Murdoch and the Search for Human Goodness* (Chicago: University of Chicago Press, 1996), 190–208.

[27] Iris Murdoch, *Metaphysics as a Guide to Morals* (London: Penguin Books, 1992), 419.

(73). More specifically, prayer is attention to the Good, which allows one to escape self-deception and egocentric attachments.

I venture to state the core theory of Murdoch's ethical system as follows: there is no end, no reward for human life. Thus, morality has no point beyond itself. The goal of life, therefore, must be to recognize and accept this fact, along with the facts of the frailty and unreality of the ego and the emptiness of worldly desires. Or, more briefly, to be moral is to recognize full well that morality, though necessary, has no point.

The resignation, the disillusionment, the bowing to necessity that characterize the good life for Murdoch are in sharp contrast to the virtues given place in Hauerwas's system. Hauerwas connects his account of the Christian moral life to Christian theology by means of the metaphysical doctrine of creation ex nihilo (out of nothing). The Christian teaching of the ex nihilo character of the divine creative act was intended to underscore God's freedom in creating—God acted out of love rather than necessity—and hence the contingent character of all created being. Hauerwas says:

> From the perspective of creation ex nihilo, Murdoch's account of necessity and contingency is reversed. The task, therefore, is not to see the particular as necessary, but to see the contingent as just that—contingent—or more accurately in Christian language, as created. . . . The task is not to see the purposelessness in the sheer existence of the contingent, but rather to see the contingent as "gift" whose purpose is to praise the creator. . . .
>
> Respect of and care for all of God's creatures is the primary means of doxological acknowledgement of God the Creator in creation. . . .
>
> In contrast to Murdoch's account of the absolute pointlessness of existence, Christians believe that God means for all creation to worship God.[28]
>
> Christians believe that our lives are at once more captured by sin and yet sustained by a hope that cannot help but appear false given Murdoch's account of the world. A Christian understanding of sin and hope is, moreover, correlative to an account of creation that sustains a teleological account of the world and our place in it. Accordingly Christians as such ask more of ourselves and our world than, I think, Murdoch can believe is warranted. . . . [We] are creatures with purposes that we did not create. (194–195)

Along with Murdoch, Hauerwas argues for the importance of pursuing clear moral vision, but, in line with his own core theory, he believes such knowledge comes from being part of a community with its exercises in communal prayer, reconciliation, and care for others—communal practices that form characters that reflect the recognition that *life is a gift*.

---

[28] Hauerwas, "Murdochian Muddles," 204–205.

How is one to choose between these two starkly different attitudes or approaches to life: Murdoch's purposeless dedication to morality versus Hauerwas's emphasis on hope? Hauerwas himself expresses puzzlement: "I wish I knew better how to engage her in argument. There are surely metaphysical issues that would be worth pursuing. . . . Yet how that is to be . . . done has been made difficult by Murdoch because she rightly, I think, refuses to separate metaphysics and morality. So it is finally not a question of how to characterize 'what is' but how 'what is' reflects as well as is determined by what we are or should be" (207–208).

I differ with Hauerwas here; the difficulty in settling the issue between himself and Murdoch is not failure to separate ethics from metaphysics. If I am correct that an ethical system can be construed as a scientific research program with a metaphysical core theory, then the inseparability of the metaphysics from its ethical consequences is crucial for the testing of the metaphysical claims. Instead, the question is how to test the ethical claims themselves. My proposal, in brief, is that the lower-level theories of an ethical program are at least implicitly means-ends statements: if you are to achieve your telos, then under circumstance c you should do x. Excepting cases where the purpose of human life is conceived exclusively in otherworldly terms, such statements are testable by means of the same sorts of research employed by social scientists to test more mundane sorts of means-ends claims.[29]

6. Theology and the Social Sciences

Taylor concludes his Introduction to *Philosophy and the Human Sciences* as follows:

> If, as I said above, the ultimate basis of naturalism turns out to be a certain definition of agency and the background of worth, does the critique terminate with the proof that this is so (supposing I finally bring it off), or is there a way we can go on and rationally assess this and other definitions of worth? This is, in fact, a particular way of putting the general question: what are the capacities of practical reason? Is it quite helpless before such basic differences in spiritual outlook, like that between the disengaged identity and its opponents? Or is there, at least in principle, a way in which this kind of question can be rationally arbitrated? I am fiercely committed to the latter view, and I recognize that the onus is on me to come up with a good argument. I am working on it, and I hope at not too remote a date to be able to publish something convincing (at least to some) on this. (12)

---

[29] See Murphy and Ellis, *On the Moral Nature*, chap. 7, where we examine social-scientific consequences for our social ethic, commenting on their empirical testability.

Let us see if we can translate Taylor's project, both conclusions and aspirations, into the language of this chapter. Taylor's point about the failure of naturalistic social science can be stated as follows: human behavior needs to be understood from the perspective of a hierarchy of social sciences. It cannot be understood solely in terms of bottom-up causation. It can be fully understood only when we recognize the role that interpretations play in determining human action—that is, in terms of concepts at home in the higher levels of the human-science hierarchy.

If ethics is counted as the science at the top of the hierarchy of the human sciences, then Taylor's concern that social science not neglect agents' attributions of worth (including moral worth) shows up as a natural corollary to the hermeneutic view of social science methodology. That is, top-down explanation involving moral concepts will be as much a regular aspect of social science as top-down explanations employing legal, political, or economic concepts.

In addition, counting ethics as the topmost social science, I believe, provides important guidance for the task to which Taylor aspires: the rational arbitration among "basic differences in spiritual outlook." It is worth noting that Taylor here describes these as spiritual, rather than moral, differences. I suggested previously that ethical theories turn out to presuppose accounts of ultimate reality, which belong to the realm of metaphysics or theology.

Thus, we return to Milbank's theme of the implication of theological positions in the social sciences. In fact, we have already seen that Niebuhr's position on violence in society is an implication of his theological eschatology. Milbank traces crucial assumptions of political science, economics, and sociology to theological roots.

One of the purposes of Milbank's book is to "demonstrate that all the most important governing assumptions of [secular social] theory are bound up with the modification or the rejection of orthodox Christian positions. These fundamental intellectual shifts are . . . no more rationally 'justifiable' than the Christian positions themselves."[30] In his account of Auguste Comte's positivism, Milbank traces the genesis of a major form of secular reason in order "to unearth the arbitrary moment in its construction" (3).

Comte's sociology grew out of the "social theology" of counter-Enlightenment thinkers such as Joseph de Maistre and Louis de Bonald. De Bonald based his claim for the positivity of society on the fact that it had been created and revealed by God. Comte stood de Bonald on his head, arguing that society creates views about God. However, Milbank argues, "the reversal leaves intact the metaphysical framework within which the reversal occurs" (59). That is, Comte keeps in place the Catholic theorists' views of the primacy of the social over natural science and the affirmation of

---

[30] Milbank, *Theology and Social Theory*, 1.

the primordial character of social affection. However, all of this, for de Bonald, was a consequence of the creation of God. Comte's reversal, his substitution of sociology for theology, strips away the original justification for this entire approach to the social.

The theological genesis of modern secular political theory is more complex. Milbank argues that Hobbes's account of human nature as the will to self-preservation was theologically promoted. It depended on taking human nature to be a reflection of the divine nature as it was conceived by late medieval voluntarists. Thus, the account of human nature as the exercise of unrestricted will could be justified as the *imago dei*. The modern de-ethicization of the public sphere that followed from Hobbes's and others' view of human nature as intrinsically self-interested depended, as well, on a privatization of religion already begun in the Reformation and continued in seventeenth-century Augustinianism (cf. Latour in section 1).

The theological dependence of modern economics is much more obvious. James Stewart and Adam Smith both employed "heretical theodicy" to justify economic systems based on self-interest rather than benevolence. Milbank writes:

> God [is] regularly and immediately present to human society, holding it together, just like the Newtonian God among the planetary bodies in Newtonian space.
> . . . The appeal to a more 'immediate' God does not reverse the 'de-ethicization' of political theory already set in train. On the contrary, it confirms and extends it, because in political economy the field of social relations between individuals falls under a 'providential' discourse about how bad or self-interested actions can have good long-term outcomes, rather than under traditional 'ethical' discourse. Hence the de-ethicization of the economic domain does not, as one might suppose, coincide in any straightforward way with 'secularization.' Here again, the institution of the 'secular' is paradoxically related to a shift *within* theology and not an emancipation *from* theology. (29)

Milbank notes the irony in the fact that while late modern theologians such as Harvey Cox are attempting to reconcile theology with the secular, thinkers as diverse as Milbank himself, MacIntyre, René Girard, and post-Nietzschean social theorists are recognizing that all thought is grounded in some sort of metanarrative and that the mythic-religious can never be left behind (3). We could add Taylor to Milbank's list. So the question is not *whether* one's thought will have theological presuppositions but *which* theology one will presuppose.

7. Conclusion

A variety of thinkers in a variety of disciplines are calling for review of modern assumptions. One set of such assumptions has been the disconnection of the social sciences from the natural sciences, the disconnection of ethics from science, and the exclusion of God from all spheres of intellectual discourse.

In this chapter, I have proposed a model for thinking about the relations among theology, ethics, and the sciences that understands them as hierarchically ordered and intrinsically interconnected. There are aspects of reality at each level of complexity that can be explained reductively in terms of lower levels. But there are also boundary questions requiring explanation from higher levels of discourse. Cosmology and physics raise boundary questions that can appropriately be answered theologically. The social sciences raise questions that can be answered only by turning to ethical systems. Ethical systems, in turn, raise theological or metaphysical questions.

Now, some who read a chapter such as this are likely to suppose that this questioning process, which ends in both cases with theology, means that all knowledge is ultimately grounded in theological claims—that it is all based on faith. Lutherans might like that conclusion. Others will object that it is relativistic since there are countless theologies. Here we come back to the epistemological concerns of Part I: is Anglo-American postmodernity (or postmodernity in general) synonymous with relativism, or are there ways to make rational assessments of large-scale traditions with their explicit or assumed accounts of ultimate reality? The answer suggested in Chapter 3 is that, although such judgments cannot be made quickly or easily, they are not always impossible.

10 • • •

Supervenience and the Nonreducibility of Ethics to Biology

1. Introduction

The purpose of this chapter is to consider claims for the relevance of evolutionary biology to ethics. I argued in the previous chapter that ethics belongs in the hierarchy of the sciences, placed above the social sciences and below theology. If this is the case, then arguments pertaining to the reducibility of one science to another will be relevant to the question of the reducibility of ethics to biology.

I argued in Chapter 1 that reductionism in science is but an instance of a ubiquitous pattern of thinking that has dominated the modern intellectual world—in ethics, political theory, epistemology, philosophy of language. I mentioned there several earlier attempts, such as Hobbes's, to locate ethics in the hierarchy of the sciences. I also claimed in Chapter 1 that there have been important conceptual developments in recent philosophy that shed light on the topic of reduction. In this chapter, I intend to use these developments to provide an account of how it could be possible for various levels of analysis (here the theological, the ethical, the social-scientific, and the biological) to be analyses of the same (or nested) systems, but without the higher being reducible to the lower. To escape the pitfalls of inappropriate reductionist thinking, we need a new *concept* to describe the relations among properties, predicates, or event descriptions that belong to different levels of analysis and yet apply to roughly the same entity or event. Until recently, only two concepts were available: *identity* and *causation*. For example, if we take mentalistic language to be a higher-level description of neurological events, then the two options were to say that mental states or properties are identical with brain states or that they are caused by brain states.[1] Both options are reductionistic.

We now have a new concept, *supervenience*. Its proper definition is still a matter of debate, but I have argued that the right definition will allow us to state unambiguously the difference between reducible and nonreducible levels of analysis (see Chapter 1, section 3.2). It is a short step, then, to show that ethical properties are (ordinarily) not reducible to biological properties.

In this chapter I look at some specific claims for the reduction of ethics to evolutionary biology. I believe that many of these proposals exhibit a common modern failure to appreciate the true nature of the ethical itself. The work of Alasdair MacIntyre, I argue, provides a *nonreductive* account of ethics in that ethics is essentially dependent on a yet higher level of analysis, namely, theology or metaphysics.[2] Some current proposals relating ethics to biology, then, will be seen not as the reduction of ethics to biology but as the attempt to derive ethics from an ungrounded naturalistic metaphysic.

2. Nonreductive Physicalism

A major thesis of this chapter is that an understanding of the proper relation between ethics and biology requires a thorough reevaluation of the modern reductionist pattern of thought. Many of the resources are already in place.

2.1. Roy Wood Sellars

At the same time that the logical positivists were refining and promoting their reductionist program for the sciences, the American philosopher Roy Wood Sellars was developing a nonreductionist view of the hierarchy of the sciences. He has called his view by a variety of names, including "emergent realism," "emergent naturalism," "evolutionary naturalism." A more common term today, and the one I employ here, is "nonreductive physicalism."[3] Sellars began in 1916 to explicate a conception of the mental as an emergent property in the hierarchy of complex systems,[4] and he ultimately developed a conception of nature as forming a nonreducible hierarchy of levels.

---

[1] Some theorists have maintained causal interaction between mind and brain, of course, but have never satisfactorily explained how a nonmaterial mind or mental state could have causal impact on the brain.

[2] This is nonreductive in a different sense from my claims in Chapter 1, section 3.5. There I argued that MacIntyre's ethic employs a nonreductive account of the relation of the social level to the individual level; here I argue that the ethical level cannot be reduced to either the social or the psychological level.

[3] This latter term has the advantage both of being widely recognized in contemporary philosophy of mind and of avoiding the atheistic connotations of 'naturalism' and 'materialism.'

[4] See Roy Wood Sellars, *Critical Realism: A Study of the Nature and Conditions of Knowledge* (1916; reprint, New York: Russell and Russell, 1966).

Sellars's position is expressly opposed to three competitors: Cartesian mind-matter dualism, absolute idealism (the view that the mental and its products are the only reality), and reductive materialism, as he designates the logical positivists' program for the reduction of all sciences to physics. According to Sellars, the natural world is one great complex system, displaying levels of complexity, which have emerged over time. In this regard, he agrees with the reductive materialists as against the idealists and dualists. However, he criticizes the reductionists for having a view of nature that is overly mechanistic and atomistic. "The ontological imagination was stultified at the start by [the picture] of microscopic billiard balls."[5]

In rejecting this reductive materialism, Sellars argues that "organization and wholes are genuinely significant"; they are not mere aggregates of elementary particles. Reductive materialism overemphasizes the 'stuff' in contrast to the organization. But matter, he claims, is only a part of nature. "There is energy; there is the fact of pattern; there are all sorts of intimate relations." "Matter, or stuff, needs to be supplemented by terms like integration, pattern, function."[6] "It will be my argument that science and philosophy are only now becoming sufficiently aware of the principles involved in the facts of levels, of natural kinds, of organization, to all of which the old materialism was blind. I shall even carry the notion of levels into causality and speak of levels of causality."[7]

The levels that Sellars countenances are the inorganic, the organic, the mental or conscious, the social, the ethical, and the religious or spiritual. So here we have an early version of the claim that ethics takes its place in the hierarchy of the sciences between sociology and theology. However, I would argue that Sellars's claims notwithstanding, his accounts of both ethics and religion *are* reductive. Moral values express judgments regarding the role of an object or act as it connects with human needs or desires.[8] Thus, ethical judgments are merely prudential judgments. Sellars's view of religion is purely humanist: religion is loyalty to the values of life (pt. 5).

Despite Sellars's belief that science and philosophy were already in his day becoming adequately aware of the facts of levels and natural kinds, there are still a large number of ardent reductionists, and theirs has been by far the predominant position in philosophy and science up to the present.[9] However,

---

[5] Roy Wood Sellars, *The Philosophy of Physical Realism* (1932; reprint, New York: Russell and Russell, 1966), 5.

[6] Roy Wood Sellars, *Principles of Emergent Realism: The Philosophical Essays of Roy Wood Sellars*, ed. W. Preston Warren (St. Louis: Warren H. Green, 1970), 136–138.

[7] Sellars, *The Philosophy of Physical Realism*, 4.

[8] Sellars, *Principles of Emergent Realism*, pt. 4.

[9] For a current example, see Hartry Field, "Physicalism," in John Earman, ed., *Inference, Explanation, and Other Frustrations: Essays in the Philosophy of Science* (Berkeley and Los Angeles: University of California Press, 1992), 271–291.

I believe that the balance is beginning to shift from reductive to nonreductive physicalism, as evidenced by developments in the philosophy of mind, as well as by the recognition in science of emergent levels, decoupling, and top-down causation (see Chapter 1, section 3.1). A variety of authors have begun to make clear that, despite astounding scientific advances brought about by means of reductive thinking, there is growing *scientific* evidence for the nonreducibility of higher levels.

2.2. Supervenience

It is fairly clear at this point that reductionism in science has its limits. What is not clear is how to *explain* this fact. That is, our multilayered analysis of reality is all an analysis of *one* reality. How can it *not* be the case that ultimately the laws of physics govern everything? I have emphasized the ubiquity of reductionist thinking in the modern period; what we need to defeat causal reductionism, as well as to understand the independence of ethics from biology, is a new 'thinking strategy.' The concepts of *supervenience* and *multiple realizability* seem to provide essential ingredients for this move.

I defined supervenience in Chapter 1 (section 3.2) as follows: for any two properties A and B, where B is a higher-level property than A, B supervenes on A if and only if something's being A in circumstance c constitutes its being B. The concepts of supervenience and realization are related in that there are often a variety of subvenient states or properties, each of which is capable of realizing the supervenient state or property. The value of recognizing both the supervenience relation and the multiple realizability of subvenient states is that together they allow us to understand how properties (actions, events) of a *single* system, but pertaining to *different* levels of analysis, are related to one another. In particular, these conceptual resources allow us to distinguish between cases where reduction is and is not possible:

1. A clear case where reduction *is* possible is in a limiting case where something's being A constitutes its being B in any and all circumstances.
2. If a higher-level property is multiply realizable, and there is no finite disjunctive set of realisands, then the supervenient property is not reducible. The reason for this is clear. To reduce the higher-level description, one needs to *define* the relevant supervenient property in terms appropriate to the subvenient level. For example, there is no closed set of actions that count as cruelty, so we cannot define 'cruelty' as wanton killing of animals, torturing of children, or turpentining of cats.
3. In the cases where circumstances matter, the supervenient property or description will be reducible only when the circumstances can be described in terms germane to the lower level. Consider here two related examples from the legal realm. Killing another person constitutes murder

only when it is "unjustified." However, the circumstances that constitute justification can themselves be defined in nonlegal terminology:
in cases of accident, self-defense, insanity. In contrast, the legal
description 'guilty of murder' supervenes on the description 'mur-
derer' only under the circumstances of the person's having been tried
in a competent court of law and found guilty according to proper procedures. There is no way to reduce the concepts of *competence* and of
proper procedures to the nonlegal (everyday) level of description.
They are sui generis. So although the property of being guilty of murder supervenes on the property of having unjustifiably killed a person,
it is not reducible to that lower-level description.

This is an appropriate point to mention an oversimplification that often
appears in discussions of the hierarchy of complex systems. It is often said,
for instance, that a society is a complex organization of individuals. In a sense
it is true that a society is nothing but the individuals making it up—there is,
in addition, no metaphysical entity such as a *Zeitgeist*. However, it is not the
case that everything pertaining to the social level is constituted by things pertaining to the individual level. In addition to the individuals, there are social
entities such as marriages and contracts and debts and rules. It will generally
be these entities with no correlates at the level of individual persons whose
involvement constitutes nonreducible circumstances.

3. Ethics in the Hierarchy of the Sciences

I suggested in the previous chapter that the hierarchy of the sciences cannot
be unambiguously ordered above biology and that it is helpful to think of a
branching hierarchy, with one branch given over to the human sciences (psychology and the social sciences) and the other to the physical sciences that
study increasingly more encompassing wholes above biology (ecology and
cosmology).[10] I then suggested that theology be viewed as the topmost science in the hierarchy.[11] I showed that the social sciences provide an incomplete account of the human world insofar as they omit ethics, and thus I add
ethics to the hierarchy above the social sciences but below theology. Thus,
the hierarchy can be pictured as in Figure 10.1.[12] A different way of approaching

---

[10] See also my "Evidence of Design in the Fine-tuning of the Universe," in Robert J. Russell,
Nancey Murphy, and C. J. Isham, eds., *Quantum Cosmology and the Laws of Nature: Scientific
Perspectives on Divine Action* (Vatican City State and Berkeley, Calif.: Vatican Observatory and
Center for Theology and the Natural Sciences, 1993), 407–435, esp. 424–425.

[11] See also Nancey Murphy and George F.R. Ellis, *On the Moral Nature of the Universe:
Theology, Cosmology, and Ethics* (Minneapolis: Fortress Press, 1996).

[12] See ibid., chap. 4, for an explanation of the ordering of the social sciences.

FIGURE 10.1   A model of the hierarchical relations among the sciences

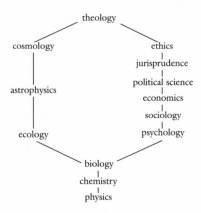

the question of order would be to consider possible supervenience relations between any two disciplines. With this approach, it is clear that the social supervenes on the individual. However, the political and the economic each supervenes on the social but neither on the other in any regular way, so these could be placed side by side in the figure. The legal then supervenes on both the economic and the political.

Examples of supervenient but nonreducible relations among levels in the social science hierarchy are easy to come by. An act describable at the biological level can be redescribed at each of the supervenient levels. Consider again the example of killing an animal (from Chapter 1, section 3.2). The animal's death and its cause are biological facts. It is only at the psychological level that the event becomes an action, that is, under the circumstances of its being done intentionally. The intention (along with other circumstances) constitutes it as one sort of action rather than another—for example, putting the horse out of its misery.

At the social level, the act can bear a variety of meanings. For example, putting an animal out of its misery may or may not be socially acceptable within a given culture. The same act may be economically sound practice or not, depending on the value of the animal and the cost of veterinary care. It may be legal or illegal, depending, for instance, on whether one owns the horse or not.

Circumstances such as ownership and economic value are not reducible to the level of the physical sciences. Ownership may be represented in the physical world by an artifact such as a bill of sale, but it is the social and legal systems that make the piece of paper a bill of sale, not the physical composition of the paper or the chemicals in the ink.

If the moral sphere is indeed a more encompassing sphere, supervening on the psychological, the social, the economic, the political, and the legal, then we should not be surprised to find moral properties that are not reducible—especially not to the biological level. It is not necessary here that the argument of the previous chapter for the *scientific* status of ethics succeed;[13] rather, it is necessary only to show that the moral does in fact supervene on the biological, as well as on the other levels I have placed between biology and ethics. That is, I need to show that properties pertaining to each of these levels can *constitute* moral properties *under proper circumstances*. This can be seen from the fact that we can ask of an intentional action, a social arrangement or practice, an economic transaction, a political order, or a legal system if it constitutes a moral or immoral action, practice, and so forth under proper circumstances. For example, killing is a moral or an immoral act in virtue of its being intentional or not; an economic policy is moral or immoral in virtue of its fairness.[14] So it does appear that the moral level supervenes on these various other levels of description, and this suggests, prima facie, that insofar as the social-scientific is not reducible to the biological, neither will the moral generally be reducible to the biological. However, the claims of biologists to account for morality in evolutionary terms need to be heard.

4. Sociobiology and Ethics

The thesis of this section is that claims to be able to reduce ethics to biology do not turn in any interesting way on new developments in biology but can be attributed instead to metaethical ignorance. That is, the arguments depend on the absence of any clear sense of what is distinctive about the moral level of analysis—what makes the good *morally* good as opposed to any other sort of good.

Biologists are not alone, however, in this predicament; it seems to be a pervasive feature of modern Western culture. MacIntyre claims that our moral language is in a state of grave disorder. I quote him at length:

Imagine that the natural sciences were to suffer the effects of a catastrophe. A series of environmental disasters are blamed by the general public on the scientists. Widespread riots occur, laboratories are burnt down, physicists are lynched, books and instruments are destroyed. Finally a Know-Nothing political movement takes power and successfully abolishes science teaching in schools and universities, imprisoning and executing the remaining scientists. Later still there is a reaction against this destructive movement and enlightened people seek to revive science, although they have largely forgotten what it was. But all

---

[13] See also ibid., chap. 5.

[14] Of course, we can ask, for instance, if it is economically sound practice to act morally, but the *constitutive* relation does not hold here. That is, the economic soundness of the policy is not in virtue of its morality; if there is such a relationship, it is merely an empirical correlation.

that they possess are fragments: a knowledge of experiments detached from any knowledge of the theoretical context which gave them significance; parts of theories unrelated either to the other bits and pieces of theory which they possess or to experiment; instruments whose use has been forgotten; half-chapters from books, single pages from articles, not always fully legible because torn and charred. Nonetheless all these fragments are reembodied in a set of practices which go under the revived names of physics, chemistry and biology. Adults argue with each other about the respective merits of relativity theory, evolutionary theory and phlogiston theory, although they possess only a very partial knowledge of each. Children learn by heart the surviving portions of the periodic table and recite as incantations some of the theorems of Euclid. Nobody, or almost nobody, realizes that what they are doing is not natural science in any proper sense at all. For everything that they do and say conforms to certain canons of consistency and coherence and those contexts which would be needed to make sense of what they are doing have been lost, perhaps irretrievably.

In such a culture men would use expressions such as "neutrino," "mass," "specific gravity," "atomic weight" in systematic and often interrelated ways which would resemble in lesser or greater degrees the ways in which such expressions had been used in earlier times before scientific knowledge had been so largely lost. But many of the beliefs presupposed by the use of these expressions would have been lost and there would appear to be an element of arbitrariness and even of choice in their application which would appear very surprising to us. What would appear to be rival and competing premises for which no further argument could be given would abound. Subjectivist theories of science would appear and would be criticized by those who held that the notion of truth embodied in what they took to be science was incompatible with subjectivism.

This imaginary possible world is very like one that some science fiction writers have constructed. We may describe it as a world in which the language of natural science, or parts of it at least, continues to be used but is in a grave state of disorder. . . .

What is the point of constructing this imaginary world inhabited by fictitious pseudo-scientists . . . ? The hypothesis which I wish to advance is that in the actual world which we inhabit the language of morality is in the same state of grave disorder as the language of natural science in the imaginary world which I described. What we possess, if this view is true, are the fragments of a conceptual scheme, parts which now lack those contexts from which their significance is derived. We possess indeed simulacra of morality, we continue to use many of the key expressions. But we have—very largely, if not entirely—lost our comprehension, both theoretical and practical, of morality.[15]

I say a bit about MacIntyre's explanation for the disorder in modern moral language later in the chapter, but I presently wish to point out that the goal

---

[15] Alasdair MacIntyre, *After Virtue*, 2d ed. (Notre Dame, Ind.: University of Notre Dame Press, 1984), 1–2.

of most modern philosophical ethics has been specifically to *reduce* morality to something else. That is, in the attempt to justify moral claims, philosophers have frequently redefined morality in terms of lower levels of analysis— utility, pleasure, enlightened self-interest, feeling, social convention—and thus have lost sight of the truly moral element. The most extreme case of reduction is emotivism: the claim that moral judgments merely express one's attitudes or feelings toward an action or state of affairs. It is clear that something of traditional moral discourse has been lost here since moral *argument* no longer makes sense if moral claims are merely expressions of preference. It is like arguing that vanilla is objectively better than chocolate.

Utilitarianism is probably the most influential form of 'moral' reasoning in our pragmatic American culture, but this, too, is ultimately reductive. If the moral is *defined* as that which results in the greatest good for the greatest number, and good is defined (as for Jeremy Bentham) in terms of pleasure, then morality reduces to a strategy for increasing pleasure. Utilitarianism has not won the day in metaethical debate since it is too easy to find circumstances wherein the act in question *does* result in the greatest pleasure for the greatest number, yet we still consider it immoral. The classic example is a situation in which consent to the torturing of one child results in great good for many others. Even though utilitarians have responses to such cases, this suggests prima facie that utilitarianism has in general gotten it wrong concerning the very nature of the moral.

Another reductive understanding of morality is cultural relativism—moral norms are nothing but the conventions of the particular societies in which they are found. Thus, the moral level is reduced without remainder to the social level. More complicated social contract theories from Hobbes to John Rawls,[16] I suggest, have the same result.

In light of this history we should not be surprised to encounter attempts to reduce ethics to biology since this is but further pursuit of the typical modern reductionist strategy. Furthermore, the *appearance* of successful reduction on the part of evolutionary biologists depends on having already redefined ethics in a reductionist manner.

E. O. Wilson is explicit about his desire to promote reduction: "It may not be too much to say that sociology and the other social sciences, as well as the humanities, are the last branches of biology waiting to be included in the Modern Synthesis [neo-Darwinist evolutionary theory]. One of the functions of sociobiology, then, is to reformulate the foundations of the social sciences in a way that draws these subjects into the Modern Synthesis."[17] In

---

[16] John Rawls, *A Theory of Justice* (Cambridge, Mass.: Harvard University Press, 1971).

[17] E. O. Wilson, "The Morality of the Gene," in Paul Thompson, ed., *Issues in Evolutionary Ethics* (Albany: State University of New York Press, 1995), 156.

an often-quoted passage, Wilson makes equally clear his intention to reduce ethics to biology:

> Self-knowledge is constrained and shaped by the emotional control centers in the hypothalamus and limbic system of the brain. These centers flood our consciousness with all the emotions—hate, love, guilt, fear, and others—that are consulted by ethical philosophers who wish to intuit the standards of good and evil. What, we are then compelled to ask, made the hypothalamus and limbic system? They evolved by natural selection. That simple biological statement must be pursued to explain ethics and ethical philosophers.[18]

Philip Kitcher has already offered a penetrating criticism of Wilson's metaethical position:

> Stripped of references to the neural machinery, the account Wilson adopts is a very simple one. The content of ethical statements is exhausted by reformulating them in terms of our emotional reactions.
> . . . Wilson's rush to emotivism depends on slashing the number of alternatives. Only two possible accounts of ethical objectivity figure in Wilson's many pages on the topic. One of these, the attempt to give a religious foundation for ethics, does not occur in my list of options. Wilson mentions religious systems of morality only to dismiss them; his reason is spurious: "If religion . . . can be systematically analyzed and explained as a product of the brain's evolution, its power as an external source of morality will be gone forever."[19]

Kitcher himself then goes on to endorse Rawls's account of justice as based on social agreement.

R. D. Alexander in "A Biological Interpretation of Moral Systems" defines morality as nothing but social convention: "A moral system is essentially a society with rules. Rules are agreements about what is permitted and what is not, about what rewards and punishments are likely for specific acts, and about what is right and wrong."[20] The content of morality, according to Alexander, is altruism: "Generally speaking, then, *immoral* is a label we apply to certain kinds of acts by which we help ourselves or hurt others, while acts that hurt ourselves or help others are more likely to be judged moral than immoral. As virtually endless arguments in the philosophical literature attest, it is not easy to be more precise in defining morality *per se*" (180). So here

---

[18] Wilson, *Sociobiology,* 153.

[19] Philip Kitcher, "The Hypothalmic Imperative," in Thompson, ed., *Issues in Evolutionary Ethics,* 207, 211.

[20] R. D. Alexander, "A Biological Interpretation of Moral Systems," in Thompson, ed., *Issues in Evolutionary Ethics,* 179.

Alexander is making specific reference to the lack of consensus on metaethical issues and argues that biological knowledge can help "take the vagueness our of our concept of morality" (188).

Michael Ruse presents a more sophisticated argument for evolutionary ethics than many of his predecessors. He is specific about the metaethical problem: "A full moral system needs two parts. On the one hand you must have the 'substantival' or 'normative' ethical component. Here, you offer actual guidance as in, 'Thou shalt not kill.' On the other hand, you must have (what is known formally as) the 'metaethical' dimension. Here, you are offering foundations or justification as in, 'That which you should do is that which God wills.' Without these two parts, your system is incomplete."[21]

Ruse is to be commended for recognizing the difference between 'altruism' as a moral term and 'altruism' as it is used in biology to describe animal behavior that contributes to the survival of the group. I use Francisco J. Ayala's terms: 'altruism^m' for the moral concept; 'altruism^b' for the biological concept.[22] Ruse suggests that whereas insects and lower animals are genetically programmed for altruism^b, humans have instead been selected for a disposition toward altruism^m. Thus, he is able to argue for an evolutionary source for altruism^m without confusing it with altruism^b.

However, having properly distinguished moral behavior from superficially similar animal behavior, he then goes on to argue that morality, thus properly understood, has no possible rational justification: "The evolutionist is no longer attempting to derive morality from factual foundations. His/her claim now is that there are no foundations of any sort from which to derive morality—be these foundations evolution, God's will or whatever."[23] Since there can be no rational justification for objective moral claims, what is needed instead is a causal account of why we believe in an objective moral order. Ruse's answer is that the survival value of altruism^m does in fact provide such an explanation. "In particular, the evolutionist argues that, thanks to our science we see that claims like 'you ought to maximize personal liberty' are no more than subjective expressions, impressed upon our thinking because of their adaptive value. In other words, we see that morality has no philosophically objective foundation. It is just an illusion, fobbed off on us to promote [altruism^b]" (234). So Ruse's account, while more sophisticated than Alexander's or Wilson's in that he fully appreciates the conceptual difference between morality and sentiment, convention, and so on, is most starkly reductive: moral objectivity is merely an illusion.

---

[21] Michael Ruse, "Evolutionary Ethics: A Phoenix Arisen," in Thompson, ed., *Issues in Evolutionary Ethics*, 226.

[22] See Francisco J. Ayala, "The Biological Roots of Morality," in Thompson, ed., *Issues in Evolutionary Ethics*, 293–316.

[23] Ruse, "Evolutionary Ethics," 234.

These are but a sampling of the positions of evolutionary ethicists, but I hope the sample is adequate to illustrate the following points:

1. There is pervasive lack of clarity on metaethical issues; it is not clear at all what is the nature of the moral itself. As MacIntyre says, our moral discourse is in a state of grave disorder.
2. One important motivation for the attempt to reduce ethics to biology is the hope of clarifying or justifying moral or metaethical claims.
3. The reduction of morality to biology generally depends on a prior reduction of morality to emotion or social convention.

5. A Nonreductive Account of Ethics

If ethics is not to be reduced to the psychological (pleasure, emotion) or to the social (social conventions, rules) or to the political (social contracts), then what is its true nature? I suggest that we can answer this question best by considering again the proposal that ethics is a science (or discipline) that falls between the social sciences and theology (or metaphysics) in the hierarchy of the sciences.

It has been argued vociferously during the past decades that the social sciences are value-free. However, the burden of proof seems now to have shifted; it is widely recognized that economics, sociology, political theory, jurisprudence, all involve what can only be called *moral* presuppositions. For example, there is the assumption in economics that self-interest, rather than benevolence, is normative and if left unchecked will lead to greater good in the end. There is the assumption in sociology, criticized in the previous chapter, that all social order is based on violence or the threat of violence. There is the assumption in political theory that justice, as opposed to love, is the highest good at which government can aim; that freedom is an ultimate human good; that life, liberty, property, and the pursuit of happiness are *natural* rights.

When called into question, these assumptions all raise ethical questions, which cannot be answered by any scientific means. The social sciences are suited for studying the relations between means and ends (e.g., if the goal is to avoid surpluses and shortages, the best economic system is the free market), but they are not suited for determining the ultimate ends or goals of human life. This is, instead, the proper subject matter of ethics.

MacIntyre argues that modern ethics is in disarray because what ethics used to be was a discipline that taught how to act in order to reach humankind's ultimate goal. The concept of humankind's telos was provided by either a metaphysical or a theological tradition, which informed the ethicist of the nature of ultimate reality. Two contrasting examples are (1) the purpose of human existence is to know, love, and serve God in this life and to be happy with God in the next (cf. *The Baltimore Catechism*); or (2) a good life consists in courage in the face of the absurdity of it all since the human race is a small-scale accident in a meaningless cosmic process.

When Enlightenment ethicists severed all ties between morality and tradition (here, largely the Christian tradition), they kept fairly traditional lists of moral prescriptions but lost all concepts of the end for which those prescriptions were the means of achievement. So a consequence of the "autonomy of morals" was confusion about the very nature of ethics as a discipline, about the very nature of moral truth. Modern representational theories of language and knowledge led ethicists to ask what kind of 'objective realities' moral prescriptions or ascriptions might represent. Failing to find any such 'realities,' ethicists reduced moral claims to some other kind of claims that could be verified (e.g., utility); yet there was the cultural memory that moral claims must be something more than that, and so we memorize and repeat Hume's law as an incantation—"one cannot deduce an 'ought' from an 'is'"—and worry about committing "the naturalistic fallacy."

All of this confusion—taken up directly into discussions of biology and ethics, as we have just seen—is due to having forgotten that the 'ought' statement—"You ought to do (or be) *x*"—is only half of a moral truth. The original form of an ethical claim (implicitly, at least) is, "If you are to achieve your telos, then you ought to do (or be) *x*." This latter sort of ethical claim can be straightforwardly true or false; the 'ought' is no more mysterious than the 'ought' in "A watch ought to keep good time." Furthermore, it can and in fact *must* be derived from certain sorts of 'is' statements: about the nature of ultimate reality, about regularities in human life regarding the achievement of ends as a result of adopting certain means—the latter being amenable to empirical study.

Let us now consider the sorts of supervenience relations that obtain as we work up the scale from the personal (psychological) level to the theological. MacIntyre's own constructive ethical work involves the restoration of the ancient and medieval approach couched in the language of the virtues. The supervenience relations here are clear.

A virtue is an acquired human characteristic (psychological level). However, what constitutes that characteristic as a virtue, rather than a vice or a morally neutral characteristic, is a set of circumstances or contexts that can be described only at a higher level. The first level of relevant context is a "social practice," in MacIntyre's technical sense (see Chapter 1, section 3.5). Practices are found throughout the hierarchy of levels of complexity studied by the social sciences and include at the social level games, marriage, medicine, science; at the economic level, businesses and regulatory practices; at the political level, legislation and campaign management; at the legal level, the practice of law itself, the interpretation of the Constitution.

An acquired characteristic necessary for attaining goods internal to a practice (e.g., *fidelity* in the practice of marriage, *honesty* in business) is a *candidate* for a virtue. However, practices themselves require moral evaluation,
and here we reach the level of ethics itself. Each such practice (as well as an
individual's decision to participate in it) must be evaluated according to its
contribution to the telos of human life.

So we may ask questions such as, Does the practice of marriage contribute
to the ultimate goal of human existence, and if so, what is its proper purpose?
For those who believe that the natural world is itself the ultimate reality, the
only answers can be propagation of the species and personal support and
pleasure. However, for those who believe that the Christian tradition provides a more adequate account of ultimate reality, marriage is a practice with
an additional goal, perhaps even superseding those of the naturalists'
account—to witness to the faithfulness of God to God's people.

So the predicate 'is a virtue' supervenes on some psychological characteristic such as fidelity or humility only in the (nonreducible) circumstances of
its being essential for attaining goods internal to social practices that in turn
further the ultimate goals of human existence. Furthermore, a chosen end
(survival of the race, the glorification of God) is in fact an *ultimate* goal only
if it is congruent with the true (ultimate) nature of reality itself.[24]

Now, let us go back to the question of the relation between ethics and
biology. We can extend the subvenience relations of virtues downward in the
hierarchy to the biological level. MacIntyre emphasizes that virtues are
acquired human characteristics, and so, on his definition, a genetically determined trait is not a candidate for a virtue. However, the habit of acting on a
genetically produced capacity or propensity (say, for altruism) is a candidate
for a virtue, but whether or not it is in fact a virtue depends finally on one's
theological or metaphysical account of reality.

G. Simon Harak has proposed that virtues are realized physiologically or
neurologically. That is, the practice of virtuous behavior actually brings about
changes in one's physical makeup or functioning such that further virtuous
behavior comes closer to being automatic. If this is the case, it is an interesting example of top-down causation from the ethical to the biological level.[25]

---

[24] MacIntyre recognized that the dependence of ethical systems on accounts of ultimate real-
ity would lead to relativism if no account could be given of the rational evaluation of these larger
traditions. For his answer to this epistemological problem, see Alasdair MacIntyre, *Whose
Justice? Which Rationality?* (Notre Dame, Ind.: University of Notre Dame Press, 1988); and
Alasdair MacIntyre, *Three Rival Versions of Moral Enquiry: Encyclopaedia, Genealogy, and
Tradition* (Notre Dame, Ind.: University of Notre Dame Press, 1990); and my summary in
Chapter 3.
[25] See G. Simon Harak, *Virtuous Passions: The Formation of Christian Character* (New York:
Paulist Press, 1993).

There are some important parallels and differences between the position developed here and the views of Francisco Ayala.[26] I want to endorse his distinction between the evolution of a capacity for moral reasoning and behavior and the evolution of the content of moral codes. I also endorse his claim that the premises of our moral judgments are received from religious and other social traditions. I hope I have made some valuable elaborations on this claim. However, I take issue with his further claim that there is no logical connection between religious faith and moral principles—that religion provides no rational justification for moral norms. In the account presented here, the moral level of analysis definitely depends (logically, not motivationally) on top-down justification.

I claim that, in fact, all moral systems are dependent, either explicitly or implicitly, on beliefs about the nature of ultimate reality. Thus, I come to a second sort of claim that has been made for the relevance of evolutionary biology to ethics—claims, such as those of Jacques Monod, that because the evolutionary process shows no evidence of intelligent direction, we must adjust our views of human nature and behavior to take account of the ultimate meaninglessness of human existence. It seems clear that this is no direct argument from biology to ethics; rather, it is an argument (a fallacious one) from biology to metaphysics or theology ("There is no intelligent creator directing the process") and then *downward* from the (a)theological view to ethics.

However, such an argument is terribly naive when we consider the many levels of analysis involved. The shift from Aristotelian to modern biology can be described as the recognition that *purpose* (in the sense of an intended goal) is not a category that applies at the biological level at all, but only begins to apply at the psychological level. We might say to Monod and company: You have not made an empirical discovery that evolution has no purpose or goal; to think that you could make such a discovery involves a category mistake. It is necessarily true (a conceptual claim) that evolution is purposeless. So this recognition cannot be a significant fact about the universe; it is not a fact, strictly speaking, at all (i.e., except in the strained sense that it is a fact about language). Nothing of metaphysical interest clearly follows from it. And it is no more to be lamented than the claim that plants have no economic interests.[27]

---

[26] Ayala, "The Biological Roots," esp. 302–303.

[27] Before the reader objects that surely I cannot dismiss this whole area of debate so quickly, let me say that I do not deny that there are important issues regarding the consistency of a metaphysical or theological worldview with the findings of science, including evolutionary biology. My point is only that one has to recognize the differences in levels of discourse and relate them much more carefully.

6. Conclusion

It is not surprising that attempts should be made to reduce ethics to biology since reductionism has been a central 'thinking strategy' of the modern period not only among the natural sciences but also in all intellectual disciplines. Such attempts are even less surprising if we agree with MacIntyre that moderns have lost earlier conceptions of the very nature of the ethical. The rejection of reductionism in ethics requires two moves. One is the restoration of the 'top-down' connections from theology (or metaphysics) to ethics. The other is a recognition of the limitations of reductionist thinking in general, which in turn depends on an adequate account of the nature of the supervenience relation.

Postscript

It would be naive to expect to be able to characterize in a few lines an entire era in Western history (or to expect all critics to agree, even if one had succeeded!). But I believe several of the authors mentioned in the preceding chapters have done well in calling our attention to important and widespread features of the intellectual world just ending.

Stephen Toulmin emphasizes the quest for certainty that grew out of the chaos of the Thirty Years' War—seeing the counter-Renaissance preoccupation with the theoretical, the universal, the timeless, the written, as pervasive features of the modern world. These anxieties show up in the assumption that knowledge must have unquestionable foundations.

Bruno Latour says that no one is truly modern who does not agree to keep God from interfering in the laws of the republic, as well as in the laws of nature. He also recognizes as peculiarly modern the attempt to compartmentalize the natural and the cultural: the objective versus the subjective, the given versus the made, facts versus values.

Jeffrey Stout characterizes modernity as the flight from authority—originally the attempt to free morals and politics from traditional religion but ultimately, according to Alasdair MacIntyre, the rejection of the role of tradition in all reasoning. I claim that the individualism of the Enlightenment—dare to think for *oneself*—is but one manifestation of atomistic and reductionistic tendencies arising in early modern science but ultimately pervading all aspects of modern thought.

In light of these characterizations, it appears that much of what is called postmodern in contemporary Western culture is nothing but pure modernity finally hitting the streets. The fragmented "postmodern self" is but a further *atomization* of the modern individual and was already discussed by David Hume in the eighteenth century.

Much of the relativism associated with 'postmodernism' is nothing like a MacIntyrean recognition of competing traditions of enquiry, but merely the skepticism that comes from a frustrated quest for *foundations*. Textual relativism results from recognition of the failure of the *referent* to stabilize meaning in an intellectual milieu blind to the grounding provided by social convention. Moral relativism is a predictable result of the denial of the transcendent in all its forms, and this rejection, too, goes back to the very beginning of modernity, at least to Thomas Hobbes's replacement of the notion of the *divine* right of kings with his social contract theory.

However, the intellectual moves that I have countenanced in this volume as truly postmodern have not (yet) hit the streets. If they do, Toulmin suggests, our culture will return to the intellectual values of the Renaissance, in particular, to a contentment with more modest expectations for the powers of human reason and, consequently, with more openness to those who see things differently.

If MacIntyre is correct, we will see an increased sense of the role of our communities in the epistemological and the ethical. We will recognize our dependence on one or more of the large-scale traditions that have shaped our culture, seeing them as resources for intellectual *progress* rather than as fossils for the museum of intellectual history.

If John Milbank has his way, theology will become again a respected participant in public discourse, and social scientists will have to come clean and admit that they, too, are making assumptions about the ultimate nature of reality and what that has to say about how we can live together. I would include some of the natural scientists with their popular writings as well—the Monods and Sagans.

Looking back, we can see many of these changes gestating in midcentury Anglo-American analytic philosophy—in W.V.O. Quine's "Two Dogmas of Empiricism," with its epistemological holism and the all too briefly mentioned fact-value holism. Quine, of course, would disavow any influence on many of the developments surveyed in this volume. He is likely to wish that theologians would stop using his work! It will be interesting to see the extent to which Ludwig Wittgenstein's posthumous publications anticipated and shaped many of these postmodern developments, as interpretations of his enigmatic writings appear that are less steeped in a Fregean mind-set—and less influenced by atheism.

The year of Descartes's death, 1650, is taken by philosophers to mark the beginning of the modern era. A good date to mark its end would be 1950 since 1951 was the year of Wittgenstein's death and of the publication of Quine's "Two Dogmas." Historians might also want to note that it was the year the present author was born.

About the Book
and Author

The term 'postmodern' is generally used to refer to current work in philosophy, literary criticism, and feminist thought inspired by Continental thinkers such as Friedrich Nietzsche and Jacques Derrida. In this book, Nancey Murphy appropriates the term to describe emerging patterns in Anglo-American thought and to indicate their radical break from the thought patterns of Enlightened modernity.

The book examines the shift from modern to postmodern in three areas: epistemology, philosophy of language, and metaphysics. Murphy contends that whole clusters of terms in each of these disciplines have taken on new uses in the past fifty years and that these changes have radical consequences for all areas of academia, especially philosophy of science, philosophy of religion, and ethics.

Nancey Murphy is associate professor of Christian philosophy at Fuller Theological Seminary.

Index

Absolute idealism, 195
Absolutism, 49–50, 60, 128
Aesthetics, 2, 11
Affective fallacy, 136, 137
Alexander, R. D., 202–203
Allen, Diogenes, 2
Altruism, 202–203, 206
American Protestant Christianity. *See*
　Protestantism; Theology
Anabaptists, 147, 164
Anarchism, methodological, 50n
Anglo-American postmodernity
　distinguished from Continental
　postmodernism, 1, 7
　See also Postmodernity
Anomaly, 53, 79, 84
Antifoundationalism, 3, 4. *See also*
　Holism
Anti-individualism, 17, 117. *See also*
　Society, corporate view of
Antinaturalism. *See* Social sciences
Antirationality, 61–62
Antirealism, 3, 39, 43, 46, 136
　postmodern, 43, 46, 136
Antireductionism, 5, 19–22, 30–35,
　174, 176, 193–199, 204–208
　role of context/environment in,
　32–34, 174
　See also Nonreductive physicalism
Antirelativism, 49–62
Approximation to reality/truth, 47, 64
Aquinas. *See* Thomas Aquinas
Aristotle, 12, 13, 28, 29, 55, 123
Artificial language. *See* Language
Astronomy, 12
Atheism, 210
Atomism, 2, 8, 12–18, 99, 209

in epistemology, 14, 16, 18, 159
in ethics, 14
linguistic, 10–11, 14, 16, 17–18, 23,
　26, 132
in metaphysics, 2, 8, 12–18, 28
in philosophy of language. *See*
　Atomism, linguistic
in political theory, 14, 28
in science, 8, 12–14, 55, 56
social. *See* Individualism
in textual interpretation, 14
See also Logical atomism
Augustine, 180
Austen, Jane, 28
Austin, J. L., 2, 4, 23–25, 41–42, 131,
　132–133, 134, 138, 140,
　141–144, 145, 151
Author, the, 135, 143
Authorial intent, 136, 139–140, 143
Authority, traditional, 209
Autonomy of morals, 185, 205, 209
Auxiliary hypothesis, 52
Axes of modern thought, 2, 8, 29, 40,
　45, 46, 49
Ayala, Francisco J., 203, 207
Ayer, A. J., 11

baptist Vision, 146–149, 151
Barlow, David H., 82–83
Barnes, Barry, 44
Barrow, John, 176n
Bedeutung (reference), 11
Bellah, Robert, 2
Benn, Stanley I., 15n
Bentham, Jeremy, 201
Berger, Peter, 181
Bible. *See* Scripture